Understanding Human Values

Understanding Human Values

Individual and Societal

MILTON ROKEACH

THE FREE PRESS
A Division of Macmillan Publishing Co., Inc.
NEW YORK

Collier Macmillan Publishers
LONDON

Copyright © 1979 by The Free Press
A Division of Macmillan Publishing Co., Inc.

The Free Press
A Division of Macmillan Publishing Co., Inc.
866 Third Avenue, New York, N.Y. 10022

Collier Macmillan Canada, Ltd.

Library of Congress Catalog Card Number: 78-24753

Printed in the United States of America

printing number
1 2 3 4 5 6 7 8 9 10

Library of Congress Cataloging in Publication Data
Main title under entry:

Understanding human values.

    Includes index.
    1. Social values--Addresses, essays,
lectures. 2. Life--Addresses, essays, lectures.
3. Values--Study and teaching--Addresses,
essays, lectures. I. Rokeach, Milton.
HM73.U52 1979   301.2'1   78-24753
ISBN 0-02-926760-9

Copyright Acknowledgments

Contents

PART THREE: VALUE CHANGE THROUGH SELF-AWARENESS

PART FOUR: VALUE EDUCATION THROUGH SELF-AWARENESS

Preface

Understanding human values is a never-ending process—a groping toward an ultimate objective that can be attained only by a method of successive approximation. In this volume, I have attempted to bring together recent contributions from several social science disciplines that in my judgment advance further our understanding and appreciation of the ubiquitous role that human values play in everyday life.

The main criterion that I employed when selecting a contribution for inclusion in this volume is that it advances theoretical, methodological, or empirical knowledge about human values. Thus I included contributions—from my own work and the work of others—that attempt to go beyond earlier work in several directions. The study of human values is extended from the individual to organizational, institutional, societal, and cultural levels of analysis. Attention is drawn to several ways in which supposedly enduring, stable, centrally located individual values naturally undergo continual change in everyday life, and an attempt is made to identify several individual and social antecedents and consequences of value and value change. Explanations of naturally occurring value change are related to explanations of value change in experimental studies. I include experimental studies that suggest that, by increasing self-awareness about one's own and others' values, it is now possible to envision enduringly affecting the values of large numbers of people in socially desirable directions via interactive computers and the mass media. The ethical question as to whether it is possible to manipulate people's values for evil purposes, a question raised in my earlier work, is further pursued.

Finally, I include several contributions that deal with implications for education and value education.

Chapters 3, 5, 12, 14, 15, and 18 are new contributions published here for the first time. Other chapters are elaborations, extensions, or integrations of previously published works. Chapter 2 by Robin Williams is an updated version of a paper previously published in *Stability and Social Change,* edited by B. Barber and A. Inkeles. Chapter 6 is a further elaboration and theoretical integration of Norman Feather's work on cultural assimilation of Ukrainians and Latvians in Australia, reported in his *Values in Education and Society.* Chapter 8 by Carol Ryff is a more detailed report of research that she co-authored with P. B. Baltes that appeared in *Developmental Psychology,* 1976. Chapter 10 by Cochrane, Billig, and Hogg is a fuller report of research concerning the equality–freedom model of political ideology in England than the one they published in the *British Journal of Social and Clinical Psychology,* 1979. And Chapter 16 is revised and extended from my earlier paper in *Values Education,* edited by J. Meyer, B. Burnham, and J. Cholvat. The remaining chapters—4, 7, 9, 11, 13, and 17—are reprinted with permission, with minor editing, from various sources.

The papers authored by myself and collaborators were supported by Grant No. GS-3045 from the National Science Foundation, and preparation of this volume was further facilitated by Grant No. 1 RO1 MH29656-01 from the National Institute of Mental Health. I am deeply grateful to both of these agencies for their support.

Finally, I wish to thank Ann Dougherty for the many ways she helped in preparing this manuscript for publication. Her considerable secretarial skills intermingled so greatly with her considerable interpersonal skills that I was unable to tell which exceeded the other, and which I appreciated more.

1

Introduction

Milton Rokeach

This volume presents recent theoretical, methodological, and empirical advances in understanding, and also in the effects of understanding, individual and societal values. These advances come from contributors trained in a number of disciplines—sociology, psychology, political science, philosophy, management, and communications. Empirical advances are based upon data obtained by survey research methods, content analysis, and controlled experiments. The fact that these diverse contributions come from such a variety of fields testifies to the central position of the value concept across the several disciplines concerned with the understanding of human behavior. Moreover, it suggests that the value concept, perhaps more than any other in the social sciences, is meaningful at all levels of social analysis, and that a substantive interest in the antecedents and consequents of human values is not likely to be co-opted by any one discipline.

This volume undertakes to elaborate and to extend previously published reports of research programs concerned with human values (Feather, 1975b; Rokeach, 1968, 1973) in four main directions: first, it attempts to go beyond the conceptualization and measurement of individual values to the conceptualization and measurement of supraindividual values, and to a consideration of the reciprocal relationship and fit between individual and supraindividual values; second, it attempts to draw attention to what appear to be some major determinants and consequences of value organization and change that can be observed to occur naturally within the individual and society; third, it attempts to extend in several directions earlier experimental work concerned with the effects of inducing self-awareness about one's own and others' values on long-term changes in values, attitudes, and behavior; and fourth, from an analysis of the crucial role that values play in all institutional settings within a society, special attention is directed to the role that values and value education should play within the context of the educational institution.

As indicated in the next chapter, which is authored by sociologist Robin Williams, values are core conceptions of the desirable within every individual and society. They serve as standards or criteria to guide not only action but also judgment, choice, attitude, evaluation, argument, exhortation, rationalization, and, one might add, attribution of causality. Values, according to Williams, are complex "pre-codings" that are a result of learned fusions of "cognitive–conceptual with imperative elements." They are, moreover, capable of being structurally organized within the individual and the society not only in terms of priority, but also in terms of extensiveness, universality of application, and consistency. Williams' analysis points up the embarrassing fact that, despite all that has been written by social scientists on the subject of human values, conceptualizations of values and value systems are still poorly understood, yet continue to improve in clarity and precision with continued analysis. Better than any other student of the subject, Williams has succeeded in drawing our attention to the fact that values are multifaceted cognitions and affections representing far more than mere standards or criteria for action.

> We cannot safely underrate any value merely because it seems characterized by lip-service, or more honored in the breach than in the observance, or is advocated primarily by hypocrites. For all these activities serve to maintain the value as valid currency or acknowledged benchmark—whereupon it can be used at any time to praise or blame, to honor or bring into disrepute. We must never lose sight of the fact that values continually are used as weapons in social struggles. (p. 26)

All the contributions in this volume, I believe, share certain assumptions that make possible the interdisciplinary and cross-cultural study of stability and change in individual and supraindividual values: that the number of human values are small, the same the world over, and capable of different structural arrangements, that they are the resultants of societal demands and psychological needs, that they are learned and determined by culture, society, society's institutions, and personal experience, that they are determinants in turn of attitudes, judgments, choices, attributions, and actions, that they are capable of undergoing change as a result of changes in society, situation, self-conceptions, and self-awareness, and finally, that changes in values represent central rather than peripheral changes, thus having important consequences for other cognitions and social behavior.

Supraindividual Values. Part I focuses attention on supraindividual values. The chapters included in this section make it apparent that it is just as meaningful to speak of societal values, institutional values, organizational values, ideological values, and the value-transmitting functions of social movements as it is to speak of individual values. Williams focuses his main theoretical attention on the role that values play in the affairs of a society, and his chapter also provides us with a good summary of what is known about the values of American society in particular. His chapter is rich in ideas about the variables that may affect values and value change, at the individual as well as at the societal level.

The next chapter, by Rokeach, is primarily methodological. In what sense can those supraindividual entities we identify as institutions be meaningfully and unanthropomorphically characterized as "possessing" values? What methods are available to social scientists interested in the measurement of the values of supraindividual entities that cannot be interviewed? Is it possible to conceptualize and study within a single universe of discourse the interactions and consistencies between supraindividual entities and individuals? The key to all this, it seemed to me, is that all persons raised within the context of society are caught from the moment of birth between their own individual needs and society's goals and demands. A person's individual needs somehow become cognitively represented as values, and so also do societal goals and demands. Thus, we may come to view the value system that each person internalizes to be just as much a reflection of individual needs as of societal goals and demands—a resultant of internal psychological and external sociological forces acting upon the person. At the same time, as Feather's analysis in Chapter 6 suggests, the fit between the individual and various components of the individual's environment is not always perfect; there is a tendency on the part of the individual to select social environments to minimize value discrepancies.

Connor and Becker's main focus in Chapter 4 is on organizational values. They point out that, despite a long interest in human values, few investigators have focused on the role that values play in organizational processes. Questions regarding how values relate to organizational reward structure, upward mobility within organizations, goal commitment, conflict, cooperation, group cohesion, communication, and leadership effectiveness remain unresolved. Within a general-systems framework, they offer a model to identify the reciprocal effects of values and various organizational variables, and within such a paradigm they propose a series of testable hypotheses. The focus of these hypotheses is not so much on individual values and behavior as on organizational values and behavior.

In Chapter 5, Ball-Rokeach and Tallman attempt a theoretical analysis of the cognitive functions served by social movements. They view social movements primarily as value-exhorting consciousness-raising movements that, through five moral confrontation strategies, attempt to increase individual awareness about positions taken with respect to certain positive or negative values, in order to expose internal contradictions and hypocrisies implicating one's values and self-conceptions, and thus to induce people to become dissatisfied with themselves. In this way, social movements attempt to increase the priority of exhorted values, and thus to pave the way for active participation and the success of the social movement.

Some Major Determinants and Consequences of Value Organization. The selections in Part II are recent empirical contributions that identify some major variables present in most societies that may affect, or that may be affected by, value orientations. These contributions report cross-cultural data obtained in Australia, Britain, and the United States. Chapter 6 by psychologist Norman Feather combines theoretical analysis with methodological innovation to report research findings concerning the effects of migrant assimilation on value change. He provides us with an analysis of processes of cultural assimilation within the framework of discrepancy theory, which is an elaboration and application of a theory about person–environment consistencies that he had put forward in an earlier monograph (Feather, 1975b). At the empirical level, his chapter is a report of the extent to which second-generation Ukrainians and Latvians have assimilated into Australian society. He reviews various types and approaches to the study of cultural assimilation and proposes several methods for measuring the degree to which there is assimilation. Two of them are new and rely on value comparisons: (1) comparison of the degree of similarity in value priorities between second- and first-generation immigrants with the degree of similarity between second-generation immigrants and representatives of the host culture; (2) comparisons of the accuracy of perception of one another's values as an index of subjective assimilation. He relates such findings to other findings concerning perceptions of ethnic identity and attitude similarity, to provide us with a broad array of methods and findings that should prove useful to those interested in studying the manifold effects of cultural assimilation.

In Chapter 7 Rokeach reports on the values, the value priorities, and the factorial structure of the values of adult Americans considered as a whole, and of various subgroups of Americans. His research demonstrates that the values of a representative sample of Americans can be easily and economically obtained, and that they are stable. It also demonstrates that meaningful changes in American values can be detected even over a short period, and that these changes can reasonably be attributed to changes in the salience of such issues confronting Americans in the sixties and seventies as civil rights, women's liberation, and concerns about ecology. Thus, we see both stability and change in American values and can anticipate continuing changes in American values as a result of the ever changing salience of societal issues.

In Chapter 8, Carol Ryff proposes a novel "instrumentality-terminality sequence" hypothesis to account for changes in value organization among adult Americans undergoing a transition from middle to old age. Her methodology is equally novel: she employs what she calls concurrent, prospective, and retrospective techniques to measure changes from instrumental to terminal value orientations. Her findings have important implications for a deeper understanding of the processes and consequences of aging and should, moreover, lead us to ponder whether it is possible and desirable to inhibit the aging process by finding ways to inhibit or delay the transition from instrumental to terminal value orientations.

In Chapter 9, political scientist Donald Searing describes the procedures that he employed to ascertain the values of several hundred Labour and Conservative Members of the British Parliament. His findings on this elite sample of politicians can be compared with those reported by Cochrane, Billig, and Hogg in Chapter 10 on the values of less elite partisans identified with the Labour, Conservative, Communist, and National Front parties in Britain. Taken together, these two chapters shed light not only on the values underlying British politics in the 1970s, and on their ability to predict political identification, but also tell us about the validity of the two-value model of political ideology (Rokeach, 1973). This model proposes that the four major ideologies of the twentieth century—communism, fascism, socialism, and capitalism—differ most fundamentally from one another in the distinctive positions they take with respect to two political values, *equality* and *freedom*. Socialism is hypothesized to be an ideology that holds both of these values in high regard, whereas fascism holds them in low regard; communism values *equality* but not *freedom*, whereas capitalism values *freedom* but not *equality*. The two chapters on British values and politics not only identify certain clusters of values as determinants of political activism, but also point to the differences we may expect when analyzing the values underlying identification with abstract political ideologies, on the one hand, and participation in concrete political parties, on the other. These differences are considered more fully in Chapter 11, wherein I present my reactions to the findings and conclusions of Cochrane, Billig, and Hogg.

Value Change.   Values are standards that are to a large extent derived, learned, and internalized from society and its institutions. These
standards guide the development of a socially defined sense of self as a
competent and moral member of society. Many different kinds of definitions of what it means to be competent and moral are possible; these
will vary, depending upon the structural position of the individual
within the social system, the relative influence and importance to any
given person of the various social institutions, of institutionally related
organizations, and of reference groups. Definitions of what it means to
be a competent and moral person will also vary with such factors as
occupational role, sex role, and changes in the life cycle through which
the individual passes (Erikson, 1950), which make different demands
upon the individual, and which are associated with differences in the
range of possibilities of which one can become aware (Smith, 1969).
Moreover, definitions of self can be affected by changes in the salience of
societal issues—for example, increases or decreases in the salience of
racial justice, sex-role equality, involvement in an unjust war, or threats
to health from pollution. As different issues become salient in day-to-day
affairs, say, through mass media coverage, they become consciousness-
raising—that is, they raise people's awareness of themselves with respect
to their stand on such issues and make possible changes in self-
conceptions. Other ways of increasing salience, and thus providing an
impetus for changes in self-conceptions, would include sudden and drastic changes in personal circumstances. Examples of the former would
include natural catastrophes, invasion, declarations of war, widespread
unemployment, energy shortages, or changes in laws forbidding discrimination; examples of the latter would include illness, accident, loss of
job, change in occupational role, or mandatory retirement.

Value change, and related changes in attitudes and behavior can
come about either as a result of (1) changes in self-conceptions or definitions of the self or because of (2) increases in self-awareness—about
hypocrisies, incongruities, inconsistencies, or contradictions between
self-conceptions or self-ideals (Leff, 1978), on the one hand, and one's
values, related attitudes, and behaviors, on the other. In the former case,
the value changes are naturally occurring changes that come about as a
result of changes in individual needs and perceptions of societal goals
and demands. In the latter case—increases in self-awareness concerning
internal contradictions—value change is motivated by a need for the
maintenance and enhancement of self-esteem and by a need for consistency between one's conception of self and one's beliefs, attitudes, values,
and behavior (Aronson, 1968, 1969; Rokeach, 1968; Greenwald and
Ronis, 1978). Thus, value change following self-awareness becomes
synonymous with value reeducation, a process removed from persua-
sion- and manipulation- oriented theory and research on attitude

change, and thus more relevant to the concerns of education, psychotherapy, counseling, and religion than to the concerns of advertising and propaganda. In either case, whether we are dealing with changes in self-conceptions or with increases in self-awareness about internal contradictions, a process of value, attitude, and behavior change is assumed to be initiated as a result of some felt experience of self-dissatisfaction, the origin of which is specific enough to be felt, experienced, or identified by the person concerned.

Experimental investigations of the effects of changes in societally defined and societally imposed self-conceptions are still far off in the future, and difficult to envision because of ethical considerations. For this reason, we have been content to study value *differences* rather than value *changes,* as a function of naturally occurring differences in self-conceptions, as indicated by differences in race, sex role, social status, age, religion, and the like. Differences (or changes) in social status or age, for instance, are accompanied by and thus imply differences (or changes) in self-conceptions, and such differences (or changes) in self-conceptions are in turn expected to lead to differences (or changes) in value systems and in value-related attitudes and behavior.

Experimental work has concentrated, instead, on the second of the two main determinants mentioned above—value, attitude, and behavioral changes as a function of increasing self-awareness—about contradictions between self-conception, on the one hand, and values, attitudes, and behavior, on the other. The method advocated and typically employed in previous experimental work to increase such self-awareness is the method of *self-confrontation,* and the psychological mechanism that this method is intended to activate is the arousal of a state of *self-dissatisfaction.* The arousal of self-dissatisfaction by self-confrontations designed to provide awareness of internal contradictions implicating one's sense of self and one's standards is posited to initiate a process of cognitive and behavioral change.

The focus on inducing self-awareness via a wedding of method to process—the method of self-confrontation to activate the psychological mechanism of self-dissatisfaction—is a deliberate one. Such a focus was designed to overcome a number of ethical problems that plague contemporary experimental research in social psychology. First, the emphasis on the effects of self-awareness is education oriented rather than persuasion oriented. Second, deception cannot be employed to induce self-awareness; indeed, it would be a contradiction in terms to say that one wishes to increase self-understanding, self-awareness, or self-insight by employing deceptive techniques. Third, the state of self-dissatisfaction that is activated is *aroused* rather than *induced.* Internal contradictions are assumed to exist chronically below the level of awareness in many persons, and such persons are merely made aware of internal contradictions that already exist. Thus, the state of self-dissatisfaction is aroused rather than artificially induced. Respondents are not experimentally manipulated to say things they do not believe in, or to do things they would not otherwise do. Those who, as a result of self-confrontation, do not experience or perceive any internal contradiction are not theoretically expected to experience self-dissatisfaction and are therefore not expected to undergo value, attitude, or behavioral change. Fourth, the method of self-confrontation allows us to respect the respondent's right to privacy since the experimenter is not required to know how any particular person is responding or whether he or she is exhibiting some internal contradiction. Fifth, informed consent is now possible since respondents can be informed beforehand that they will be provided with information about their own and about others' values, and that they are possibly at risk in discovering something unpleasant about themselves in exposing themselves to such information.[1] Sixth, respondents in our experiments receive something in return for their participation. They find out something important and true not only about themselves but also about others. Thus, respondents who feel they are learning something important from their participation are more likely to perceive the experiment as personally and socially relevant.

But previous experimental work has thus far been limited in a number of ways. It has confined itself primarily to the experimental induction of self-awareness about contradictions implicating one's position with respect to two values in particular (*equality* and *freedom*), and it has typically confined itself to face-to-face interactions between an experimenter and a relatively small number of students in classroom contexts. This work has also been limited by the fact that specified target values had been selected in advance for experimental treatment and, moreover, by the fact that the data communicated to respondents required additional interpretations deliberately designed to needle students to make them feel uncomfortable, such as: "The finding that most college students rank *freedom* far ahead of *equality* suggests that they generally care more for their own freedom than for the freedom of others."

In the present volume, this work is extended to consider the effects of self-awareness on other values, particularly those that have implications for health-related public policy. William Conroy's Chapter 12 is a contribution to what might be called the field of value therapy—an approach to behavior modification that offers an alternative to Skinner's operant approach, one that proposes that health-related behavior modification can be brought about as a result of changes first brought

---

[1]In previous work, this point was not made explicitly enough to respondents. There is no methodological or moral reason, however, why it should not be made in future work.

about in the values that underlie a particular behavior. While Conroy's main experimental concern is on changes brought about in smoking behavior, by acting upon and arousing self-dissatisfaction about certain values underlying smoking, he focuses his analysis more generally to point up the potential of value therapy for reducing all sorts of health-destroying behaviors. Thus, behavior modification through value therapy is seen to have implications for and applications to such problems as obesity, alcoholism and drug abuse, achievement-related tension, unsafe driving, and physical inactivity.

Experimental work is further extended by considering whether value change can be induced not only by human experimenters who interact face to face with students in classroom contexts, but also by computers interacting with respondents (Chapter 13). The computer study further extends earlier work by studying the effects of self-awareness on bringing about persisting value change under conditions wherein there are no preselected target values and, moreover, wherein interpretations of findings are not offered to respondents.

Chapter 14 by Sanders and Atwood takes us beyond the question as to whether computers can affect human values to the effects of television and the written word. Their research will be of special interest to those concerned with mass media effects. The implications of their work will be obvious when we keep in mind that large numbers of people can be reached by television and the written word, that the experimental treatment is a single treatment lasting less than an hour, and that the values affected are political values.

All such experimental work suggests that values can be affected, and that value changes can persist and can lead to related and persisting changes in attitudes and behavior. Inevitably, such findings give rise to an ethical uneasiness and apprehension about those who might be tempted to change our values in one or another direction for evil reasons (Schwartz, 1974). Is it possible to manipulate people's values arbitrarily to conform to whatever are the whims of an ethically insensitive experimenter, a power-hungry demagogue, a repressive government, or a profit-seeking advertising industry? Who will decide which value to change and in which directions to change them? The unidirectional hypothesis, originally put forward in 1973, proposes that although people can be induced to change their values by arousing a state of self-dissatisfaction, their values cannot be arbitrarily manipulated. Value change, and other cognitive and behavioral change that might follow from value change, is inherently unidirectional rather than bidirectional in nature:

A person should undergo an increase or decrease in regard to any given value in only one direction—whichever direction will provide . . . self-conceptions with a certain mileage—and not in the other direction. In the final analysis, self-conceptions reflect social definitions of the self. (Rokeach, 1973, pp. 328-329)

Two studies described in Chapter 15 by Rokeach and Grube attempt to address themselves to this issue of unidirectionality. In the first study, respondents are asked to imagine that they have unlimited power to change other people's values, and then to imagine that certain others have such unlimited powers. Which values would the respondents want to see increased or decreased, if they had the power to do so? And which values would they resist having increased or decreased if others initiated them? How powerful are the norms or the consensus about increasing or decreasing specified values? And will people respond consistently about themselves wanting to increase certain values, yet resist others' attempts to decrease them, and vice versa? A second study, carried out by Joel Grube, is more experimental in design, and builds on the first study. Two groups of antiegalitarian respondents are compared with one another in an experiment explicitly designed to increase their value for *equality*. The first group was selected because, notwithstanding their antiegalitarian position, they had previously indicated that they would increase the importance of *equality* to others if given the chance, and would moreover resist attempts by others to decrease *equality*. The second group had previously indicated, consistent with their antiegalitarian position, that they would decrease the importance of *equality* if given the chance, and would resist attempts by others to increase the importance of *equality*. The unidirectional hypothesis predicts that the former group of antiegalitarians would be vulnerable to value change by information about their own and others' values designed to increase value for *equality*, whereas the latter group would be invulnerable.

The ethical question, Can values be arbitrarily manipulated?, is, however, too complex to be settled by one or two studies. The most that I can reasonably hope for, in publishing these studies, is that it will pave the way for others to pursue this question further.

Value Education.   Theory and research on the effects of increasing understanding about one's own and others' values has educational implications, and is particularly relevant to the field variously identified as value education, values clarification, moral education, or moral development. Chapter 16 by Rokeach provides an analysis of the role that values necessarily play in all institutional settings, with special reference to the role that values do and should play in educational settings. Consistent with the analysis of institutional values offered in Chapter 3, the position taken in Chapter 16 is that the educational institution has a special stake in certain values that are broadly identified as educational values, that the educational institution has an obligation to inculcate students with educational values, and, therefore, that the educational institution cannot be value-neutral. Educational values pertain to issues of competence development no less than to issues of moral development. Both kinds of development, I argue, would be advanced by a mandated program of value inculcation, on the one hand, and by a program of substantive value education, on the other.

An emphasis on increasing understanding about one's own and others' values in educational settings is desirable not only for its own sake but also because it can lead to increases in student perceptions of personal and social relevance of course content. Such increases in perceptions of relevance are widely sought after in educational circles because they are believed to lead to increases in academic motivation. In Chapter 17, philosopher Ronald Epp discusses how he has employed the technique of increasing such understanding to heighten student interest and participation in a course dealing with traditional ethical theories. And in the final chapter, Lundy and Rokeach report on their experimental studies designed to ascertain the effects of increasing personal relevance by increasing self-understanding on the short- and long-term academic performance of students in a social psychology course. These findings about the effects of self-understanding have implications for the teaching of social science courses more generally.

Judging from the diversity of the various contributions to this volume, it may be anticipated that theory and research on the antecedents and consequents of human values will be especially receptive in the years ahead to genuinely fruitful interdisciplinary thinking and collaboration.

PART ONE

Societal, Institutional, and Organizational Values

2

Change and Stability in Values and Value Systems: A Sociological Perspective

Robin M. Williams, Jr.

This chapter represents a revision and elaboration of ideas that have been developed in various publications over a period of some twenty-five years (Williams, 1951, 1967, 1968, 1971; Goldsen, Rosenberg, Suchman, & Williams, 1960). Some overlap and duplication is inevitable, especially in the case of the closely related treatment of the topic in Barber and Inkeles (Eds.), *Stability and Social Change* (1971). Our presentation deals briefly with background questions about the nature of values and their place in the determination of behavior, but focuses mainly on theory and data concerning change in values, especially macrochanges in American society.

We start with the observation that all continuing human groupings develop normative orientations—conceptions of preferred and obligatory conduct and of desirable and undesirable states of affairs. Such normative orientations are highly diverse across different societies, and are concretely very complex. Essentially, however, the most important types of normative elements are *norms* (specific obligatory demands, claims. expectations, rules) and *values* (the criteria of desirability).

THE NATURE OF VALUES

The term "values" has been used variously to refer to interests, pleasures, likes, preferences, duties, moral obligations, desires, wants, goals, needs, aversions and attractions, and many other kinds of selective orientations. To avoid such excessive looseness, we have insisted that the core phenomenon is the presence of *criteria or standards of preference* (Williams, 1968, 1970). The beginning point or substrate is preference (Pepper, 1958). But sheer preference alone leaves out the conceptual and directional qualities that are of greatest interest and importance for explaining human social behavior. Values merge affect and concept. Persons are not detached or indifferent to the world; they do not stop with a sheerly factual view of their experience. Explicitly or implicitly, they are continually regarding things as good or bad, pleasant or unpleasant, beautiful or ugly, appropriate or inappropriate, true or false, virtues or vices. A comprehensive initial view of the field of valuing must identify the generic characteristics; for specific purposes, more restrictive conceptions should be formulated as needed. All values have cognitive, affective, and directional aspects. Values serve as criteria for selection in action. When most explicit and fully conceptualized, values become criteria for judgment, preference, and choice. When implicit and unreflective, values nevertheless perform "as if" they constituted grounds for decisions in behavior. Individuals do prefer some things to others; they do select one course of action rather than another out of a range of possibilities; they do judge their own conduct and that of other persons.

As we examine evidences of *values,* we find them appearing in various admixtures with *knowledge* and *beliefs.* For our judgments of what *should be* are always related to our judgments of what *is.* Thus our present view of mental illness as illness (rather than as possession by demons, or as the result of morally culpable behavior) points to humane medical treatment rather than punishment as a "good." The change from older orientations is partly a change in biological, psychological, and sociological knowledge, but in the long run the changed beliefs profoundly affect evaluative standards even as, in turn, changes in values will affect our conceptions of reality.

Values are not concrete rules of conduct; nor can values be merged into the concept of institution. Rather, institutions must be conceived either as complex sets of rules (Williams, 1970) or as "value-integrates" (Parsons, 1951, pp. 36–45); in either formulation, some consistent or systematic *combinations* of concrete criteria and objects of preference are implied. One must avoid the trap of confusing value *standards* with *objects of cathexis,* and values cannot be assimilated to either existential beliefs or to concrete evaluations (such as ideologies). Beyond question, then, values are defined by analytic constructs; they are not object-bound.

But if this conception is held, what can values possibly *be*—if, indeed, the existential verb makes any sense here? Can the social actor be "committed" to or come to "internalize" a particular value? If so, values must be characterized by some quality of "entitivity" (Campbell, 1958)—some boundedness or object quality. And if a value may be likened in some way to an "object" (of regard, of affect, etc.), this conclusion would appear to rule out a sheerly nominal status, that is, a concept of a value as *purely* a "tendency," "vector," or "principle" as inferred by an external observer. Otherwise, values would be analogous to principles of syntax wholly unknown to the speakers of a language. In this event, the particular manifestations of correct or appropriate values would be positively regarded, to be sure, but one would be stretching the point to assert that the values themselves were objects of positive regard.

But the implied problem is not really so difficult. Observation of processes of evaluation makes it quite clear that some values are, indeed, highly explicit, and appear to the social actor as phenomenal entities: the person can state the value, illustrate its application in making judgments, identify its boundaries, and the like. Other standards of desirability are not explicit; and social actors may even resist making them explicit. Nonetheless, some criteria of this kind can be inferred from selective behavior, and when such inference is presented to the behaving actor some individuals can recognize in their own conduct a value of which they had previously not been aware. In the enormously complex universe of value phenomena, values are simultaneously components of psychological processes, of social interaction, and of cultural patterning and storage (Parsons, 1951, 1968; Albert, 1968, pp. 287-291).

PATTERNS OF VALUES

Rokeach has indicated that differences among individuals may be not so much in the presence or absence of particular values as in the arrangement of values, their hierarchies or priorities (1973; Chapter 3). Certainly differences in values across total social systems and across major distinctive "cultures" or "civilizations" typically do not consist of the total absence of some values in one case as over against their presence in another. In every full-fledged society, every one of Rokeach's 36 values will appear—as will each of the values or themes listed by C. Kluckhohn, F. Kluckhohn, R. F. Bales and Couch, C. Morris, M. Opler, and R. Williams. Yet as total systems, societies differ radically in their patterns of values. The differences reside not only in hierarchies or priorities—the ordering of values according to importance, in some sense—but also in other important modes of relationships among values.

What are these other modes of relationships among values? What we have just said is that out of a very nearly universal or constant list of values, societies (and other less inclusive collectivities) differ in the *patterning* of the values. In addition to *hierarchical ordering* (usually imperfect and partial), societies differ, second, in the extensiveness of adherence to any particular values (Williams, 1970, Chapter 11). Thus, equality may be an elite value in an aristocratic city-state: all oligarchs agree that oligarchs are equal, no one else counts. In a modern parliamentary democracy, equality may be much more widely shared as a value among the total population. A related but not identical mode of patterning, is, third, the degree of *universality of application,* for example, "all Americans must be free"—when "Americans" may mean white, adult, Protestant, property-owning males, or, in contrast, when the value is extended to more and more inclusive categories of the population. Values may be patterned in a fourth mode, that of *consistency:* in one society, a metavalue emphasizes logical or "deontic" consistency among various values; in another society, little attention is paid to consistency, or else there is a positive appreciation of ambiguity, paradox, and irony. "Inconsistency" may be prized as "richness," as indicative of scope and grandeur in experience.

Beginning with a sociological definition of institution as "a set of institutional norms that cohere around a relatively distinct and socially important complex of values" (Williams, 1970 p. 39), Rokeach suggests in the following chapter that institutions be regarded as "social arrangements that provide frameworks for *value specialization,* that is, frameworks for the transmission and implementation mainly of those subsets of values that are especially implicated in their own particular spheres of activity" (p. 51). This is a useful perspective, particularly because it provides for the structural articulation of individuals' values with macrosocial arrangements. In highly differentiated modern societies, such diversity of values is compartmentalized in the major specialized institutions (kinship, stratification, economy, polity, education and science,[1] religion), and contradictions and incongruities are often dealt with by specialized collectivities and social statuses (e.g., those specialized in adjudication, mediation, conciliation, arbitration, therapy, suppression, or diversion).

---

[1]By questionnaire surveys and content analysis, Rokeach shows that various samples of respondents and of editorials in *Science* agree in giving top ranks to *wisdom, freedom, self-respect, a sense of accomplishment, a world at peace,* and *equality.* Lowest ranks went to *salvation, pleasure, national security, mature love, true friendship,* and *a comfortable life* (Chapter 3).

HOW VALUES ARE STUDIED

Data, concepts, and research methods for the study of values have been drawn from several major fields of study—ranging across philosophy, the behavioral and social sciences, cybernetics, and several branches of the biological and physical sciences (Wiener, 1954; Pepper, 1958; Deutsch, 1963; Williams, 1967; Rokeach, 1968; Buckley, 1968; Parsons, 1968). The study of values cannot be confined to a single discipline or a narrow range of methods of research.

In the behavioral and social sciences, the discovery of the relative ease with which "attitudes" could be measured and manipulated in the laboratory probably has encouraged a concentration upon "problems of persuasion" rather than "problems of education and re-education" (Rokeach, 1968, 1973). The apparent usefulness of studies of opinions and attitudes to the advertising industry, to government and political leaders, to political propagandists of various kinds, and to business management probably also contributed heavily to this emphasis. At any rate, the American psychological research of the last few decades has apparently emphasized short-term effects, group conformity, and techniques of presentation and persuasion—rather than the possible long-term effects of "socialization, educational innovation, psychotherapy, and culture change on values" (Rokeach, 1968, p. 159). It is indeed very likely that a focus of attention upon quite short-range effects on relatively docile laboratory subjects would not supply a clear view of the long-range causal importance of pervasive values—which partly define the very limits of what is "possible" and "thinkable" in human conduct.

The dilemmas of defining value for research purposes are many, but the most crucial in many ways is the choice between a broad and a narrow definition. Highly specific definitions fail to deal with important phenomena that we are forced to recognize as having value properties. Very broad definitions tend to equate "value" with preference, desire, liking, or satisfaction (Fallding, 1965)—thus passing over the most distinctive feature of valuing, that is, the partial autonomy of *criteria* of desirability from desire or wish.

The growing attention now given to values in research may help to reduce the confusion in thinking about human social behavior that has often resulted from the absence of a clear discrimination between *energy* and *information* (Ackerman & Parsons, 1966, p. 37 ff.). Lacking an adequate conceptualization of values, some theorists have argued as if one could simply decide *in general* whether "ideas" or "material factors" were stronger determinants of behavior or whether "sexual drives" were more influential than "moral norms," and the like. Such debates amount to elaborations of pseudoproblems, failing to deal with the relations between information and energy. Is a radar pulse stronger than a quart of gasoline? The question is manifestly absurd, unless further specified—and so are the equivalent psychological and social questions. For ideas, moral norms, values, beliefs, and symbols represent information, not energy. The energy of human action, which comes from the biological organism, and the environmental energies that the organism draws upon and that human action may release, are controlled by information, by signals, by symbols (Vickers, 1968, Chapter 7). The main *cultural* controls of action consist of (1) systems of knowledge and cognitive beliefs, and (2) systems of values and norms (Parsons, 1959, pp. 612–711). Without *both* energy and information, there is no social behavior.

A value system is an organized set of preferential standards that are used in making selections of objects and actions, resolving conflicts, invoking social sanctions, and coping with needs or claims for social and psychological defenses of choices made or proposed. Values are components in the guidance of anticipatory and goal-directed behavior; but they are also backward-looking in their frequent service to justify or "explain" past conduct.

Criteria of evaluation are always interdependent with beliefs, which orient actors to the putative realities of their existence. Such beliefs about existential realities are not wholly "arbitrary," but they are surely open to a wide range of variation, within which they are not rigidly restrained by environmental imperatives. Actual selections of behavior result from concrete motivations in specific situations; both the motivations and the definitions of the situation are partly determined by the prior beliefs and values of the actor. A good illustration is provided by the relatively well-studied area of occupational choices. Such choices have been shown to be constrained by awareness of actual personal and environmental conditions, by values, and by beliefs about opportunities for value realization (Laws, 1976). In American society, for example, there are widely shared and somewhat stereotypic beliefs concerning occupations and employing organizations. There is some evidence that the image of the job in the large corporation is that of high pay, rapid advancement, and (somewhat less) a secure future, but of little initial responsibility or social recognition and of little development of lasting friendships (Braunstein & Haines, 1968). The preliminary testing on small samples so far reported show strongly patterned conceptions of the values prevailing in different types of organizations and occupations.

Valuations may refer to any existential objects whatsoever, including ideas and symbols as such. And social structures and processes may be affected by variations in those values held by social actors that concern nonsocial matters—physical objects, cultural objects, personalities as biopsychic entities, and so on. Not surprisingly, however, special importance for any analysis of social systems attaches to values which serve as criteria *for judging social systems themselves.*

The values which come to be constitutive of the structure of a societal system are, then, the conceptions of the desirable type of society held by the members of the society of reference and applied to the particular society of which they are members. The same applies to other types of social systems. A value *pattern* then defines a *direction* of *choice,* and consequent commitment to action. (Parsons, 1968, p. 136)

Thus, values constitute what Vickers (1968) calls "an appreciative system." The total set of affective–conceptual criteria for preferential behavior not only is essential to deal with the world, but is constitutive of any enduring society. Any society must change in its value constitution to cope with changing adaptative problems, yet it must retain some coherence in its appreciative system (based on some minimal consensus) or the social order will break down (Vickers, 1968, p. 35). As components of the black box of the human social actor, values may be said to be complex precodings for behavioral choice—precodings that also continually change in response to current inputs.

Thus, values operate as constituents of dynamic systems of social action because of their *interconnectedness,* their *informational* or *directive effects,* and their capacities to serve as *"carriers" of psychological energy.* Values always have a cultural content, represent a psychological investment, and are shaped by the constraints and opportunities of a social system and of a biophysical environment. Changes in values are constrained and limited both by the external "reality constraints" of the aforementioned interpenetrating systems and by the "internal" dimensions of consistency, congruence, or appropriateness among values and beliefs themselves.

When we can identify interconnected sets of values and beliefs which describe a preferred or "obligatory" state of a social system, we speak of an *ideology.* Actual concrete specifications of preferred conduct are *norms,* which in turn are referred to values for legitimation, for boundary-setting, for redefinition, and for linkage to other norms.

Because concrete social action necessarily occurs in particular situations, generalized value commitments can become effective in behavior only through quite precise interpretation and adaptation to enormously varied situations. It follows that continuous fidelity to the essential meaning of evaluative standards *requires* a basic commitment by the social actor—most commonly a particular person who has internalized the value as a basic component of his personality as well as of his social status or social *persona* (Parsons, 1968, p. 144).[2]

If these considerations are valid, a scientific approach to values must analyze the empirical weights of varying preferential precodings in relation to the immediate, fluid, ambiguous situations which are typically the

---

[2]Specifically, "the primary sanctions that back value-commitments must be internal to the responsible unit" (Parsons, 1968, p. 144).

settings for our behavior. There would seem to be no doubt that the value space of human life necessarily becomes filled with standards relating to all the significant types of objects of experience. Values, accordingly, are always mapped on to the physical world, the human organism, other organisms, the biopsychic personality, social actors and relationships, cultural items, and cosmic or transcendental realms. Accordingly, the specifically *social* value orientations are embedded in a much larger setting of value and may be interdependent with any of these other orientations.

In each main area of the total value space, many different dimensions (modes) of valuing may be developed. For the field of *social relations*, for example, the *criteria of desirability* may emphasize:

equality or *inequality;*
collectivity or *individual interest;*
acceptance or *rejection of authority;*
individual autonomy or *interdependence;*
expressiveness or *restraint* (affectivity/neutrality);
diffuseness or *specificity;*
ascribed qualities or *excellence of performance* (ascription/achievement);
particularistic relationships or *categorical memberships;*
personalized or *universalistic standards;*
hostility or *affection* or *indifference;*
dominance or *submission.*

A relatively few major value dimensions can constitute the organizing principles for thousands of specific beliefs and attitudes (Rokeach, 1968, 1973). For example, Bales and Couch (1969) have shown that a densely filled "value space" can be represented reasonably well by four orthogonal factors: (1) the extent of acceptance of authority, (2) need-determined expression or value-determined restraint, (3) acceptance or rejection of egalitarianism, and (4) extent of acceptance of individualism (pp. 3–17).

We know that values are learned. This means that they are developed through some kind of experience—of pain or pleasure, deprivation or gratification, goal attainment or frustration or failure, social approval or disapproval, love or hate. Even very short-term experiences may appreciably influence evaluations and beliefs concerning both concrete objects and abstract concepts (Breer & Locke, 1965). Similar repeated and pervasive experiences are often characteristic of large numbers of persons similarly situated in society; such experiences are described, discussed, and appraised by the persons involved. The communication of common appraisals eventually builds value standards, which often become widely accepted across many social and cultural boundaries (Inkeles, 1960; Lipset, 1963; Kohn, 1969; Williams, 1970, Chapter 11; Inkeles & Smith, 1974).

RELATIONSHIPS BETWEEN VALUES AND BEHAVIOR

Values make a difference; they are not epiphenomenal. With this assertion, we flatly reject all reductionist formulations that would by fiat rule out values as significant causes of behavior in advance of specific investigation of particular empirical problems.

Evidence that values do influence subsequent behavior is not available in the quantity and with the decisiveness we would prefer, but the total research-based data are nevertheless quite impressive. College students make occupational choices consistent with their values and change their occupational choices in directions consistent with their values as expressed at an earlier time (Goldsen, Rosenberg, Suchman, & Williams, 1960, Chapter 2; Rosenberg, 1957). Changes in vocational choices as recorded six years after a training program, followed closely changes in broad types of values, as indexed by the Allport–Vernon scale (Kemp, 1960, pp. 335–345). The rank ordering of "salvation" in a set of 12 values is highly predictive of church attendance (Rokeach, 1968, p. 169). Differences in values have been shown to be associated with significant differences in the following kinds of attitudes or behavioral outcomes:

1. speed of recognition of words presented by means of a tachistoscope. (Postman, Bruner, & McGinnies, 1948);
2. occupational-career choices (Goldsen, Rosenberg, Suchman, & Williams, 1960) and occupations actually followed (Strong, 1955; Rosenberg, 1957);
3. cheating on examinations (Henshel, 1969, 1971);
4. political attitudes and behavior (Wickert, 1940a, 1940b; Smith, 1949; Levine, 1960; Almond & Verba, 1963; Baum, 1968);
5. anti-Semitism (Evans, 1952);
6. juvenile delinquency (Clark & Wenninger, 1963; Lerman, 1968);
7. choice of friends (Williams, 1959; Beech, 1966);
8. frequency of religious participation (Rokeach, 1960);
9. participation in civil rights activities (Rokeach, 1973);
10. public interracial behavior (Rokeach, 1973).

Data indicating that values are consequential for behavior have come both from experimental studies (Breer & Locke, 1965; Rokeach, 1968, 1973) and from nonexperimental studies using the most diverse methods and settings (Caudill & Scarr, 1962; DeCharms & Moeller, 1962; Hamblin & Smith, 1965).

All major theories concerning the development of values through learning in early life suggest that the causal linkage between values and overt behavior should become tighter with increasing age. This result is predicted both because of the increasing scope and organization of moral cognitions and because of the greater integration of internalized values with patterns of motivation. In a carefully designed study, Henshel (1971) has confirmed the central hypothesis, showing that among schoolchildren the negative correlation between generalized honesty and number of cheating incidents increased sharply from the lower to the higher grades. (Further, at all age levels, fourth through seventh grades, adherence to honesty values as found by prior testing predicted to subsequent noncheating behavior.)

Values, our theoretical orientation would predict, should enter into motivation in two main ways: first, by defining the *gratifications* which establish and reinforce motives; second, by defining the *sources* of gratification. Conversely, a particular kind or type of motivation should affect behavior in different ways, depending upon the presence and the particular content of relevant values (Kohlberg, 1968, p. 484).

An analysis of the latter expectation is available for the case of the relation between achievement motivation (n Achievement) and occupational preferences. In a study of 394 entering freshman males at five two-year community centers of a state university, Lueptow found that scores on the McClelland test of n Achievement were essentially unrelated to occupational preferences. Yet n Achievement is positively related to a generalized goal of career accomplishment, whereas there is (as expected) no relationship to "extrinsic" goals of status success, security, or luxury. Therefore, "n Achievement appears to be related to 'career salience' but not to conscious intrinsic value-orientations" (Lueptow, 1968, p. 307). Students with high achievement motivation tend to prefer occupations with primary intrinsic rewards *only* when their value orientations define the occupation as a locus for intrinsic satisfaction. When occupational roles are defined in terms only of intrinsic gratifications, the tendency to choose intrinsic-satisfaction occupations is strong among students of high n Achievement. Therefore, it appears that the choice of occupation is affected by the motivational component only when there is present a mediating value standard which identifies the occupation as an appropriate avenue for expression and gratification of the need. The value orientation is essential, that is, in providing a basis for defining an appropriate goal-object (Lueptow, 1968, p. 311).

Although there are errors and inadequacies in some theories which have posited fixed stages of development of value orientations and moral judgments from early childhood to adulthood, there is evidence that some broadly invariant sequences do exist. Piaget seems to have formulated cross-culturally valid principles in pointing to the tendencies in young children to judge acts as wrong if they are punished, to judge consequences without regard to intentions, and to make absolute and total judgments of right and wrong. On the other hand, there is not a universal age-graded trend from obedience to authority toward peer-oriented egalitarian moral judgments. However, the general order of development is from premoral to conventional conformity to self-accepted principles (Kohlberg, 1968).

Of course, the particular norms to which an individual conforms may remain essentially unchanged throughout the individual's life course even while the relation of the rules to the metaorder of values changes greatly. Such changes appear to follow a fixed sequence from (1) requirements based on power and external consequences, to (2) those based on exchange and gratifications, to (3) those based on maintenance of legitimate expectations, to (4) those based on values, ideals, or logical principles of social organization. Value commitments become increasingly stabilized by systematic conceptualization.

But, obviously, neither conceptual clarity nor individual commitment are sufficient to guarantee particular behavioral outcomes. Only when norms or values are "activated" can they influence conduct, and activation requires some cognitive linkage between the normative component and other aspects of the behavior setting (Schwartz, 1968, p. 355). For example, when social disapproval is expected to result from a value-conforming action, anticipated public disclosure of the action will reduce the rate of conforming responses (Warner & DeFleur, 1969, p. 164). Similarly, when behavior in accordance with a particular value is costly to the individual (by requiring sacrifices in other values or interests), and especially when the individual cannot count on a compensatory future realization of the value, the sheer internalization of the value is not likely to be a sufficient condition for the requisite conforming behavior. As Firey has indicated in a study of the conservation of natural resources, two other conditions appear to be necessary—namely, the institutionalization of sanctions and the linkage of conformity to the welfare of individuals and collectivities to which the social actor is strongly attached (1963, esp. p. 152).

The importance of this proposition for a theory of values has been somewhat neglected by those sociological and psychological analyses which tacitly assume that values are not determinants of conduct unless they operate in an immediate, unmediated way directly through the motivation of the individual. But the causal influence of values is much more complex than that, although we certainly grant that under some conditions individuals do express their strongly internalized values—for example, "follow the dictates of conscience"—in the absence of either negative sanctions or social support. The more frequent pattern, however, is that specific norms which express the behavioral implications of a value become established and enforced through the actions of persons who reap advantages therefrom—or, at least, who do not incur excessive costs in so doing. Once the norms are effectively institutionalized, nearly everyone may conform because it is now "in their interest," even though few would have conformed in the absence of the superadded incentives of social sanctions and group attachments.

Values conceptualize needs and desires that can be represented to other persons as valid claims (Rokeach, Chapter 3); this means that values are conscious and capable of explicit statement, even when shaped to some degree by inchoate, unconscious, or socially condemned desires and needs. Accordingly, values are used socially to present claims, to evaluate other people, to evaluate oneself, to attack others, to gain revenge, to gain instrumental advantage. This means that we cannot safely underrate any value merely because it seems characterized by lip-service, or is more honored in the breach than in the observance, or is advocated primarily by hypocrites. For all these activities serve to maintain the value as valid currency or acknowledged benchmark—whereupon it can be used at any time to praise or blame, to honor or bring into disrepute. We must never lose sight of the fact that values are continually used as weapons in social struggles.

Once a given criterion has been learned and has become reinforced by vivid cues linking it to personally consequential rewards and punishments or deprivations, then, to a very large extent, the evaluation of particular objects of appraisal often becomes quasi-automatic or nonvoluntary. Persons being inducted into an academic profession, for example, learn the criteria of excellence in their field, learn that their futures depend upon being able to produce evidence of these qualities of excellence in their own attainments, and are exposed to persons who are vivid exemplars of the appropriate values. Given these conditions, it is difficult to imagine how an inductee could possibly withhold attributions of prestige or respect to a person who manifests the proper qualities—even though the object of appraisal might be intensely disliked on other grounds—for example, "he is an awful so-and-so—but he is a great physicist." Indeed, Hamblin and Smith (1965) have reported that professional status imputed to professors increased with attributed merit of publication, merit of teaching, "negative cordiality" (maintaining social distance), and length of service or experience in the discipline; the increase corresponded to a multiple-stimulus power function, $(R - {}_c S_1{}^{n1} S_2{}^{n2} \ldots S_i{}^{ni})$, and accounted for an extraordinary 98 percent of the variance.[3] The authors propose:

> Genuine status-giving is problematic because having feelings of approval, respect, or esteem for someone appears to be beyond the individual's direct choice. (Hamblin & Smith, 1965, p. 184)

The sheer correlation of values with beliefs, opinions, attitudes, and other observed behavior shows only that there is a structure, a nonrandom patterning. To be able to infer causal sequences from values to other items, we need some evidence that the value or value system was present prior to or simultaneously with the explicandum, that its presence is associated with a heightened frequency of the phenomena to be

---

[3]Efforts should be made in other research to replicate this well nigh unprecedented result.

explained, and that there is a theoretically compelling connection. Varying degrees of "strong inference" are, of course, to be expected.

A consistent and plausible pattern of findings, analyzed by Kohn (1969), suggests that child-rearing practices derive in part from parental values, and that these parental values are substantially a joint result of social class and of class-linked characteristics of particular types of occupations. Analysis of data from a national (U.S.) survey indicates that social class is the most important single variable accounting for differences in patterns of values. Among the components of "class," education is the most important, followed by occupation; income adds little to the predictions of values from education and occupation. The relationships of these variables to values are continuous, linear, and additive. The study finds no evidence that disparities between education, occupational level, and income have any important effect upon values (Kohn, 1969, Chapter 8).

The relations between occupations and values have been explored in several other significant ways. There are consistent and marked differences between educational and occupational levels of the American population in the criteria of desirability invoked in judging the "ideal" and "worst" features of occupations. Emphasized by persons of lower education and occupational position are security, fringe benefits, physical conditions, and nature of supervision. Mentioned more frequently at the higher levels are self-expression and development, creativity, active personal relationships, worthwhileness of work, challenge, and opportunity for personal achievement (Kilpatrick, Cummings, & Jennings, 1964, pp. 82–83).

If nonmonetary values were to play no part at all in the selection of an occupation, the proportion of persons freely choosing an occupation, of course, would be a linear function of anticipated earnings. However, if nonmonetary elements do enter into selections, the tradeoff curve between income and other criteria of occupational desirability is not likely to be linear. Specifically, there are likely to be some occupations which most individuals would reject even were the income extremely high (e.g., executioner, prostitute), because of social stigma, danger, disagreeableness, or moral repulsion. At the other extreme, some occupations may be so desirable in terms of prestige, freedom, pleasure, opportunity for creativity, and other nonmonetary rewards that they frequently will be chosen even though low paying. Over a wide intermediate zone, the nonincome rewards may be "psychologically equivalent," that is, choice will be essentially responsive to expected income (Braunstein & Haines, 1968, p. 381).

A comparison of academicians and nonacademicians by major fields of specialization showed that, even though persons in academic employment were *more* highly trained and worked as many hours as their nonacademic counterparts, they generally earned less. Persons who have foregone the higher incomes in business and industry in order to stay in academia emphasize "professional" values in their work; others emphasize "acquisitive" values; furthermore, there is a positive correlation between level of education and emphasis on the professional values of originality, independence, and freedom. Analysis of specific types of work activities shows that those of high academic emphasis are associated with low income. It is concluded that nonmonetary values actually do constitute a tradeoff with money income for the choice between academic and nonacademic employment (Marsh & Stafford, 1967, pp. 740-754).

A beginning has been made in the empirical study of courses and consequences of differences in value consensus in specified settings (cf. references in Williams, 1971). Illustrative of findings and hypotheses are the following reported by Bowers (1968): Among American college students (a sample of 5,422 persons at 99 colleges and universities), (1) the likelihood that an individual will violate a norm of behavior is lower in those colleges where group disapproval is frequent, independently of the person's own sense of approval or disapproval; (2) the seeming effect of the group disapproval is greatest for individuals who themselves do *not* disapprove of norm violations; (3) the contextual effect does not appear, on the average, until the proportion strongly disapproving reaches a level between 40 and 60 percent; (4) the most pronounced drop in norm violation among individuals who do *not* personally disapprove appears only when as many as 80 percent of their fellows strongly disapprove. Thus, the individual behavioral correlates of consensus seem to depend upon both the individual's own attitude toward the group and the extent of consensus in the local social environment.

Without citing the many other relevant studies, we believe that enough material has been presented to show that under appropriate conditions values are important determinants of social behavior. But it would be well nigh incredible were values, that is, *generalized* criteria of desirability, to predict such behavior precisely and regularly in all its delicate responsiveness to specific situations. If we could simply "deduce" such behavior by deontic logic from the *a priori* relevant values, it would follow that we would be dealing either with a world of "fanatics" and "psychotics" or else with a set of astonishingly simple and nonresistant situational realities. In a world of continually varying realistic exigencies and of multiple values, only a maniac or a saint will always act "consistently" in terms of a (1) simple, (2) prearranged, (3) hierarchy of (4) fixed desiderata.

In short, to hypothesize an influence of values upon social behavior under specified conditions is not to make the absurd claim that all behavior is merely an expression of values and has no other determinants.

Any suggestion that value theory implies such a naive emanationist view must be rejected as grossly incorrect.

The *anchoring effects* of value systems can rarely be seen by analyses that are restricted to a particular local culture or set of processes—for the local ecological, demographic, technological, and social–structural factors *already will have been "saturated" with numerous effects from prior social actions which themselves had been partly determined by value components.* To detect these cumulative–diffuse effects, *comparative* analyses are required. On the basis of a single society (or type of society) one may find, for example, that rules of kinship, marriage, and affinity seem rather clearly to derive from systems of land tenure and property. But comparisons with other societies may then show that similar effects can be correlated with equally stable and definite features of values as embodied in law and rules of morality (Wijeyeswardene, 1966). Thus, the "material" relations to the means of production are not independent of prior value patterns.

This basic point is also illustrated in the historical hypothesis that the antislavery movement's unity on behalf of black equality disintegrated in the 1870s, not merely because of the formal abolition of slavery, but because black equality was one among many values. Prior to 1860, other strongly held values of the antislavery proponents had not been in conflict with the preeminent position given to black equality; during the War, and increasingly thereafter, other values did come into opposition or contradiction. By 1877, many of the advocates of black equality were ready to acquiesce in the withdrawal of federal troops from the South—not merely "on grounds of expediency," but because other high-ranking values were at stake (Carroll, 1969).

And Hammond (1974) has presented data that strongly support the proposition that certain nineteenth-century revival movements definitely increased political support for abolitionist parties in Ohio.

Value analysis in studies of social change can help to protect us from a mistaken readiness to attribute complex historical sequences to a few simple and sovereign causes. Thus in the United States, the history of relationships of black and white people, which in the 1930s and 1940s was often so simply explained as "economic exploitation," was in the 1960s even more simply explained as due to something called "white racism." Such overly simple formulations, so detrimental to accurate diagnosis, can be avoided by historical value analysis, which shows that the controversies over slavery are inexplicable without reference to exceedingly complex and deep interrelations and incompatibilities of beliefs and values. As David Brion Davis says:

> Slavery, of course, was an economic institution closely tied to various social and political structures. . . . Yet the fact remains that it was a shift in value orientations that made possible the first organized protests against the in-

stitution . . . the very act of questioning brought deep conflicts to the surface and opened fissures in the prevailing ideologies . . . . Abolitionism furnished a new basis for social organization and a new means for simplifying and socializing individual moral perceptions. (1968, p. 706; cf. Davis, 1966)

The nonobvious implications of sociological analyses of values are further illustrated by the proposition that opposition of interests and struggles among individuals and collectivities within a continuing polity and societal system actually can contribute to the establishment and elaboration of generalized values and symbols. In such contentions, each party will appeal to those values that are presumably accepted by third parties to legitimate its position and to attempt to recruit support or to disarm potential opposition. If successive contests and conflicts are then successfully resolved *without repudiation of the values which legitimate the conflict-resolving process or mechanisms,* the more highly generalized values will come more and more to be regarded as axiomatic or unchallengeable. Although the specific social implications of the general value principle will be changed through successive occasions, nevertheless, all parties come to have a stake in maintaining the complex value referent as a resource for the future.

VALUES AND SOCIAL CHANGE IN AMERICAN SOCIETY

With these illustrative materials in mind, let us now turn to a more systematic review of value patterns in the United States.

The Mid-century Inventory

In repeated earlier analyses (1951, 1960, 1970) we drew upon a large and diverse body of data from historical, economic, political, and sociological studies to describe some 15 major themes of value–belief orientations that have long been salient in American society. The list is as follows:

1. Activity and work
2. Achievement and success
3. Moral orientation
4. Humanitarianism
5. Efficiency and practicality
6. Science and secular rationality
7. Material comfort
8. Progress
9. Equality

10. Freedom
11. Democracy
12. External conformity
13. Nationalism and patriotism
14. Individual personality
15. Racism and related group superiority

Taken as a total set, these complex orientations imbue the culture as a whole with the tendency to emphasize active mastery rather than passive acceptance of events, an external rather than an inward view of the world; an outlook that perceives society and history as open-ended, not static, a faith in rationalism as opposed to traditionalism; an interest in orderliness; a universalistic rather than a particularistic social ethic; horizontal or egalitarian rather than hierarchical social relationships; a high evaluation of individual personality rather than collective identity and responsibility; and an exceedingly strong emphasis on an expansive instrumental society rather than one devoted to consummatory or expressive activities and experiences.

Modes of Change in Values and Beliefs

Among the ways in which values and beliefs can change, the following are noteworthy:

1. *Creation.* A new standard or belief is developed out of experience and becomes effective, at some level, in regulating behavior.

2. *Abrupt destruction.* There are some instances in which a massive event results in the relatively sudden disappearance of previously accepted orientations. But this is an extremely rare outcome. What may appear to be an abrupt rejection of a hitherto prevailing value or set of values usually turns out upon closer inspection to have been preceded by long-term diminution in strength of commitment and by a gradual withdrawal of attention and effort. To be maintained, values require "investment"—of time, attention, effort, affect. Unless "exercised," values atrophy.

3. *Attenuation.* Relatively slow withdrawal of affect and commitment; intensity diminishes; fewer and fewer persons will promote, support, teach, or defend the belief or value orientation.

4. *Extension.* Application of the orientation to objects and events in addition to those included in the original sphere of relevance.

5. *Elaboration.* The value or belief is progressively rationalized, symbolized, dramatized, documented, and otherwise made more complex or more embedded in its sociocultural context.

6. *Specification.* A generalized orientation increasingly is defined in terms of the particular contexts in which it is considered applicable, as

when compulsory school attendance, military conscription, and compulsory vaccination come to be defined as compatible with freedom, or equality is redefined as (competitive) equality of opportunity.

7. *Limitation.* Through confronting *other* values, any given value position necessarily comes to be altered. Although the change may be in the direction of rigid absolution, a more frequent outcome is that the challenged value comes to be bounded or limited by the recognized claims of other values. In this way, for instance, American democratic philosophies and practices have always been obliged to accommodate a persisting strain between *freedom* and *equality:* each is necessary for the other, but neither can be pushed to extremes without negating its companion.

8. *Explication.* In the form of folk virtues, values are typically implicit. At the opposite extreme, highly detailed explicit values are stated in creedal or philosophical systems. American society has long been characterized by a vast proliferation of explicit value statements. The last half century seems to have brought increasingly explicit articulation of major values—partly a result of rapid changes in norms and by direct challenges, including the rise and spread of totalitarian political movements as well as internal social conflicts.

9. *Consistency.* It comes as no surprise that two sharply opposed diagnoses are with us: (a) American values are becoming more consistent; (b) American values are becoming less consistent. Our suggestion is that neither global generalization is warranted. Greater systematic explicitness at the level of national political assertions and mass media creeds almost certainly implies "contradiction," "inconsistency," and "hypocrisy" when viewed against the daily realities of behavior in particular localities. And the structural separation of collectivities and groups permits the coexistence of many incompatible values within the same political and economic order.

10. *Intensity (absolutism).* A value formerly accepted as one among many *desiderata* may become so intensely held and promoted as to become the center of life. A value formerly the focus of all other criteria may lose its central intellectual and emotional *raison d'être,* become relativized, and recede into the ranks of the ordinary criteria of daily life.

The above outline presents *types* of changes. But how do these changes occur? What are the conditions for stability or change? In the space available here we can illustrate only a few of the dynamics.

Both stability and change in values and value systems are affected by the interaction between the degree of consensus in the relevant social collectivity and the intrinsic characteristics of the values themselves. Thus, a hypothesis consistent with much evidence is that the more frequently a given value is opposed or challenged, the more elaborate (numerous, varied, and interrelated) will be the beliefs and symbols connected with the value (Rokeach, 1968, p. 21).

The greatest change in a total matrix of values should be induced whenever two or more "central" and "terminal" values are brought into relations of inconsistency or incongruity of some kind. Three main ways in which such incongruity is brought about are:

1. persons are induced to behave in a manner incompatible with their values;

2. persons are exposed to new information, including evaluations, from significant others that is inconsistent with one or more central values; and

3. persons are exposed to information about inconsistencies already present among their values (Rokeach, 1968, p. 167).

Elsewhere in this volume, the detailed results of studies are presented demonstrating the strong change-inducing effects of revealing to individuals how certain of their values, attitudes, and behaviors are incongruent with their positively valued self-conception. Parallel studies are needed to show the effects of importance, centrality, connectedness, and consistency in value patterns of social collectivities.

It is reasonable to accept the three major assumptions concerning beliefs (and, in our terms, values) suggested by Rokeach: (1) different values have differing degrees of importance to any given individual; (2) resistance to change is strongest for beliefs and values that are most important ("central"); (3) if a particular value or belief is changed, the more central it is, the more numerous will be changes in other beliefs and values. We might suppose, for instance, that it is differences or similarities in the more important values and beliefs that will have the greatest effect upon relationships among individuals or collectivities, for example, of different ethnic categories. But careful attention will need to be given to such other dimensions as intensity of commitments, structural location of value carriers, networks of communication, and other system characteristics (Williams, 1970, chapters 13–15).

Clearly, predictions of any changes resulting from incompatibilities, dissonance, or incongruities will depend upon some estimate of the *relative* weights of *relevant* differences in (1) cognitive beliefs, (2) values, (3) positive or negative cathexis of persons, (4) positive or negative evaluation of reference individuals or groups, and (5) instrumental interests. Thus, a very strong value congruity might be determinative of a friendship, even when many of the cognitive beliefs are dissonant, or a strong cathexis may override sharp differences in instrumental interests.

Values especially resistant to change at the individual level seem to involve psychologically *"primitive"* beliefs for a high proportion of social

actors, and are highly *interconnected* with other values for a high proportion of the individuals who endorse them. In the social system, change-
resistant values are high in *centrality, pervasive,* and supported by powerful *sanctions* and high *consensus;* supporters of these values hold positions
of high *prestige* and authority. In the cultural system, the most resistant
values are *congruent* with many other values and beliefs, and are *symbolized* in many different ways. Values having these 10 characteristics will
be strongly sanctioned and actively defended and promoted.

We have said that values emerge from learning; hence, by implication, they are generalized from experience. It follows that substantial
and long-continued shifts in the conditions of social life will produce
changes in the ordering, arrangement, intensity, and so on of values.
Ascetic–instrumental values are subject to attenuation under conditions
of great affluence and security. The value of *freedom* tends to diminish in
rank and intensity of commitment under conditions of great economic
and political insecurity. *Equality* diminishes in attractiveness among the
winners in competitive activities. Achievement is likely to be stressed
among populations experiencing high levels of richly rewarded opportunities for individual attainment. And so on.

Two major qualifications must be added to this thesis of the long-run
responsiveness of values to behavioral reinforcements and changed
realities of adaptation and goal attainment. First, change is slowed by the
processes of conformity within established social orders and by the numerous interdependencies within a complex value–belief system. Second, the generalized character of values permits a great amount of rein-
terpretation before drastic change has to occur in the legitimizing value
commitments. Thus, we should not be too surprised to find that many
local communities show considerable persistence in value patterns over
long periods (Du Wors, 1952), and that a list of the most prominent
values in the United States has changed little over a span of two cen-
turies.

Evidence Concerning Changes

Let us, then, review a few sets of data illustrating stability and change
in values and beliefs.

At the most generalized level, it seems correct to say that during the
twentieth century no completely new major value orientations have appeared, nor have any main values completely disappeared (Lipset,
1963). On the one hand, the most important changes have been changes
in beliefs and, on the other, changes in emphasis, accent, and arrangement of values. Yet these changes are filled with consequences for
human experience and the direction of societal development. On this
ground, we are reassured that we may legitimately deal with real and

important changes in both beliefs and values (Kluckhohn, 1958). In the long run, values are responsive to changes in social experience; change in values can result from changes in information about oneself and one's social environment. Even within an interval as short as three years, the relative ranking of certain values—e.g., *equality*—changed appreciably in a national sample of American adults (Rokeach, 1974a, p. 235).

In Charles Morris' "Ways of Life" inventory of values and beliefs, way number 7 is a flexible multivalued approach to living. It is the single way of life most often chosen by samples of respondents in the United States. A comparison of responses in 1950 and in 1970 showed very little change (Morris, 1956).

Samples of persons in various occupations have been tested with the Strong Vocational Interest Blank at various times from the 1930s to the present. For persons in the same occupations, those tested in the 1930s were quite similar in measured interests to comparable samples studied in the 1960s (Campbell, 1971, p. 325). However, the mean cultural change scores increased from 1925 to the 1960s (p. 332), suggesting a general trend toward lesser stability. Also, for both men and women, the changes have been toward "extroverted, outgoing, people-oriented activities" (p. 337).

Evidence of both long-term and recent decreases in the frequency or salience of achievement comes from studies that have used quite diverse sets of data. Imagery in children's readers, examined by DeCharms and Moeller (1962) for the period 1800–1950, shows a rapid and continuous decrease from about 1890 to 1950. Other scattered studies of cultural products consistently suggest a long-term decline in expressed achievement values. Analysis of a random sample of editorials in the *National 4-H Club News* from 1924 to 1958 showed a significant decline in emphasis on the values of achievement (and no significant change in *affiliation* or *cooperation* values) (Straus & Houghton, 1960). Similar results were found in an analysis of advertising in the *Ladies Home Journal* from 1890 to 1956 (Dornbusch & Hickman, 1959). Magazine fiction and mass heroes (e.g., entertainers) also show indications of lessened stress on excellence of achievement and more on the rewards of being successful.

Our own impression from all the bits and pieces of information that are available is that "achievement" has receded in salience and intensity in relation to "success," but that the change is a shift in emphasis rather than a reversal of values and that achievement remains an outstanding value orientation.

Lessened veneration of efficiency and practicality has developed, along with disillusionment concerning both the inevitability and desirability of progress in the traditional sense.

Wright and Wright (1976) conclude that between 1964 and 1973 (the dates of two NORC surveys that provide basic data), there were substantial changes in value orientations of parents for children—most clearly a decrease for "obedience" (down 10 percentage points) and "acts like a boy or girl" (5 points). Second, the later analysis confirms Kohn's earlier finding (1969) that social class (indexed by education and occupation) is the single most important factor accounting for differences among parents in self-direction values (Kohn, 1976). Substantial amounts of variance in self-direction (about three-fifths) remain when class is controlled; the factors of city size and region, ethnicity and religious background remain substantially correlated with differences in self-direction.

The tremendous growth in scientific activity over the last hundred years has entailed the spread of scientific values more and more widely through the social system (Merton, 1957). The emphasis upon applied science and technology has strengthened and extended the theme of instrumental activism in nearly every area of human interests, eventually including society and social man himself. In the systematic pursuit of empirical validity, science has produced highly desired by-products in mastery of the physical environment, with greater material comfort, progress in the conquest of diseases, and increases in social power. At the same time, there is inevitably resistance and value incompatibility. Life-saving discoveries appear side by side with environmental pollution, population explosions, and nuclear, chemical, and biological weapons. Economic growth through technology has undesired side effects. And the scientific modes of thought are often felt to threaten cherished beliefs and values.

Many bits of evidence point to a process of secularization of certain aspects of religious beliefs, values, and practices. For instance, Barnett has traced the way in which Easter came to be treated in the popular press as a commercial opportunity rather than as a sacred occasion (Barnett, 1949). A study of the changing content of hymns over the century beginning in 1835 showed a marked decrease in transcendental and supernatural topics and references and a marked increase in social and ethical content (Crawford, 1938). Many topics formerly defined and discussed in a religious context have come under the sway of scientists and other professionalized secular agents.

With many reservations and qualifications, we can say that religiously connected beliefs and values have, over the last half century, moved from personal salvation to social ethics, from a concern with the supernatural order and the afterlife to a greater interest in the pressing problems and sufferings of the here and now,[4] from sacramental and ritualistic activities to social service and involvement in the great domestic and

---

[4]As one small illustration, Crawford (1938) found that hymns dealing with sin, salvation, evangelism, death, and judgment were 44 percent of the Methodist hymnal in 1836 but had declined to 12 percent by 1935.

international issues of the times. Personal fulfillment in devotion and service is more often emphasized, and asceticism, sacrifice, and impersonal duty is less often stressed.

An obviously central part of American value orientations are bound together in a distinctive moral orientation, including the idea of obligatory moral principles that transcend expediency and apply to everyone. Because moral principles of this kind run counter to very strong interests, impulses, and *other* values, the record shows much deviant behavior and violation. In our judgment, there has been some decrease in the binding power of such "absolute" values as "honesty," but a probable increase in the effective implementation of humanitarian values. The prevailing ethic in personal relations is perhaps less stern and rigid, and possibly more kindly, than previously. "Moral teaching," in the sample of children's readers studied by DeCharms and Moeller (1962), declined from 1830 onward, and had practically disappeared by 1950, the last year analyzed. A tendency to move from a punitive–moralistic to a humanitarian–medical approach is prominent in many areas—for example, the evaluation and treatment of mental illness (Woodward, 1951).

A general movement to apply universalistic criteria and to accept humanitarian values seems evident in public policies toward ethnic and racial minorities, poor people, the physically disabled, children, women workers, and others subject to special stresses, disabilities, and discrimination (Rooney, 1973; Rodham, 1973; Erskine & Siegel, 1975). Such sensitivity does not seem marked, on the other hand, with regard to enemies in war, or to those who dissent radically from prevailing beliefs. The complexity of relationships between humanitarianism and other values can be appreciated only by close inspection of concrete issues. A remarkable example is the case of blood donations. Surveying the high cost and unequal distribution of health services in the United States, Titmuss (1971) concludes that the commercialization of blood and donor relationships represents the crucial example that shows the society to be inhumane. Comparison with Great Britain, where blood is donated, not sold, is said to show greater efficiency and far more disinterested humanitarian concern in the British case. Titmuss puts the appraisal bluntly:

> The commercialization of blood and donor relationships represses the expression of altruism, erodes the sense of community, lowers scientific standards, limits both personal and professional freedoms, sanctions the making of profits in hospitals and clinical laboratories, legalizes hostility between doctor and patient, subjects critical areas of medicine to the laws of the marketplace, places immense social costs on those least able to bear them— the poor, the sick, and the inept—increases the danger of unethical behavior in various sectors of medical science and practice, and results in situations in

which proportionately more blood is supplied by the poor, the unskilled, the unemployed, Negroes and other low income groups and categories of exploited human populations of high blood yielders. (1971, p. 245)

On the whole, although the evidences are fragmentary and sometimes contradictory, it seems that the value of *equality of opportunity* has received increased attention and implementation during the last generation. There has not been a steady or continuous movement, but two great periods of change, that is, the early New Deal and the developments associated with the civil rights movement of the 1950s and 1960s (Williams, 1973). At the level of national law and administrative policy there has been substantial movement toward establishing equality of political and civil rights for segments of the population formerly subject to discrimination and disadvantage—women, the propertyless, blacks, aliens, unpopular religious sects, and so on. To this extent, a universalistic ethic has become more firmly institutionalized. On the other hand, there has been no actual increase in substantive economic equality of income or wealth.

Decreases in racism and in militant expansionist nationalism have been evident and large.

The changes in the values of *freedom* and *democracy* have been so varied as to preclude any adequate brief summarization. Both remain strong at the level of generalized creeds—as does the value of *individual personality*—but are severely strained by organizational centralization and the categorical and impersonal character of much of national life.

For fuller discussion, we must refer readers to chapters 11 to 15 of *American Society* (Williams, 1970).

Below is a modified summary taken from that work (p. 636).

Although appraisals of this kind have only suggestive value—because of their highly aggregated character and because of the gaps and inadequacies in the data—the broad directions of change do seem well attested. The main features of change certainly include an increased emphasis upon expressive and consummatory values, relative to both absolute–transcendental values and to instrumental activism. At the same time, changes in the cognitive aspects of valuations seem to have produced a greater emphasis on the empirical consequences of values, for example, the questioning of the "growth ethic," and more favorable attitudes toward legalized abortion. A parallel development is lessened emphasis on sheer doctrinal consistency or upon the rigid adherence to value-based rules. In a broad sense, accordingly, there has been a relativizing of rules in favor of evaluations that represent *judgments*—not merely rule-following behavior—that take into account multiple values and the particular circumstances of varying situations. Implied by these changes is lessened emphasis upon any one fixed hierarchical ordering of values which is regarded as obligatory under all circumstances.

TABLE 2.1. Impressionistic Estimates of Major Changes

VALUE–BELIEF COMPLEXES	DIRECTIONS OF CHANGE— PERIOD (APPROXIMATE)*	
	1900–1945	*1945–1976*
Activity	Indeterminate	−
Work	−	−
Achievement	−	+
		(post–Sputnik I); after 1965
Success	+	+
Material comfort	+	+
Humanitarianism (domestic)	+	+
Humanitarianism (war)	+	−
"Absolute" moral orientation	−	Indeterminate
Practicality	+	−
Efficiency	+	−
Science and secular rationality	+	Indeterminate
Progress	+	−
Freedom	Indeterminate	−
Equality	+	+
Democracy	+	Indeterminate
Conformity (to social pressure)	+	+
Individual personality	+	Indeterminate
Nationalism	+	−
Racism—group superiority	−	−
Totals		
Increase	13	6
No change or indeterminate	2	4
Decrease	4	9

*(−) is decrease; (+) is increase.

A necessary note of caution must be added: (1) the changes sketched are net statistical tendencies, and numerous counterchanges coexist; (2) resistance to the changes is strong in some important segments of the society; (3) conditions of massive social threat and deprivation, as in a major war or depression, would reverse many of the recent trends, encouraging greater absolutism and authoritarianism.

PROBLEMS OF VALUE CHANGE IN MODERN SOCIETY

Values which at the same time are isolated or compartmentalized within the individual's psychological system and are held by persons scattered more or less randomly across the units of a social system should be most accessible to change through mass communication. Induced changes in such values, however, would be expected to have minimal structural consequences in the social system.

Prediction of short-run social changes from knowledge of values will require accurate mapping of patterns of values and beliefs onto specific statuses (Neal, 1965) and collectivities (Hyman, 1953; Rosen, 1959; Rodman, 1963; Rokeach, 1973). Only through linking values to specific social positions and changes therein will it be possible to identify points of tension and the size and power of consensual and dissenting components of the society.

A differentiated society necessarily has a complex set of specifications of its main values (Parsons, 1968, p. 147); furthermore, rapid social change continually brings unpredicted effects. Complex specificity together with unanticipated changes necessarily generate numerous new problematic relations between the generalized value system and the "operating" values and norms applicable to specific practical situations. Tendencies then arise, on the one hand, toward alienated criticism of alleged hypocrisy and cynicism, and, on the other hand, toward absolutistic or fundamentalistic reassertion of the generalized values and of their *identification* with the concrete values to which the advocates are committed. If these tendencies are empirically important, as they seem to be, the stability of complex societies may depend strongly upon (1) continuous and rapid respecification of generalized values, (2) ability to frequently create new formulations of generalized values, and (3) insulation of absolutistic reactions in the form of nonpolitical activities.

High levels of structural differentiation, if successfully stabilized, produce *generalized and explicit* values. The more pronounced the process of generalization, the greater will be the number of different types of specific value content and of levels of concreteness or generality that must be legitimized by reference to the master generalized values. But the larger the number and the more diverse the connections between concrete, particular values and generalized standards, the more points at which value absolutism may challenge the legitimacy of existing social arrangements as "hypocritical" or "decadent" and call for a return to absolute and concrete commitments. In another direction, the legitimacy of the prevailing value system as a whole is challenged in the name of a revolutionary change. The third possibility is the integrative process of institutionalizing new generalized values which resolve the primary oppositions and conflicts. The crucial empirical problems are to specify the combinations of conditions which determine the relative importance of the three main outcomes—that is, *fundamentalistic regression, schismatic revolutionary outcomes,* or *institutionalization of new integrative value-generalizations* (Parsons, 1968, p. 159).

Systems of social stratification, insofar as they are systems of *ranking* rather than merely factual orders of distribution of scarce values, involve consensus on values; and changes in such consensus will lead to changes in the structure of the system (Berreman, 1968). Any *sectioning* of a society by limits upon social interaction results, in the long run, in the growth of cultural differences. When the closure of interaction runs along lines of social stratification, the growth of such cultural divergence always contains potentialities for social change.

If there are marked divergencies and incompatibilities of values and beliefs concerning criteria of distribution and ranking, as among the main strata of an inegalitarian system, any marked change in economic position or political power among the strata or ranked groupings will produce conflict and widespread challenges to the authority of the upper strata (Williams, 1975a, 1975b).

There does not appear to be available as yet a firm, empirically based theory which would permit us to predict *in general* that values change "more slowly than" norms or social structures. However, there does seem to be agreement among most analysts of social values that the values which *legitimate and provide generalized direction* for *particular* institutions generally change only after the structure or the functioning of the institutions has changed. Although this proposition is highly general (and has not been tested by systematic attempts to falsify it in a series of concrete instances), it is illustrated by enough historical cases to show that the sequence frequently does occur.

An important form of long-term change is the case in which conviction and commitment is gradually withdrawn from an institutionalized set of beliefs, values, and symbols. Eventually, individuals no longer engage in the practices and social relationships which formerly expressed the set, and they no longer assent to the explicit beliefs and values. Still, even individuals who have thus withdrawn from the specific content will, if originally socialized in the institutional complex, often and perhaps typically retain a set of implicit and unacknowledged beliefs and values consonant with its major assumptions—for example, avowedly secularized persons who continue to react to success, achievement, and enjoyment as "gifts" and to express gratitude for good things and for the avoidance of disaster. In short, they still "thank God" long after specific myths and symbols of traditional religion have been avowedly discarded.

Because moral values—by definition—stand near the top of the hierarchy of "cybernetic" cultural controls, and because their control operates only through internalization and the commitment of the individual personality, innovations of moral values as such or major changes in their social applications have quite special characteristics. For one thing, change at this level will involve especially strong psychological tensions and ambivalences. Advocates of change are likely to retain some attachments to the older values that they are striving to displace; in reaction, they are likely to exaggerate the "absoluteness" of the change. In the same way, defenders of the threatened values are likely to emphasize the threat as total. These psychological processes are stimulated and then accentuated by social processes of polarization. Were only these components operative, moral value innovation would always result either in severe social conflict or in quick extinction of the incipient change. The severe conflict would ensue when there is substantial, even if latent, continuity between the new and the old value positions, and when both are held by large numbers of strongly committed and socially powerful members of the society. Quick extinction, on the other hand, would result if there were essentially *no* continuity between new and old values, so that the innovators *must* initially constitute a very small and highly aberrant, repulsive, and dangerous element of the collectivity (Parsons, 1968, p. 157).

Social movements which stress value absolutism counter to some aspects of the established system tend to generate processes of social dedifferentiation. Given a commitment to a highly rigid set of values, the range of social statuses and activities that are clearly legitimate tends to narrow; at the same time, the value absolutism eventually favors centralized leadership and control. The commitment to the value innovation tends to displace or reduce other value commitments and to preempt a large proportion of resources (time, energy, money, skills, "social credit") of the members or adherents. If the struggle is very intense, the members may repudiate family obligations and normal work, rejecting orderly procedures, rational processes, search for empirical knowledge, long-term prudence, and so on. A single-valued ethic of sentiment tends to take precedence over a multivalued ethic of consequences (Parsons, 1968, p. 157).

The fluctuation between a pluralistic and a monolithic emphasis can occur in any part of a society's value system. Thus, when the theme of instrumental activism in the United States has been controlled and moderated within an integrated system of moral and political values, it has served to support and implement many expressive and socially integrative values. But instrumental activism has at times, among some elements of the society, become an intense central preoccupation, largely divorced from control by other values. Then it changes qualitatively into a *different* world view, becoming an overriding or ultimate value, and a transformation occurs: the theme becomes one of *acquisition* and *omnipotence*. In terms of acquisition, it becomes a final goal to have all we want, whatever we want, whenever we want.

> Existentially, we may describe it as never accepting the fact that we must die and that we have only what we have, right here and right now. It is not only that we want, we want supremely and absolutely. There is always something out there to reach for with the promise that this time it will be what we really

wanted.... We believe it and make ourselves miserable in the impossible quest for fulfillment. (Brogadir, 1967, p. 1996)

Any value orientation accepted as one among many values in a culture will, if pressed to extreme limits, disregarding other values, produce unexpected and undesired implications and consequences.

EXAMPLE 1:
Who does not want freedom?
Who does not believe in some aspects of equality of human rights?
But what happens if we demand instant and total freedom, or instant and total equality? Total freedom is chaos, and the end result always is a dictatorial order. Total substantive equality requires a tight system of social control.
EXAMPLE 2:
Strongly oriented as it is to social mobility, activity, individual achievement, and the future, American society could not fail to place a high value on youth as a life stage and upon young people as "the hope of the future." A society which has so greatly emphasized progress and which has developed a cult-like stress upon being up to date provides a setting especially favorable to efforts to define the beliefs, values, goals, and norms of the adult generation as anachronisms, mere survivals of an outmoded past.

As these examples suggest, the fusion of conceptual and affective elements is a distinctive mark of value phenomena, in contrast to sheer matters of belief. But it is the direct fusion of *cognitive–conceptual* with *imperative* elements that is even more striking. Given some concepts of preferred states, the most important act of evaluation is to identify and define the relevant entities: for example, "fetal tissue" versus a "living fetus" versus "a baby," or juvenile delinquent versus "criminal," or "murder" versus "nonnegligent manslaughter," or "democratic centralism" versus "totalitarian dictatorship."

As we observe the extremely rapid and widespread shifts in attitudes and opinions in American society since the end of World War II one crucial implication seems unmistakable, although it is often ignored. What are often called major changes in values (Yankelovich, 1974), when attention is restricted to the short run, are typically *not* changes in the criteria of desirability or even in the ordering of preferability of abstract valued states (such as kindness or cruelty, freedom or equality, justice or love). Rather, the change may *consist* of a change in the cognitive–conceptual components of valuing—a redefinition of what exists, what can exist, what causes what, what are the concomitants of desired actions, and the like.

Once one is sensitized to the possible significance of classificatory assumptions in directing value judgments, illustrations of the most diverse kinds are easily found at every hand. The author's own prolonged observations of federal budgeting, appropriations and expenditures for social research and development, suggest that the *initial categorization* of budget items is one of the most important types of political action in Washington, D.C., today. Thus a line of government action that Congress has judged to be too politically hazardous to fund as a separate program may be "tucked in" under a series of "demonstration projects," or the enemies of an educational program may insure its death by combining severe underfunding with massive requirements for evaluative research on outcomes. A similar political metaphysics of naming appears prominently in controversies concerning conservation, ecological protection, and a great variety of regulatory activities mandated to serve the public interest.

In controversies concerning major environmental decisions, it has been observed that "contrary to what one might naively expect, the existence of disparate (e.g., contradictory) analyses does not help to resolve the debate" (Socolow, 1976, p. 11). The continuation or exacerbation of controversy following additions of facts and logical analysis arises through several distinct processes. Disagreements continue concerning the *boundaries* of the system or event under consideration. Advocates of a specific "project" may resist any widening of the scope of analysis to include indirect, long-term or widely ramified consequences. Advocates of stronger regulation may wish to broaden the scope—for example, the problem of the ozone layer, the long-term genetic consequences of chemicals, effects of a proposed river dam on recreational opportunities of low-income versus high-income strata. Other conceptual boundary problems include controversies about the range or scope of the factors to be included in a value-relevant analysis. For example, a public regulatory commission may insist that its decisions deal only with the economic, allocational effects of rates charged for electric power—and, further, that the only rule allowable is that rates to different classes of consumers reflect the marginal private costs of supplying the power each consumes. Controversy arises when this rule is challenged, as by insisting that marginal social costs (including environmental externalities) be the basis of pricing, or that minimum equity considerations be introduced—for example, that no person be allowed to freeze in the dark as a consequence of automatic cessation of service following failure to pay a utility bill. Analysis of the Tocks Dam controversy leads Socolow to suggest that advocates who use cost-benefit analysis develop arbitrary rules to restrict such uncertainties about boundaries:

> Those costs and benefits which it is permissible to include in analysis become codified, as do many of the procedures for evaluating their dollar magnitudes. The warping effect on discourse is substantial. (Socolow, 1976, p. 14)

Boundaries are further restricted by an insistence on "golden numbers"—fixed numerical elements that are assumed to be immune to question—and by setting fixed ratios of risk–damage that are regarded as acceptable (e.g., 55,000 highway deaths a year versus none at all), or by refusing to acknowledge that any tradeoffs are being accepted in public policy.

It is a clear implication of the functional theory of social systems that the more highly differentiated societies will necessarily have the most advanced separation of cultural from social systems, and of the specific norms from the more generalized sets of values. Both of these developments directly imply enhanced variety and lability in particular social structures—hence, greater flexibility and change, especially in adaptive and goal-attainment activities. Particularly in such societies is the character and extent of value consensus highly problematic. In terms of the stability of authority and of stratification, it may turn out that the most crucial kind of consensus is not awareness of agreement on values but consensus of knowledge and belief—for example, what power exists, how it is exercised, who controls what, what the authority-holders are doing and why, how they will react to challenges, and the like (Berreman, 1968, p. 55). In the broadest sense, this is a cognitive–conceptual consensus, and it need not involve high agreement of evaluations.

Within recurring situations in societies of a particular kind—such as agricultural–feudal versus urban–industrial–democratic—particularly value orientations, repeatedly experienced and reformulated by large numbers of persons over extended periods, will eventually become intellectualized as components of a comprehensive world view. Linked with numerous other existential and evaluative conceptions, a given subset of value orientations may so monopolize attention and legitimacy as to constitute the very *context* (or framework) *within which* more particular ideologies and major societal and political issues are defined, discussed, and fought over. A crucial contemporary case seems to be the axiomatic quality of the value orientations of *equality* and *freedom*—in contrast to classical conceptions of order and hierarchy.

Most "ancient" and "medieval" political orders developed out of a long background of violence and misery; were maintained with violence, although internal misery may have been alleviated for considerable periods; and disintegrated with great violence and misery. In preindustrial societies, most persons perforce saw the world as one of limited resources, unavoidable scarcity, inevitable hardship. For many people through most of recorded history, even minimal safety of life and limb depended upon authoritative protection by the strong, and even minimal subsistence depended upon an enforced order. Out of countless experiences with scarcity, violence, and acute social dependence, there evolved such hierarchic evaluative world views as the medieval Christian doctrines or the developed Hindu views of caste.

What appears to be distinctive about the modern outlook is the spread, over a great deal of the world, both West and East, of a value–belief system which: (1) *rejects the postulate of scarcity;* (2) *posits the unconditional desirability of freedom;* and (3) *posits the unconditional desirability of equality,* in contrast to hierarchy. Perhaps no more explosive a combination has thus far confronted political man in complex, large-scale societies. To the extent that equality is stressed, the great and growing inequalities among different parts of the world and the grave difficulty of eradicating or even reducing the conspicuous inequalities within our own national society generate severe tensions, oppositions, and conflicts.

An essential immediate problem in the highly dynamic industrialized societies of the late twentieth century is to *guide* or *channelize* their enormous physical and social energies. The complex high-energy society is an intricate thing, and its survival in anything like the form of a pluralistic-liberal democracy is very much open to question. Clashes of values resonate with speed and force in a permeable social structure, suffused with mass communication. Increasing demands are made upon existing social arrangements. The growth of the public sector increasingly makes societal allocations a highly visible *political* process. It remains to be seen what the consequences will be in a world of energy crises, explosive population growth, basic interdependence, serious political instability, and incessant change. Greater understanding of the place of values in social systems surely warrants intensified intellectual effort in the years just ahead.

3

From Individual to Institutional Values: With Special Reference to the Values of Science

Milton Rokeach

Is it possible to identify the values of highly abstract, supraindividual social systems that sociologists identify as social institutions? What is the relation between institutional values and individual values? Satisfactory answers to these and related questions presuppose, at the very least, that it is scientifically meaningful to characterize abstract entities such as social institutions, no less than concrete individual persons, as having or possessing values, and that objective methods are available for measuring them. My purpose in this chapter is to propose an approach to the conceptualization and measurement of institutional values, an approach which is also applicable to the study of other kinds of supraindividual values—cultural values, organizational values, or group values.

INDIVIDUAL VALUES

A main point of departure to the proposed conceptualization and measurement of institutional values is earlier work concerned with the conceptualization, organization, measurement, and change in individual values (Rokeach, 1973). Individual values are socially shared "conceptions of the desirable" (Kluckhohn, 1951), conceptions that are the learned resultants of external and internal forces acting upon a person. Values can be regarded as the cognitive representations of internal "needs" mediated by external "presses" (Murray, 1938). Put another way, values may be conceived as cognitive representations of underlying needs—whether social or antisocial, selfish or altruistic—after they have been transformed to also take into account institutional goals and demands. In this way, all of a person's values, unlike all of a person's needs, are capable of being openly admitted, advocated, exhorted, and defended, to oneself and to others, in a socially sanctioned language.

Values serve as standards (Williams, 1951) that we learn to employ transcendentally across objects and situations in various ways: to guide action; to guide us to the positions that we take on various social, ideological, political, and religious issues; to guide self-presentations (Goffman, 1959) and impression management (Tedeschi, Schlenker, & Bonoma, 1971); to evaluate and judge ourselves and others by; to compare ourselves with others, not only with respect to competence (Festinger, 1954), but also with respect to morality. We employ values as standards, moreover, to decide what is worth and not worth arguing about, worth and not worth persuading and influencing others to believe in and to do. And, finally, we employ values as standards to guide processes of conscious and unconscious justification and rationalization of action, thought, and judgment. Thus, the ultimate function of human values is to provide us with a set of standards to guide us in all our efforts to satisfy our needs and at the same time maintain and, insofar as possible, enhance self-esteem, that is, to make it possible to regard ourselves and to be regarded by others as having satisfied societally and institutionally originating definitions of morality and competence.

Two main types of individual values have been previously distinguished: terminal or ends values and instrumental or means values. The former refer to beliefs or conceptions about ultimate goals or desirable end-states of existence that are worth striving for (such as happiness or wisdom); the latter refer to beliefs or conceptions about desirable modes of behavior that are instrumental to the attainment of desirable end-states (such as behaving honestly or responsibly). So conceived, "education" and "work" would not qualify as values, because they are neither end-states of existence that people strive for nor idealized modes of behavior, but "wisdom" and being "capable" would qualify. Thus defined, the universe of discourse, when considering the problem of individual and institutional values, is sharply restricted to a relatively small number of terms, numbering in the dozens rather than in the hundreds or thousands. Moreover, these value terms are assumed to be more or less universally present, for there are just so many end-states of existence that people everywhere are capable of striving for, and just so many idealized modes of behavior that are instrumental for their realization. Such a relatively small number of values can justifiably be assumed to be universally present on the same grounds that psychologists assume the same basic individual needs are universally present, and on the same grounds that sociologists assume the same basic social institutions are universally present.

We thus arrive at a conception of humans differing from one another not so much in terms of whether they possess particular terminal or instrumental values, but in the way they organize them to form value hierarchies or priorities. Even if people everywhere were conceded to possess only a relatively small number of terminal and instrumental values, it would still be possible to account for the richness and variety of individual differences in behavior, attitudes, ideologies, self-presentations, judgments, evaluations, and rationalizations. A dozen and a half terminal values, for instance, can be ordered in trillions of different ways, far more than enough to account for variations in values among individuals, groups, organizations, institutions, societies, and cultures the world over.

Value hierarchies or priorities are organizations of values enabling us to choose between alternative goals and actions, and enabling us to resolve conflict. At the individual level, for instance, value priorities guide decisions about occupational goals and interests, on how to spend our money, or for whom to vote. At the supraindividual level, value priorities guide decisions about such things as the setting of organizational goals, the allocation of resources, and the formulation of new policies.

In sum, human values are conceptualized as consisting of a relatively small number of core ideas or cognitions present in every society about desirable end-states of existence and desirable modes of behavior instrumental to their attainment that are capable of being organized to form different priorities. If the words symbolizing such a small number of core ideas were eliminated from any given language, individuals growing up in such a society would have no cross-situational standards by which to live and no linguistic tools with which to rationalize, and they would not know how to go about meeting societal demands about behaving competently or morally. They would have no principles or rules to guide them in making decisions or resolving conflicts. Most important, they would not know what to do in order to go about maintaining and enhancing their self-esteem.

A measuring instrument that identifies, or attempts to identify, major end-states of human existence and the behavioral modes for achieving them is the Value Survey (Rokeach, 1967). It also attempts to measure variations in personal value priorities. The Value Survey consists of one alphabetically arranged list of 18 terminal values and another alphabetical list of 18 instrumental values, as displayed in tables 3.1 and 3.2. Defining phrases typically accompanying these values are also shown. Respondents are instructed to "arrange them in order of their importance to YOU, as guiding principles in YOUR life." Notwithstanding the Value Survey's extreme simplicity and highly abstract nature, extensive research with it in different societies has consistently shown that it is both a reliable and valid measuring instrument (Feather, 1975b; Rokeach, 1973).

One objective of the proposed approach is to ascertain to what extent these two lists of values are indeed comprehensive for research at the institutional as well as the individual level. Readers are referred to other publications (Feather, 1971b, 1975b; Greenstein, 1976; Grube, Greenstein, Rankin, & Kearney, 1977; Rokeach, 1973, 1974a, 1974b) for a description of how these particular values were selected; for detailed reports of their reliability and validity; for the extent to which values are stable and are undergoing change in American society; for the extent to which various subsets of values distinguish significantly among groups varying in nationality, sex, religion, politics, socioeconomic status, age, and occupation; for their relation to various kinds of attitudes, behavior, and life styles; for the conditions under which individual values, attitudes, and behavior can be experimentally induced to undergo modification; and for the long-term consequences of value change for attitude and behavioral change.

INSTITUTIONAL VALUES

The value concept is an especially powerful one for all the social sciences because it can be meaningfully employed at all levels of social analysis. Values are as much sociological as psychological concepts; it is just as meaningful to speak of cultural, societal, institutional, organizational, and group values as it is to speak of individual values. If individual values are socially shared cognitive representations of personal needs and the means for satisfying them, then institutional values are socially shared cognitive representations of institutional goals and demands. Thus, institutional and individual values are really the opposite sides of the same coin. This duality of values—its societal, sociological pole and its individual, psychological pole—has been noticed by Bronowski in his admirable essay on *Science and Human Values:* "The problem of values arises only when men try to fit together their need to be social animals with their need to be free men. There is no problem, and there are no values, until men want to do both. . . . The concepts of value are profound and difficult exactly because they do two things at once: they join men into societies, and yet they preserve for them a freedom which makes them single men" (1956, p. 70). It is thus conjectured that the parallelism between societal and individual goals leads to a parallelism between institutional and individual values, and consequently that the universe of discourse will turn out to be the same, with the same array of ultimate goals and the means for achieving them meaningful when attempting to identify, describe, or measure both institutional and individual values.

There is a reasonably good consensus among sociologists that the most distinctive property or defining characteristic of a social institution is its values. Thus, Robin Williams defines an institution as "a set of institutional norms that cohere around a relatively distinct and socially important complex of values" (1951, p. 29). Eisenstadt observes that a "basic approach to comparative typology takes off from the different types of major value orientations around which the different institutions tend to become focused or integrated" (1968, p. 24).

If the most distinctive defining property of a social institution is indeed its "complex of values," then its most distinctive functions can be suggested to be value transmission and value implementation. The former implies that all social institutions can be expected to engage in value inculcation, and the latter implies that all social institutions can be expected to engage in behavior regulation (Eisenstadt, 1968) and institutional maintenance (Parsons, 1951).

Value Specialization.   A social institution cannot be expected, however, to transmit or implement the whole array of human values. Rather, there is a differentiation of function between institutions, each focusing its efforts and resources on different spheres of social activity, such as regulation of the means of production, education of the young, or protection from external attack. As a consequence of such a differentiation of function, social institutions emerge. These can be defined as social arrangements that provide frameworks for *value specialization,* that is, frameworks for the transmission and implementation mainly of those subsets of values that are especially implicated in their own particular spheres of activity. It is as if the total spectrum of human values has, through a process of evolution or historical development, been divided up and "assigned" to the several social institutions for their specialized transmission and implementation. Thus, the religious institution can be defined as one that specializes in the transmission and implementation of a certain cluster of values that we identify as religious values; the institution of science is one that specializes in the transmission and implementation of another cluster of values that we call scientific values; and so on for the remaining institutions of society. Presumably, such a division of labor is adaptive, both for the society and also for the individuals within it.

The hypothesis that the basic institutions of society are mainly frameworks allowing for specialization in the transmission and implementation of different subsets of values presupposes a competition model of social institutions (Collins, 1975; Dahrendorf, 1959; Horowitz, 1972; Lenski, 1966). The various institutions compete with one another for priority in drawing upon society's limited resources—say, how much of the national budget should go for social welfare, the military establishment, environmental control, space exploration, education, science, or the arts. Moreover, they compete with one another for influence and control over individuals. We may think of hierarchically organized individual value systems as the end result, in large part, of interinstitutional competition for influence over individual value priorities. Thus, to the extent that one particular social institution of society is the more powerful—say, religion—we may anticipate that its specialized values will become manifested as having the greatest priority within individual value systems, and the specialized values of other institutions will necessarily manifest a lesser priority (Ball-Rokeach, 1976). One major objective in systematic research that attempts to understand the interrelationships and interactions among institutions, and between institutions and individuals, is to identify which social institutions within a particular society are competing with one another over the transmission and implementation of which specific values.

Value Sharing.   There is integration as well as differentiation of function, cooperation as well as competition, among social institutions (Parsons, 1951). The cluster of values in which any one social institution specializes is by no means altogether different from those in which other institutions specialize. Several institutions may share, overlap, reinforce, or mutually support one another's specialized values—for instance, the family and religious institutions in the United States, or the two institutions that C. Wright Mills had identified as the military–industrial complex (1956). Thus, a social institution can be defined as a social arrangement that provides not only a framework for value specialization, but also for value sharing. Accordingly, a systematic study of an institution would require us to identify not only the specific values in which it specializes, but also those values shared with other social institutions.

The extent of cooperation or competition among institutions is, however, not necessarily a constant. It may vary over time and it may vary from one society to another, as a function of complexity or of economic or environmental conditions. In traditional societies, for example, the religious and scientific institutions are not usually structurally differentiated. In certain societies, there may be a sharing of the same set of specialized values between the religious and educational institutions (as in Franco's Spain), or between the family and economic institutions (as in the Israeli kibbutz), or between the political and educational institutions (as in the Soviet Union). Or, within a particular society, we may observe over time an increase in competition between institutions (as in the United States, wherein secularization has led to an increase in competition between the educational and religious institutions).

METHODS FOR MEASURING INSTITUTIONAL VALUES

Is it possible to study institutional values by quantitative procedures that are conceptually coordinated with those employed to measure individual values, yet at the same time methodologically appropriate for an institutional level of analysis? Thus far, five methods believed to be methodologically appropriate have been identified and are specified below. They are based on the following assumptions: that institutional values are substantively the same as those manifested at the individual level; that institutional values are major determinants of individual values and, like individual values, are hierarchically arranged. Closely related, social institutions are assumed to leave value traces. The idea of value trace is perhaps most similar to the traces left by an ancient civilization—artifacts from which archaeologists reconstruct or infer what life must have been like in an ancient civilization. Analogously, social institutions can be imagined to leave traces of their distinctive value patterns in institutional documents, in the personal values of institutional gatekeepers and the "clientele" served by the institution, and in the value images of the institution, as perceived by gatekeepers and clientele. Such institutional value patterns can be "recovered" by at least the following five methods:

1. *Content analysis*—by extracting the terminal and instrumental values that are exhorted in institutional documents or publications, through the method of content analysis (Holsti, 1968).

2. *Personal values of institutional gatekeepers*—by measuring the personal values of institutional gatekeepers (Lewin, 1951), such as scientists, the clergy, or military officers, on the assumption that gatekeeper values are especially likely to reflect the influence of socialization by a particular social institution.

3. *Personal values of an institution's special clients*—by measuring the personal values of certain classes of persons whom there is reason to believe have been especially influenced by one or another social institution—for instance, religiously devout churchgoers, or future gatekeepers, such as graduate students in science, seminary students, or military cadets.

4. *Perceived values of an institution by gatekeepers*—by measuring the perceived values of a given social institution (its value image) as perceived by institutional gatekeepers.

5. *Perceived values of an institution by general clients*—by measuring the perceived values of a given social institution, as perceived by virtually anyone within a society who can be regarded as the "target" or "general client" of the institution.

Each of these five methods[1] appears to have at least some degree of face validity. But each considered in isolation can be anticipated to have certain limitations. The institutional value traces tapped by any one method can be "contaminated," to one extent or another, by other influences. For instance, a content analysis of the values contained in institutional documents (method 1) may reflect the idiosyncratic values of the authors of the documents as well as those of the institution, or may inform us selectively only about the institution's most important values, or may selectively omit mentioning certain important values because they are taken for granted. The personal values of institutional gatekeepers or its special clients (methods 2 and 3) may reflect the influence not only of the dominant social institution but also of other institutions. The perceived values or value image of an institution by its gatekeepers or general clients (methods 4 and 5) may be distorted by self-interest, bias, ignorance, or misinformation. Thus, there is little reason to anticipate in advance that any one of the five methods will be superior to the others. A multimethod approach that allows for triangulation and cross-validation is therefore preferable to reliance upon any one method (Campbell & Fiske, 1959).

Employing these five methods, then, it should be possible to identify the values and value priorities of the major institutions within any given society. In work presently under way, and to be reported in future publications, we are concentrating our attention on the following 10 institutions within American society: (1) the arts, (2) the economic in-

[1]Two other methods are possible: the perceived values of any given institution by its special clients, and the personal values of an institution's general clients. These are omitted from further consideration because data on the perceived values of an institution by its gatekeepers are clearly preferable to those obtained from its special clients, and the personal values of general clients may be a reflection of other social institutions, as well as of any specific institution in which we might be interested.

stitution, (3) education, (4) the family, (5) the legal–judicial institution, (6) leisure–recreation, (7) the military, (8) politics, (9) religion, and (10) science.

MEASUREMENT OF VARIABLES

Given the present approach to the empirical study of social institutions, it is now possible to generate various objective measures, some of which characterize institutions, while others characterize individuals' relations with institutions.

Institutional Variables

1. *Similarity between institutions.* The rank-order correlation between rankings obtained for any two social institutions, given a common value set such as the one proposed herein, is a measure of institutional value similarity. Considering each of the five methods separately, and in combination, it is possible to generate a similarity matrix describing the extent to which each of the social institutions of a society is similar to each of the others. One such similarity matrix would describe terminal value similarity among social institutions, and the other would describe instrumental value similarity. These two kinds of similarity matrices would then enable us to make separate statements about the extent to which two or more of the institution's *goals* and *behavioral demands* are similar.

2. *Value specialization.* Whereas value similarity is a global measure of similarity between the value systems of two or more institutions, value specialization focuses attention on the identification of specific values that are the most distinctive of a given social institution. This can be operationalized as the values (terminal or instrumental) that are among the top-ranked three or six (or whatever) of 18 values. If our conceptualizations are valid, we would expect to find that (a) each social institution specializes in advancing some distinctive nonoverlapping subset of terminal and instrumental values, those that are most relevant to its sphere of action, and that (b) each terminal and instrumental value has been "assigned" for specialization to at least one social institution, that is, there are no terminal or instrumental values that will be "left over," that are not the focus of specialization by at least one social institution.

3. *Value sharing.* When two or more social institutions regard any specified value as important it is an indication of value sharing. Again, importance can be operationally defined as those values ranked among the top three or six (or whatever) of 18 terminal or instrumental values by two or more institutions.

4. *Institutional change.* If we assume that the main distinguishing characteristic of a social institution is its value system, then a change in this value system should be an indicator of institutional change. Two approaches to the study of institutional change are possible:

a. *Institutional change over time.* If a social institution is said to undergo natural change over time, institutional value priorities should also undergo change. Content analyses of any given institutional documents of differing time periods should enable us to demonstrate such changes, and moreover, magnitude of change can be operationally manifested as differences in value rankings.

b. *Experimental induction of institutional change.* Earlier experimental research (Rokeach, 1973, 1975, 1979) has shown that feedback of data drawing attention to contradictions between one's personal values, or between one's own values and those of significant reference groups, leads to long-term changes in personal values, and in value-related attitudes and behavior. Analogously, it is conjectured that feedback of relevant data to institutional and organizational gatekeepers (e.g., boards of directors of corporation, College of Cardinals, university administration, Pentagon officials) is one way to bring about institutional value change from within, assuming that structural conditions are supportive. Such feedback would make gatekeepers aware of discrepancies or contradictions between the personal values and the perceived value images of the social institution, or discrepancies or contradictions between the personal values and the perceived institutional values of higher- or lower-level institutional gatekeepers.

Individual Variables

1. *Subjective alienation from social institution.* The rank-order correlation between one's personal value rankings and one's perception of the value rankings of any given social institution is assumed to represent a measure of subjective alienation versus subjective identification with the social institution.

2. *Objective alienation.* We assume that the most valid index of any social institution's value system is the average value ranking of a set of values obtained by employing all five methods described above. Assuming that individuals within a society have been exposed to one degree or another of influence from all social institutions, objective alienation would then be operationalized as the rank-order correlation between one's personal value rankings and any given institution's value rankings, averaged across all five methods.

3. *Accuracy of perception of institutional values.* The rank-order correlation between one's perception of the values of an institution and a more objective measure of institutional values (as obtained, say, by the five

methods) is assumed to be a measure of accuracy of perception of institutional values.

4. *Perceived influence of social institution.* We assume that virtually all persons, by virtue of the fact that they are socialized by the several institutions of their society, can report with one or another degree of accuracy on the extent to which each social institution has exerted a positive or negative influence on their personal lives. Perceived influence can be operationalized in terms of a rating scale ranging from perceived positive to negative influence.

5. *Perceived importance of social institution.* We further assume that people will differ in their conceptions about the relative importance of various social institutions—to themselves and to society. Importance can be operationalized by asking respondents to rank or rate the several institutions for importance or, preferably, by asking respondents to allocate scarce resources to the several institutions.

6. *Participation in institutional activities.* A behavioral rather than cognitive indicator of institutional importance is the extent to which a person participates in institutional activities, such as religious, familial, recreational activities, and so on.

The above six institutionally oriented individual variables are seen to be interrelated; they should, moreover, be related to other individual variables that are important to sociologists and social psychologists. We can tentatively pose the following as examples of questions now capable of empirical investigation:

What is the relation between objective and subjective alienation from a social institution?

To what extent is objective and subjective alienation, as conceived and measured, related to or a function of the perceived negative or positive influence of an institution? perceived importance of an institution? participation in institutional activities?

Is it meaningful to think of alienation from society as being a function of alienation from each of the social institutions within the society? Assuming that total alienation is measured by the sum of subjective or objective alienation across all social institutions, to what extent will it be related to alienation or anomie, as traditionally conceived and measured (Seeman, 1975; Srole, 1956; McClosky & Schaar, 1965), and to the feeling that one is externally rather than internally controlled (Rotter, 1966; Gurin, Gurin, Lao, & Beattie, 1969)?

Is it possible to predict an individual's personal values from information about one's identification with and influence by the several institutions of a society? from information about one's participation in institutional organizations and activities?

Under what conditions will subjective or objective alienation from a social institution be positively related to social status? negatively related?

What are the determinants or correlates of accuracy of perception of institutional values? How is accuracy related to such variables as social status, subjective or objective alienation, anomie, or external control?

SOME PRELIMINARY FINDINGS ABOUT THE INSTITUTION OF SCIENCE

In research already completed, the five methods described above were employed to ascertain the values of science as a social institution. To illustrate the conceptual and methodological approach advocated here to the systematic study of institutional values, the specific procedures employed and some major findings are described in this section.

1. *Content analysis.* Extensive research by White (1951) and Eckhardt (1972) has shown that the values contained in various historical and political documents can be reliably extracted by content analysis. A content analysis employing the present scheme led to the identification of the major differences in value priorities among such political ideologists as Lenin, Hitler, Goldwater, and Norman Thomas (Rokeach, 1973). Rous and Lee (1978) have carried out a similar analysis of other ideologists, and their findings are very similar. Another content analysis (Rokeach, Homant, & Penner, 1970) enabled us to determine that the value pattern extracted from the disputed Federalist Papers was more similar to James Madison's than Alexander Hamilton's and, therefore, that it was probably Madison who was the author of these papers. This conclusion has been independently confirmed by historical evidence, and also by Mosteller and Wallace (1964).

In these content analyses, the material analyzed was typically ideological and, therefore, exhortatory in nature. More generally, it can be assumed that (a) the purpose of any exhortatory material, which would include the special literary form that we recognize as editorials, is advocacy—to argue in favor of the desirability or undesirability of one or more means or ends values—that (b) it is possible to identify the values so advocated by content analysis, and that (c) exhortatory material originating with different social institutions will focus attention on different values.

Content analysis was employed in the present instance to ascertain the values of the journal *Science*. Eighty editorials (about 46,000 words) were randomly selected from among 520 editorials published in *Science* over a 10-year period, 1964-1973. Two judges were first trained independently—to the point where the reliability of their judgments reached .95 for the terminal values and .85 for the instrumental values. They were then assigned the task of extracting the values contained in these 80 editorials, dividing the editorials up more or less evenly between them. First they decided whether each value they judged to be present in the editorial was a terminal value, if it referred to an end-state of existence, or an instrumental value, if it referred to a mode of behavior. They tallied as many values as they judged to be contained in any one editorial.

To insure maximum comparability with the data obtained with the remaining four methods, the judges assigned each value judged to be contained in the editorials, if at all possible, into one of the same 18 terminal or 18 instrumental value categories that are mentioned in the Rokeach Value Survey, as shown in tables 3.1 and 3.2. For instance, "efficient" and "competent" were coded "capable"; "prudent" and "restrained" were coded "self-controlled"; "ingenious" and "creative" were coded "imaginative." Proceeding in this manner, the judges identified a total of 134 references in *Science* editorials to various terminal values, and 154 references to various instrumental values—all told, 288 mentions of end-states or ideal modes of behavior, or an average of 3.6 values per editorial. The total frequency for any one value was the total number of separate mentions of that value in the 80 editorials. The judges succeeded in assigning 97 percent of all the values mentioned in the editorials to one of the 36 value categories of the Rokeach Value Survey, suggesting that this list of values is a reasonably comprehensive one. The remaining 3 percent were dropped from further analyses.

2. *Personal values of scientists.* Previous research has also shown that individuals employed in various occupational and professional groups exhibit different patterns of terminal and instrumental values (Rokeach, 1973). One of the groups for whom data are available is 152 faculty members at Michigan State and Wayne State universities with the rank of assistant professor or higher from various scientific disciplines: the biological sciences, which included biology, botany, and biochemistry (N = 51); the physical sciences, which included physics, chemistry, and geology (N = 51); and the social sciences which included psychology, sociology, anthropology, political science, and economics (N = 50). The value patterns obtained from these three subgroups of scientists are reasonably similar to one another (Rokeach, 1973) and, when combined, are assumed to be more or less typical of the personal values of the institutional gatekeepers to science.

The value rankings of these scientists were obtained, using Form D of the Rokeach Value Survey. Each value, with defining phrases added in parentheses (as shown in tables 3.1 and 3.2), was presented to the respondent on a removable "pressure-sensitive" gummed label. The 18 terminal value labels were initially arranged alphabetically down the right-hand side of the page, and the respondents merely rearranged them in order of judged importance to themselves by moving them to 18 boxes printed on the left-hand side of the page. Similarly with the 18 alphabetically arranged instrumental values.

3. *Personal values of graduate students in science.* These data were obtained from 86 graduate students in various fields of science at Washington State University using the same value instrument. They were selected in about equal proportions from the biological and physical sciences, on the one hand, and the social sciences, on the other (N = 39 and 47, respectively). The value patterns of these two groups of graduate students are on the whole similar, and do not vary significantly by years of graduate study. It was assumed that the personal values obtained from this group of graduate students is reasonably representative of those of future gatekeepers to science.

4. *Perceived values of science by scientists.* Measures of perceived values of science by scientists—that is, by gatekeepers of science—were obtained by modifying the standard instructions usually employed to measure individual values. The respondents were 101 faculty members of the rank of assistant professor or higher at Washington State University, from the following fields: the biological sciences, including biology, botany, and biochemistry (N = 20); the physical sciences, including chemistry, physics, and geology (N = 31); and the social sciences, including anthropology, economics, political science, psychology, and sociology (N = 50). They were instructed to "rank the values in order of their importance to *the SCIENCES as a social institution.* That is, the value which you feel is most important should be placed in Box 1, and so on. The value you feel is least important to *the SCIENCES as a social institution* should be placed in Box 18."

5. *Perceived values of science by nonscientists.* Similarly, 122 undergraduates taking an introductory course in sociology at Washington State University (general clients) reported their perceptions of the values of science as a social institution, employing the same instructions and measuring instrument employed to measure the perceived values of science by scientists (see 4 above).

Tables 3.1 and 3.2 show the value rankings obtained with all five methods, the former showing the terminal value rankings of science, and the latter showing instrumental value rankings. The first column shows the frequency of mention of the various values extracted from the *Science* editorials and, in parentheses, the rank order of these frequencies. The next four columns show the median rankings obtained by each of the remaining four methods for each of the 18 terminal and 18 instrumental values and again, in parentheses, the "composite" rankings are shown, defined as the ranking of all 18 medians from 1 to 18. For instance, the median ranking of *a sense of accomplishment* was 3.7 for the 152 scientists who were asked to rank their own terminal values. Since this median is the highest of all 18 medians, its composite rank is 1. Similarly, these same scientists show a median ranking of 17.6 for *salvation*. Since this is lower than any of the others, its composite rank is 18.

For ease of reading, the values shown in tables 3.1 and 3.2 have been arranged in order of their ranked importance to the institution of science. This was determined by simply summing the ranks for each value obtained by the five methods as shown in parentheses, and then ranking these sums from 1 to 18. These sums and rankings are shown in the last column of tables 3.1 and 3.2.

Wisdom is clearly the most important terminal value of science and, moreover, all five methods agree in placing it among the top three in importance. This is followed by *freedom, self-respect, a sense of accomplishment, a world at peace,* and *equality.* The main themes that seem to be evident in these values are those concerning personal strivings for growth, understanding, and self-realization, on the one hand, and social strivings for a peaceful, libertarian, and egalitarian world, on the other. At least three of the five methods agree with one another that these half-a-dozen terminal values are the most important ultimate goals of science.

Our procedures allow us to ascertain not only which are the most important values of science, but also which ones are not important, or are minimally important. Table 3.1 identifies *salvation* as the terminal value that is uniformly considered to be the least important to science. Other values falling into the category of the half-a-dozen least important values to science are *pleasure, national security, mature love, true friendship,* and *a comfortable life.* Thus, it would seem that the ultimate goals that are the least important to science (that are least the "business" of science) are those implicating religion, nationalism, materialism, hedonism, affiliation, and love.

Moving on next to consider the instrumental values of science (the behavioral demands of science), the several methods identify *intellectual* as the most important, followed by being *capable, honest, responsible, imaginative,* and *independent.* And not far behind this cluster of science's half-a-dozen behavioral demands are being *broadminded* and *logical,* which rank seventh and eighth. Two major themes suggested by this value pattern are a demand for competence intertwined with a demand for morality. The former is defined primarily as a nonconforming, rational competence of intellect and imagination and the latter, in terms of honesty and a tolerance for dissent.

Again, it would be helpful to know which instrumental values are least considered to be the values of science. These seem to implicate mainly instrumental values derived from religion and those that, for lack of a better term, might be called "conventional values." At least four of the five methods agree with one another in identifying *obedience* as the

TABLE 3.1. Terminal Value Rankings of Science Obtained by Five Methods

	CONTENT ANALYSIS	VALUES OF SCIENTISTS (N = 152)	VALUES OF GRADUATE STUDENTS IN SCIENCE (N = 86)	PERCEIVED VALUES OF SCIENCE BY SCIENTISTS (N = 101)	PERCEIVED VALUES OF SCIENCE BY NONSCIENTISTS (N = 122)	SUM OF RANKS
Wisdom (a mature understanding of life)	60(1)	5.3(3)	5.1(2)	2.0(1)	3.7(2)	9.0(1)
Freedom (independence, free choice)	19(2)	5.7(5)	5.8(4)	4.8(3)	5.9(4)	18.0(2)
Self-respect (self-esteem)	3(6.5)	4.4(2)	5.1(1)	6.0(5)	7.6(6)	20.5(3)
A sense of accomplishment (lasting contribution)	0(15)	3.7(1)	8.2(8)	3.0(2)	2.6(1)	27.0(4)
A world at peace (free of war and conflict)	13(4)	7.3(7)	10.7(12)	5.3(4)	5.3(3)	30.0(5)
Equality (brotherhood, equal opportunity for all)	9(5)	6.7(6)	9.4(10)	7.7(6)	8.5(8)	35.0(6)
A world of beauty (beauty of nature and the arts)	16(3)	11.2(12)	11.6(13)	8.0(8)	9.2(9)	42.0(7)

Value						
Inner harmony (freedom from inner conflict)	1(11)	9.1(9)	6.3(5)	11.7(13)	10.4(11)	49.0(8)
Family security (taking care of loved ones)	0(15)	5.3(4)	8.3(9)	10.4(10)	11.5(12)	50.0(9)
Social recognition (respect, admiration)	3(6.5)	13.0(14)	15.0(16)	8.1(9)	6.9(5)	50.5(10)
Happiness (contentedness)	2(9)	11.4(13)	5.7(3)	11.7(14)	11.8(13)	52.0(11)
An exciting life (a stimulating, active life)	0(15)	8.5(8)	10.1(11)	7.9(7)	11.8(14)	55.0(12)
A comfortable life (a prosperous life)	2(9)	14.8(15)	12.8(14)	11.6(12)	9.6(10)	60.0(13)
True friendship (close companionship)	0(15)	10.5(11)	7.3(7)	13.1(15)	14.3(16)	64.0(14)
Mature love (sexual and spiritual intimacy)	0(15)	10.0(10)	6.5(6)	16.1(17)	14.6(17)	65.0(15)
National security (protection from attack)	0(15)	15.0(16)	16.6(17)	11.5(11)	7.9(7)	66.0(16)
Pleasure (an enjoyable, leisurely life)	2(9)	15.4(17)	12.8(15)	13.6(16)	13.1(15)	72.0(17)
Salvation (saved, eternal life)	0(15)	17.6(18)	17.2(18)	17.9(18)	16.4(18)	87.0(18)

63

TABLE 3.2. Instrumental Value Rankings of Science Obtained by Five Methods

	Content Analysis	Values of Scientists (N = 152)	Values of Graduate Students in Science (N = 86)	Perceived Values of Science by Scientists (N = 101)	Perceived Values of Science by Nonscientists (N = 122)	Sum of Ranks
Intellectual (intelligent, reflective)	17(3)	6.2(4)	6.5(4)	2.3(1)	3.0(1)	13.0(1)
Capable (competent, effective)	44(1)	6.1(3)	6.8(6.5)	4.9(5)	6.5(5)	20.5(2)
Honest (sincere, truthful)	6(9)	3.6(1)	5.1(1)	4.4(4)	9.7(11)	26.0(3)
Responsible (dependable, reliable)	10(4.5)	5.9(2)	6.6(5)	8.4(9)	6.6(6)	26.5(4)
Imaginative (daring, creative)	10(4.5)	7.3(7)	7.9(8)	4.3(3)	6.9(7)	29.5(5)
Independent (self-reliant, self-sufficient)	9(6)	8.4(9)	6.1(3)	6.6(6)	9.1(9)	33.0(6)
Broadminded (open-minded)	5(10)	6.6(5)	6.8(6.5)	7.2(8)	5.7(4)	33.5(7)

64

Logical (consistent, rational)	4(11.5)	7.6(8)	9.0(10)	3.4(2)	4.2(3)	34.5(8)
Ambitious (hard-working, aspiring)	7(8)	9.2(10)	11.8(14)	7.1(7)	3.4(2)	41.0(9)
Helpful (working for the welfare of others)	20(2)	9.7(11)	10.2(11)	11.4(12)	8.1(8)	44.0(10)
Courageous (standing up for your beliefs)	4(11.5)	7.2(6)	8.8(9)	9.6(10)	10.0(12)	48.5(11)
Self-controlled (restrained, self-disciplined)	8(7)	11.9(14)	10.9(12)	10.4(11)	9.4(10)	54.0(12)
Loving (affectionate, tender)	1(15)	11.5(13)	5.8(2)	16.4(17)	16.6(18)	65.0(13)
Forgiving (willing to pardon others)	0(17.5)	11.0(12)	11.4(13)	14.4(14)	14.8(16)	72.5(14)
Cheerful (lighthearted, joyful)	1(15)	13.0(15)	12.0(15)	14.2(13)	15.8(17)	75.0(15)
Polite (courteous, well-mannered)	1(15)	15.0(16)	15.2(16)	14.7(15)	14.7(15)	77.0(16)
Clean (neat, tidy)	0(17.5)	16.1(17)	15.8(17)	15.4(16)	13.5(13)	80.5(17)
Obedient (dutiful, respectful)	3(13)	17.3(18)	17.6(18)	17.2(18)	13.8(14)	81.0(18)

least important behavioral demand of science, followed by being *clean, polite, cheerful, forgiving,* and *loving.*

While occasional inconsistencies may be noted in tables 3.1 and 3.2, there seems to be general agreement among the five methods. But it is possible to be more precise in determining the extent to which there is overall agreement among methods, and it is also possible to determine whether certain methods are better indicators of science's values than others. The correlation (rho) between the value rankings obtained by any two methods is an index of the amount of overall agreement between them. The intercorrelations between value rankings obtained using all five methods are shown in Table 3.3, the terminal and instrumental value correlation matrices being shown above and below the diagonal, respectively.

The terminal value correlations range between .24 and .89, and the mean correlation between methods is .51. For instrumental values, the correlations range between .30 and .80, and the mean correlation is .64. These findings suggest that (a) the five methods vary as valid indicators of science's values, that (b) there is at least a moderately good overall agreement among the several methods in assessing science's value hierarchy, and that (c) the overall agreement is somewhat higher in the case of science's instrumental than terminal values.

The size of the average correlation between any one method and the remaining four can be taken as an index of its relative internal validity as an indicator of science's values. Such an index of internal validity is especially useful when external validity is not readily ascertained. The data are shown in the last row and column of Table 3.3, and an inspection of these data reveals the following:

1. The least sensitive single indicator of science's values is method 3, personal values of graduate students in science (future gatekeepers). The mean correlation obtained between this method and the remaining four is .38 and .54, respectively, for terminal and instrumental values.

2. The most sensitive indicator appears to be method 4, perceived values of science by scientists, its mean correlation with the remaining four being .64 and .71, respectively. It is also worth noting that only this method places *social recognition* among the top half-a-dozen values of science, thus supporting Merton's (1967) contention that scientists are motivated by issues of priority in discovery as well as by norms of communality (Gustin, 1973; Reskin, 1977).

3. The second best indicator is method 2—personal values of scientists, the mean correlations being .57 and .71, respectively.

4. Method 5—perceived values of science by nonscientists—is a moderately sensitive indicator of science's values, not the best but not the worst either. It is highly correlated with the perceived values of science by scientists and its mean correlation with the remaining four methods is .56 and .61, respectively, for the terminal and instrumental values.

TABLE 3.3. Intercorrelations (rho) Between Five Methods of Measuring the Values of Science*

	1. CONTENT ANALYSIS	2. VALUES OF SCIENTISTS	3. VALUES OF GRADUATE STUDENTS IN SCIENCE	4. PERCEIVED VALUES OF SCIENCE BY SCIENTISTS	5. PERCEIVED VALUES OF SCIENCE BY NONSCIENTISTS	MEAN CORRELATION (TERMINAL VALUES)
1. Content Analysis		.24	.25	.56	.58	.41
2. Values of Scientists	.63		.70	.77	.57	.57
3. Values of Graduate Students in Science	.50	.78		.34	.21	.38
4. Perceived Values of Science by Scientists	.66	.79	.57		.89	.64
5. Perceived Values of Science by Nonscientists	.72	.63	.30	.80		.56
Mean Correlation (Instrumental Values)	.63	.71	.54	.71	.61	

*Correlations above the diagonal are for the terminal value systems, and correlations below the diagonal are for the instrumental value systems.

5. Method 1—content analysis of *Science* editorials—is a relatively poor indicator of science's terminal values; its correlation is only .41 with the remaining four methods. But it is considerably better as an indicator of science's instrumental values, its mean correlation with the remaining four methods being .63.

6. The data obtained by methods 2 and 4 may not be altogether independent and, therefore, may account for the high correlations obtained. Note, however, that the correlations obtained between methods 4 and 5, which are independent, are even higher.

In more general terms, our findings suggest that the most sensitive single indicator of an institution's values is, first, the value image of the institution by its gatekeepers, and, second, the personal values of its gatekeepers. Next best is content analysis and the value image of the institution by its general clients, depending on whether we are considering the institution's terminal or instrumental values. Finally, our findings suggest that the least sensitive indicator is the personal values of future gatekeepers undergoing training. It remains to be seen, however, whether these findings are peculiar to the present analysis of the values of science. It would be premature to conclude from the preliminary findings presented here that the present ordering of the sensitivity of the five methods will necessarily be replicated when other institutions are examined.

The two methods that consistently provide us with the best agreement—the perceived values of science by scientists and the personal values of scientists—both involve institutional gatekeepers. Because scientists, by virtue of their training, have had long and intimate associations with the institution of science, they are presumably in a better position than others to inform us about the values of science.

One additional way that is available to us to evaluate the merits of the present approach to the identification of institutional values is to compare the value priorities of science, as determined empirically by the five methods discussed here, with those rationally derived by Bronowski: "Truth is the drive at the center of science.... Consider then, step by step, what kind of society scientists have been compelled to form in this single pursuit" (1956, p. 77). First, Bronowski suggests, come independence and originality "and therefore dissent... the surface mark of a deeper value... freedom... free inquiry, free thought, free speech, tolerance... they are self-evident... logical needs" (pp. 78–79), and from these "first needs of science" (p. 80) Bronowski derives other values: democracy and a respect for others, which he defines as a public acknowledgment of justice, honor, and dignity. "Science at last respects the scientist more than his theories, for by its nature it must prize the search above the discovery and the thinking (and with it the thinker) above the thought. In the society of scientists each man ... has earned a dignity more profound than his doctrine.... The sense of human dignity ... is the cement of a society of equal men, for it expresses their knowledge that respect for others must be founded in self-respect ... the respect of a lucid honesty with himself" (pp. 82–84).

Bronowski's analysis interests us here for at least two reasons. First, it can be regarded as the value image of science by an unusually keen and respected gatekeeper to science. Alternatively, it may be regarded as a set of rationally derived hypotheses that are capable of being empirically tested. Either way, it would seem that there is a great deal of congruence between Bronowski's list of science's values and those found here empirically. We may note especially the congruence between Bronowski's suggestion that truth is "the first need of science" and the present finding that *wisdom* is clearly the most important ultimate concern of science. But the congruence is not complete—because of differences in terminology, because Bronowski does not venture to say which of his derived values are more and less important, because certain values (such as beauty and peace) are not included in his discussion, and because Bronowski does not address himself, as we do here, to a consideration of values that are of minimal concern to science.[2]

SUMMARY

The shift from an earlier focus on individual values to the present focus on institutional values proceeds from the observation that the value concept seems equally meaningful when employed at either level, and from the premise that personal needs, on the one hand, and institutional goals and demands, on the other, probably both end up being linguistically coded into the same set of values. Both depend upon a conceptual definition of values that delimits the universe of discourse to a reasonably small number of end-states and the means of achieving them, that are moreover capable of being differentially organized into priority systems.

The several methods proposed here for the measurement of institutional values are similar to one another in that they all attempt to tap one or another value trace or manifestation of institutional influence. They differ from one another, however, in that the value traces are of different quality or validity. Since it was not possible to predict in advance which methods would provide us with results that are the most valid indicators of an institution's values, the employment of the several methods in combination seemed the best strategy, in the expectation that

[2]For some general incisive comments about the culture, codes, norms, and values of science, but not necessarily the value priorities of science, see Merton (1957), *Social Theory and Social Structure,* and Cournand and Zuckerman (1970).

each would overcome or cancel out the limitations of the others. The fact that we found considerable convergence among the several methods, at least in our analysis of science's values, increases our confidence not only in the valid identification of the values and value priorities of science, but also that such a multimethod approach would turn out to be useful in future comparative studies of other social institutions, both within and across societies.

That we also find divergence among methods suggests a need for caution when confronted with data about the values of an institution that have been obtained with only one method. Moreover, it would be premature to conclude from the present findings that the present ordering of the sensitivity of the five methods as indicators of the values of science will necessarily be replicated when other institutions are examined. It would also be premature to conclude that the limitations of content analysis noted here, which concern specifically the recovery of values from editorials contained in *Science,* would necessarily apply to editorials written within other institutional frameworks, or would necessarily apply to other types of institutional documents.

In conclusion, the approach suggested to the conceptualization and measurement of institutional values allows us to raise additional questions that are amenable to further investigation. (1) Can other methods and improvements in the representativeness and size of sampling of respondents and institutional documents increase the accuracy of identification and measurement of institutional values? (2) To what extent can it be demonstrated that different individuals within a society are exposed to the values of different institutions, and to what extent will such exposure affect personal values, on the one hand, and institutional value image, on the other? (3) Is it possible to monitor change in social institutions over time, that is, change in institutional values? It is unlikely that the goals and demands of science as a social institution have remained the same from ancient to modern times, or that they are not now undergoing further change in this era of increasing preoccupation with problems of ethics and values. (4) Finally, to what extent can change in institutional values be regarded as a social indicator of change in the quality of our everyday life?

4

Values and the Organization: Suggestions for Research

Patrick E. Connor and Boris W. Becker

Interest in the subject of human values has ranged from abstract contemplation by philosophers and political theorists to empirical scrutiny by quantitative psychologists. With only a few exceptions, however, investigators have not concerned themselves with values and the organization. Specifically, little attention has been paid to the interaction between properties of the organizational setting and values of the actors therein. Employee and managerial attitudes, including their relationship to structural characteristics of the organization (Porter & Lawler, 1965), have been related extensively in the literature. A thorough compendium of such studies is given by Scott and Cummings (1973). Employee and managerial *values,* however, particularly as they relate to organizational performance, have received only scant treatment.

The purpose of this selection is to outline a program of systematic research to fill this theoretical gap. First, values are defined, and their distinction from, yet interrelationship to, attitudes and behavior is specified. Second, the nature of the problem in relating values to organizational properties is discussed. Third, a conceptual framework for viewing the formal organization and various processes within it is provided. Fourth, using this framework, the kinds of relationships among values and organizational characteristics that might reasonably be expected to obtain are specified.

71

VALUES, ATTITUDES, AND BEHAVIOR

There is considerable variation in the attention accorded to the general concept of value by scholars in several fields of learning. Despite this variety, some theoretical consensus regarding a definitional posture appears to be developing. Scott (1956) and Kluckhohn (1951) define values as a conception of the desirable: "A value is a conception, explicit or implicit . . . of the desirable which influences the selection from available modes, means, and ends of action" (Kluckhohn, 1951, p. 389). Building from this idea, Rokeach (1968, p. 124) defines values as "abstract ideals, positive or negative, not tied to any specific object or situation, representing a person's beliefs about modes of conduct and ideal terminal goals." Values thus are global beliefs that "transcendentally guide actions and judgments across specific objects and situations" (Rokeach, 1968, p. 160).

Attitudes, on the other hand, do focus on specific objects and specific situations. "An attitude is an orientation toward certain objects (including persons—others and oneself) or situations. . . . An attitude results from the application of a general value to concrete objects or situations" (Theodorson & Theodorson, 1969, p. 19). Indeed, one of the functions of attitudes, being object-specific, is to allow expression of more global underlying values (Katz & Stotland, 1959).

Behavior may be viewed as a manifestation of attitudes and values. In fact, attitudes have been defined by some in terms of the probability of the occurrence of a specified behavior in a specified situation (Campbell, 1950). As Newcomb notes, "Such definitions (of attitude), while relatively devoid of conceptual content, serve to remind us that the ultimate referent of attitudes is behavior" (Gould & Kolb, 1964, p. 141).

In brief, then, values may be thought of as global beliefs about desirable end-states underlying attitudinal and behavioral processes. Attitudes are seen to constitute cognitive and affective orientations toward specific objects or situations. Behavior generally is viewed as a manifestation of values and attitudes. It is contended here that behavior in organizations is no exception; indeed, although he develops a conceptual scheme different from that presented here, Churchman (1961) has argued that the *ideal* setting for the study of human values is the complex organization.

STATEMENT OF THE PROBLEM

Although little attention has been paid specifically to the study of values and the organization, the sociological, psychological, and administrative theory literature does contain numerous studies of values as a general human property. Moreover, as noted above, some consensus is developing as to the theoretical conception of "value." There is no agreement, however, as to proper operational characteristics. Although there is a lengthy list of empirical studies in various fields that purport to use values as dependent or independent variables, literature search confirms that what Kluckhohn pointed out previously is no less true today, a generation later:

> Reading the voluminous, and often vague and diffuse, literature on the subject in the various fields of learning, one finds values considered as attitudes, motivations, objects, measurable quantities, substantive areas of behavior, affect-laden customs or traditions, and relationships such as those between individuals, groups, objects, events (Kluckhohn, 1951, p. 390).

The operational ambivalence of much research is illustrated by a recent report (Locke, 1970). The investigator variously discusses values as being synonymous with emotional reactions, valuation (x is more valuable than y), goals, interests, needs, and outcomes. Even the early work of England (1967) treated managerial values and preference for specified organizational goals as interchangeable quantities; however, England subsequently has focused his attention more narrowly, developing comprehensive profiles of managerial values (England, 1973). For Churchman too, values are the valuations placed by actors on possible outcomes of behavioral acts. Thus, values are seen as inferable from behavior, or predictive of behavior, when the individual is aware of all available alternatives, can freely choose any particular one, and knows the probabilities of outcomes occurring (Churchman, 1961).

Thus the problem facing the organization theorist is twofold. First, there is a need for researchers to settle upon a commonly accepted operational definition of value. This is not a call for a standardized value-measuring instrument; the creation of such an ultimate instrument is probably not possible, or even desirable, given the variety of research questions and methodologies it would have to serve. Rather, it is a call for acceptance of the fact that values cannot fruitfully be operationalized as attitudes, or goals or objectives, or preferred outcomes. If they are to have any useful meaning apart from these concepts, values must be operationalized as parsimoniously as possible, as desirable endstates of existence underlying attitudes and behaviors. Thus, while such formulations as those by Churchman (1961) and Kluckhohn (1951) are equally appealing in their rigor and elegance, the approach advocated by the latter is the more helpful; values have importance beyond the formation and pursuit of goals—they are fundamental to, not identical with, these processes.

The second aspect of the value and organization problem is more pragmatic. A fair amount is known and more is being learned, at an accelerating rate, about relationships among various organizational properties—structural components, for example (Blau & Schoenherr,

1971; Hall, 1972). A fair amount also is known about such organizational processes as power, conflict, leadership, communication, and environment adaptation (Hall, 1972). By contrast, very little is known about the relationships among the various organizational properties and processes and the values of organizational actors.

VALUES AND THE ORGANIZATION

Of the many models of organization, the general-systems approach appears to be preferable on a large number of counts. Most comprehensive treatments of organization either embrace the systems approach totally, or at least pay homage to it. See, for example, Hall (1972), Kast and Rosenzweig (1974), and Katz and Kahn (1966). Even some critics of systems theory appear to be questioning their earlier views (Peery, 1973).

An Organizational Paradigm

Basically, the systems approach to organizations postulates that organizations acquire resources from the external environment, transform these input resources into output goods and services, and dispose of the outputs in such a way as to facilitate the continual acquisition of additional inputs. This is illustrated in Figure 4.1.

This conceptualization may be elaborated, as by James Thompson (1967), and may be illustrated in greater detail, as demonstrated in Figure 4.2.

Regardless of their precise form (the various feedback loops have been left out of Figure 4.2 for visual clarity), systems models share a conception of the organization as a resource processing entity operating under norms of rationality, which is a subsystem of larger subsystems. Probably the foremost proponent of the systems view for organizational analysis has been Talcott Parsons (1956).

For purposes of this discussion, the systems view has been reformulated, as shown in Figure 4.3, which is an expansion of an earlier formu-

Figure 4.1   Simplex Systemic Representation of the Organization

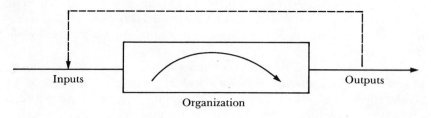

Inputs   Outputs

Organization

Figure 4.2   Complex Systemic Representation of the Organization

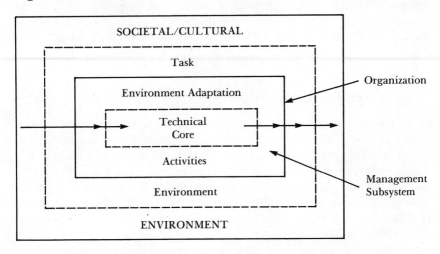

lation (Connor, Egan, & Karmel, 1973). The roncept underlying this
view is straightforward.

The organization is viewed as a resource processing subsystem. The
transformation of input resources into outputs occurs within the formal
organizational framework (*A*). The nature of this transformation is constrained by the contextual components, as well as by various organiza-

Figure 4.3   An Organizational Paradigm

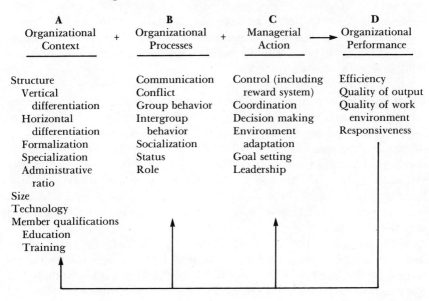

A Organizational Context	B Organizational Processes	C Managerial Action	D Organizational Performance
Structure	Communication	Control (including	Efficiency
Vertical	Conflict	reward system)	Quality of output
differentiation	Group behavior	Coordination	Quality of work
Horizontal	Intergroup	Decision making	environment
differentiation	behavior	Environment	Responsiveness
Formalization	Socialization	adaptation	
Specialization	Status	Goal setting	
Administrative	Role	Leadership	
ratio			
Size			
Technology			
Member qualifications			
Education			
Training			

tional processes (B). The transformation is then effected through managerial action (C), and is reflected in ultimate organizational performance (D). The reader is referred to Connor et al. (1973) for an extended description of the variables and processes identified in Figure 4.3.

Values and Organizational Variables

In the literature there have been occasional reports or discussions of values as they relate to the organization. Zald (1963), for example, attempted to determine whose values predict organizational performance. Sikula (1971) related respondents' values to their personal goals. DeSalvia and Gemill (1971) compared values held by students of business administration to those held by practicing managers. Hage and Dewar (1973) compared elite values and organizational structure as predictors of organizational innovation.

In addition to these studies, many investigators have concerned themselves with what Katz and Stotland (1959) call "instrumental" values, as they obtain in organizational settings. The investigations reported by Merton, Reader, and Kendall (1957) and Becker, Geer, Hughes, and Strauss (1961) are classics; they demonstrated the effects of medical school socialization on the student. Similar studies have been conducted on other occupational groups in a variety of organizational settings: teachers in public schools (Gross, Mason, & McEachern, 1958), counselors in juvenile correctional institutions (Perrow, 1966), officers in military schools (Palen, 1972), convicts in prisons (Hefferman, 1972; Thomas & Foster, 1973), patients in mental institutions (Goffman, 1961), scientists and other professionals in various organizations (Moore, 1970; Vollmer & Mills, 1966), and managers in business corporations (Dill, Hilton, & Reitman, 1962).

As a result of such investigations, a great deal is becoming known about how, for example, socialization takes place in complex organizations. Still, little is known of the impact such a process has on the organization or its operations. In particular, it is not known how values of organizational actors interact with organizational properties in effecting socialization, or how such interaction affects other processes or managerial actions. Beyond this specific consideration of socialization, little is understood about the ways in which values affect, are affected by, and interact with a multitude of organizational properties, processes, and managerial actions.

A brief parenthetical observation is in order: Organizational-member values, or value orientations, may be more accurately characterized by the concept "value profile." Probably the best methodological approach to assessing values in organizations is the use of profiles and profile analyses. Thus, the average significance attached to a particular value by a set of organizational members may be viewed and assessed in relation to the significance attached by them to other selected values. Top management, for example, or middle management in small-batch organizations, or some other such member set may be characterized by a profile of value emphases. This profile then may be used in profile analytic tests of hypotheses concerning values.

From the paradigm in Figure 4.3, it can be seen that several classes of questions are seemingly important, yet remain unanswered.

(A) Values and Organizational Context. What is the relationship between values and organizational context? Are member values affected by various contextual components? Are there reciprocal aspects to the relationship? Hodgkinson (1971) found that value orientations differ by hierarchical levels. On the other hand, he found little relationship between values and such biographic data as age, sex, and seniority. Coughlan (1969) also found no relationship between values and biographic variables. In another vein, Woodward (1965) concluded that values of top executives varied by organizational technology. Although these data clearly are insufficient to allow generalizations to be made, as a general testable proposition it is suggested that there *are* stable relationships between values of organizational members and components of organizational context. In particular, the following illustrative hypotheses are proposed:

A1. Value orientations vary systematically with hierarchical position.

A2. Value orientations vary in accordance with variation in organizational formalization.

A3. Value orientations vary in accordance with variations in education and training of members.

A4. Value orientations differ in accordance with differences in dominant technology.

(B) Values and Organizational Processes. It cannot be assumed that member values are related only to formal properties of the organization. In fact, it is suspected that values, as a variable, may explain even more of the variance in organizational processes, such as conflict, communication, and group behavior. Hodgkinson (1971), for example, found values of teachers and administrators in elementary schools to be related to their hierarchical status in the school system. He further reports variances in social-interaction perceptions of teachers as a function of value differences.

Unfortunately, little else has been reported on the relationship between values and organizational processes. For purposes of inquiring into the matter, therefore, the following hypotheses are offered:

B1. Conflict occurs more frequently and is resolved with greater difficulty, the greater the value differences among parties.

B2. Accuracy of communication among organizational members varies directly with value consensus among the members.

B3. Group cohesion is directly related to value consensus among group members.

B4. Effectiveness of intergroup cooperation is directly related to between-group consensus of member values.

(C) Values and Managerial Action. The implications of values for organizational administration are best identified by considering the ways in which member values relate to specific managerial actions. It is almost certain that decision making, for example, is influenced by the values of those involved in the decision-making process. Thus, Drake (1973) reports that the perceived usefulness of group decisions was positively related to similarity of values between the decision makers.

Other managerial actions also are likely to affect and be affected by member values. Pennings (1970) found promotion rates to be directly related to values of subordinates; whether this finding also is reflective of the *superordinates'* values is unknown. Further, Hesel (1971) reports a positive relationship between teachers' values and their pupil-control ideology. Specific hypotheses suggested by these considerations include the following:

C1. Perceived decision utility is directly related to degree of value consensus among decision makers.

C2. Leadership effectiveness is directly related to degree of value consensus between leader and followers.

C3. Emphasis placed on various organizational goals by management (goal profile) is directly related to management's value profile.

C4. Effectiveness of administrative coordination is directly related to value consensus among those whose activities are being coordinated.

C5. Type of managerial control, as exemplified by criteria used in the organization's reward system, is directly related to management's values.

C6. Means by which management performs its environment adaptation functions are directly related to management's values (example: means by which purchasing agent tasks are performed are predictable from management value profiles).

(D) Values and Organizational Performance. As a final aspect, the relationship of member values to ultimate organizational performance is considered. Although many scholars have investigated organizational effectiveness, little consensus exists as to its proper dimensions or how to measure them. A review of the literature suggests the four dimensions

indicated in Figure 4.3: efficiency, quality of output, quality of work environment, and responsiveness (Connor, Egan, & Karmel, 1973). Briefly, *efficiency* includes financial and administrative variables such as labor productivity, profit, waste control, proportion of capacity used, elimination of dysfunctional procedures, improved work flows, and appropriate information systems. *Quality of output* refers both to goods produced and to services rendered by the organization. In the manufacturing sector, a single unit of output may be of superior or inferior quality. This qualitative difference is clearly important to an assessment of organizational effectiveness. In the service sector, the quality of service rendered may be as important as the fact that the service occurred. In the health field, for example, this component may mean utility of the service to the consumer. *Quality of work environment* is reflected in member satisfaction with the organization as a whole, the job being performed, supervision, or interpersonal relationships with organizational colleagues. *Responsiveness* is the ability of the organization to adapt to its external environment and to maintain flexibility to adjust its internal operations to meet changing circumstances. Responsiveness therefore is the coping mechanism which increases the capacity or potential of the organization to survive and prosper over the long range under conditions of uncertainty.

Whether viewed as identical with or underlying the formation and pursuit of organizational goals, values are inherently critical to the organization's performance on these several dimensions. In the latter view, values are seen to lie at the heart of goal-setting and strategy-choosing processes; in the former view, values *are* the goals. Regardless of which view one holds, there are few data which allow anything except speculation about the relationship between values and organizational effectiveness. What data do exist concern that aspect of organizational effectiveness referred to here as quality of work environment, or elsewhere as organizational climate. Several investigators report findings which show a strong relationship between member values and the character of organizational climate (Coughlan, 1971; Gies & Leonard, 1971; Hodgkinson, 1971). These studies all were conducted in elementary and secondary schools, however, and they dichotomized organizational climate into "open" and "closed," following the scheme developed by Barnes (1960).

Because of the complexity of the organizational effectiveness construct, and because of the paucity of information regarding it, one is reluctant to offer hypotheses even as imprecise as those presented previously. Some illustrative questions can be posed, however, suggesting the directions that research might take in this area:

D1. Is there a direct, stable relationship between organizational performance on various dimensions of efficiency and the management value profile? Worker value profile? Management–worker value consensus?

D2. How are worker values related to output quality? Is output quality related to degree of management–worker value consensus?

D3. Is value consensus between management and workers related to properties of organizational climate (such as job satisfaction, leadership style, etc.)?

D4. Is the organization's ability to be responsive related to top management's value profile? Middle management's? Top–middle consensus? Management–worker consensus? Do the same relationships hold for both external adaptability and internal flexibility?

Questions such as these require investigation if an understanding of the ways in which values relate to the organization's ultimate effectiveness is to be developed.

CONCLUSION

It has been suggested that an important knowledge gap exists in organization theory. This gap concerns the nature of the relationships among values of organizational members and various organizational properties, processes, and activities. The merit of research into this area is relatively clear. First, values may well be more parsimonious predictors of organizational phenomena than are such variables as attitudes, perceptions, and personality traits—all of which are currently used frequently and with little thought of their relationships to underlying value systems (Connor & Becker, 1974). Second, values may supply some critical missing variance. That is, it is not expected that values will always explain 100 percent of the variance of some other variable. To the contrary, the evidence is clear that, even without considering values, there are strong relationships among some variables (Hall, 1972). It is contended, however, that such relationships may be more fully explained by including member values as a distinct variable in the analysis.

Some cautionary remarks are offered. First, the authors have been extremely vague in their operational use of the concept "value," as in the hypotheses and questions presented in the preceding section. This vagueness has been deliberate and it arises out of necessity. As Rokeach states, "Given the present state of development of the social sciences, it is not yet conceptually meaningful or technologically feasible to assess routinely . . . values" (Rokeach, 1968–1969, p. 547).

This deficiency is reflected in the vast number of value instruments available. A volume published by the University of Michigan's Institute for Social Research contains no less than 12 value instruments, plus several others that could easily be considered value measures (Robinson

& Shaver, 1969). Perusal of this volume demonstrates the variety of operational approaches extant, ranging from simple two- and three-value instruments to complex multivalue arrays. At this stage of research, the authors feel it is unwise to attempt to specify the "universal value sets." Rather, different research objectives will call for attention to different kinds of values. For example, research into the relationship between top management values and conflict resolution effectiveness probably would be concerned with value consensus along professional, social harmony, administrative, and rationality dimensions, rather than spiritual and aesthetic.

This selection has emphasized exhortation rather than specifics. However, the current state of knowledge regarding values and the organization is almost nil; thus, exhortation appears to be called for. Organizational researchers have little understanding regarding the function that member values play in organizational processes. Systematic research into such topics as those suggested here may help develop that understanding.

5

Social Movements as Moral Confrontations: With Special Reference to Civil Rights

Sandra J. Ball-Rokeach and Irving Tallman

One of the central problems faced by groups seeking social changes is how to overcome the inertia and apathy which tends to characterize the orientation of a populace toward most social issues. This problem is exacerbated for those who lack the institutional and organizational bases of authority that enable legislators, educators, jurors, and other legitimate agents of change to affect social policy. Those individuals or groups who do not have access to legitimate avenues of influence will attempt to affect policy by direct appeals to the populace; in brief, to mobilize pressure for change through means of a mass social movement. Those social movements which were able to have an impact on the popular conscience seem also to have had greater impact on the course of social events.

In this chapter we shall explore some of the mechanisms available to social movements in their efforts to overcome public inertia and appeal to social conscience. Specifically, the thesis developed in this selection is that the creation of a morality play is an effective mechanism for mobilizing support for the movement's objectives. We do not claim that the capacity to create a successful morality play is sufficient for accomplishing the larger movement goals of preventing or bringing about change. Others (Smelser, 1963; Tilly, 1964; Olson, 1965; Turner & Killian, 1972; Oberschall, 1973; McCarthy & Zald, 1973; Berk, 1974; Marx & Wood, 1975) have analyzed the critical role of historical–structural forces and organizational and material resources in movement formation and impact. However, the morality play contributes an essential impetus through its capacity to bring about belief and behavior change via moral confrontation. Further, its dramatic qualities effectively absorb the player and the audience alike into a symbolic dynamic which heightens and intensifies the interactions. This dynamic elicits the media coverage so necessary for movement visibility and success.

We shall first identify the essential players in contemporary social movement morality plays. We will then identify five strategies of moral confrontation that articulate the moral problem from the movement's point of view to pose the moral dilemma to nonmembers. Morality play construction and strategies of moral confrontation are then elaborated in a case study of one of the most successful civil rights movements in American history, the Southern Christian Leadership Conference.

THE PLAYERS

We conceive of social movement morality plays as having at least four players—the good, the bad, a chorus, an audience—and, possibly, a fifth player—decision makers—depending on whether the movement is change oriented. It is generally in the interests of social movements to be cast in the role of the "good,"[1] since it casts at least an informal legitimacy upon the movement and its goals. Such legitimacy is enhanced when the movement embellishes the good role through martyrdom or victimization at the hands of the "bad." Observers have noted, for example, the impetus given the civil rights movement by Bull Connor's brutality against black demonstrators in Birmingham in 1963, thus prompting President Kennedy to observe: "The civil rights movement owed Bull Connor as much as it owed . . . Lincoln" (Metcalf, 1968).

Individuals and groups whose values and interests are in conflict with the goals of a particular social movement will understandably resist the "bad" label and attempt to reverse the order of moral attribution. Wealthy or powerful targets usually fail to be convincing in the good or martyred role and, thus, resort to other means of avoiding the bad label. Efforts may be made to keep the issue from public awareness by avoiding confrontation, by discrediting the opposing side through challenge

[1]There are, of course, exceptions, such as terrorist and satanical movements that do not seek to be cast in the role of the "good." In the case of terrorists, however, rationales usually include the ultimate good that, unfortunately, can only be reached through "bad" means.

of credentials and motivation or by explicitly denying the moral issue. Directly confronting one or another of the moral components of the issue will be a last resort (Tallman, 1976). Thus, we see the initial struggle between the movement and its target to be over the very construction of the main substantive theme of the morality play.

In modern societies, the role of the "chorus" is frequently played by the mass media, which disseminate and interpret the morality play to the "audience." An increasingly important component of movement visibility is media coverage, because the major communication links between movements and the public or the audience are provided by the mass media (Katz, Gurevitch, & Haddassah, 1973; Ball-Rokeach & De-Fleur, 1976). It is usually in the movement's interest to establish reciprocity between it and the media, wherein the movement provides the media with a "newsworthy" event to cover and, in exchange, the media provides the movement with an audience. Since, increasingly, "newsworthy" is interpreted in terms of dramatic appeal, those movements that are characterized by conflict, violence, pathos, and uniqueness are most likely to be considered newsworthy and are, therefore, most likely to gain a media chorus. The "chorus" plays a key role in unraveling the drama, for it speaks "objectively" with the truth of an oracle.

Even if movements have all of the other essential ingredients for success (e.g., material resources and organizational skills), "decision makers" will probably not attend to movement objectives unless they perceive the movement as capturing the audience's attention and involvement. Because movements generally lack easy access to decision makers, they are forced to use dramatic means to make their issues salient matters of public opinion that decision makers must attend to (Lipsky, 1968; Turner, 1970; Klapp, 1970). The morality play is a particularly effective tactic because it can provide the drama of conflict between the good and the bad to meet media and audience requirements to be both absorbing and entertaining, and thereby heighten pressures for decision-maker involvement.

Values provide the symbolic threat that ties all these players together around a common moral theme. The values of the players may differ in their hierarchical ordering, but they come from the same value pool, a value pool that is generally known and adhered to by virtually everyone in society. The movement seeks to promote or prevent change in the name of certain universal moral values. These values are usually translated into prescriptions for change that would not only require decision makers to alter their present policies and practices, but would also bring some cost to those benefiting from the status quo. A social movement's values not only guide the articulation of such changes, but also provide justifications as to why such changes constitute moral imperatives. Likewise, the arguments of the movement's opponents are couched in value terms to justify the policies and practices that the social movement would change. The social conflict that emerges is rooted in competing value priorities that guide and justify competing policy prescriptions for resource distribution (Marx & Holzner, 1977; Oberschall, 1973).

MORAL CONFRONTATION

While the media considers itself successful if it draws a large and attentive audience, the social movement must go further: it also attempts to have an impact on the audience. To engage the heart and mind of an audience in the moral struggle, movement strategists must not only know the audience's conceptions of good and bad, but also what constitutes a genuine moral dilemma for it. With this information in hand, the movement can then set the process of moral confrontation into motion.

Our conception of moral confrontation instigated by natural social movements seems analogous to the self-confrontation technique employed in many laboratory experiments (Rokeach, 1973, 1979, and chapters 12 to 15 in this volume). Self-confrontation is brought about by the communication of information that exposes awareness to specified inconsistencies between values, attitudes, or behavior. Research has shown that awareness of such inconsistencies often produces an affective state of self-dissatisfaction, and, consequently, relevant values and related attitudes and behavior undergo change designed to remove the self-dissatisfaction. People need to see themselves and to be seen by others as moral and competent beings, and this need provides a powerful vehicle for belief and behavior change. When social movements—change agents—are able to point to specific instances in which people are violating their own conceptions of morality and competence, the mechanisms of behavioral and social change are often set in motion. We are suggesting that social movements employ self-confrontation to bring about social changes in ways which parallel the techniques used in laboratories to produce value, attitude, and behavior change. Indeed, we will attempt to show that all of the components of this technique are evident in certain civil rights struggles of recent years.

Of the many possible variations of the confrontation technique, five that are particularly suitable for social movements are identified below. These are not mutually exclusive, for a movement may use more than one strategy at the same time or over time. Letting X = an individual or group, and Y = another individual or group, the moral confrontation strategies are as follows:

1. *Hypocrisy:* Value–Behavior Discrepancy
Xs are confronted with evidence indicating that their behaviors are inconsistent with their espoused values.

2. *Forced Choice:* Value Incompatibility

Xs are confronted with the fact that one of X's cherished values cannot be fulfilled because it is incompatible with another of X's cherished values.

3. *False Consciousness:* Value Control

Xs are confronted with evidence that Ys have instilled value priorities in Xs, thus allowing Ys to control Xs.

4. *Disaster:* Behavioral Consequences

Xs are confronted with information indicating that their value priorities will lead to disaster and must therefore be changed.

5. *Purity:* Value Conformity

Xs are informed that their values do not conform to an absolute Y value system, and thus stand in danger of losing Y's approval.

It may be conjectured that all social movements are in the moral confrontation business, employing one or more of the five moral confrontation strategies—to gain public attention, adherents, and the attention of decision makers. Social movements try to bring about or to resist social change mainly by attempting to change values, or by attempting to freeze them, through one or another strategy of moral confrontation. We suspect that the effectiveness or ineffectiveness of any social movement hinges upon the clarity of the morality play and of the strategies the movement is able to employ.

To illustrate such a general "morality play" view of social movements, we will focus our attention in the remainder of this chapter on Martin Luther King's civil rights movement as a case study, in the hope of learning what made it so successful, at least at the outset, and what later led to its decline. We will first analyze the players and the strategies employed by Martin Luther King's SCLC and its opponents; how SCLC first managed to gain media attention and, through the media, the attention and support of the public; some morality play factors that led to the decline of SCLC; and a novel, emerging morality play within the civil rights movement of the late seventies. Finally, we will consider briefly some research implications.

THE SOUTHERN CHRISTIAN LEADERSHIP CONFERENCE

The formation of SCLC can be seen as a continuation and extension of a struggle that began with the American Revolution. Content analyses of the major revolutionary documents—the Declaration of Independence, the United States Constitution, and the Federalist Papers—uniformly show that the value of freedom is the most frequently mentioned of all values (Tracy, 1975). But the constitutionally guaranteed freedoms were initially restricted to landed male adults. It was this restriction that was to become the focal point for virtually all the civil rights struggles that were to follow. It set the stage for one group after another (up to and even including the movement culminating in the Bakke case) to articulate the dominant theme of all such morality plays: expressing a demand for equal access to constitutionally guaranteed individual freedoms.

In analyzing how the SCLC became one of the most potent morality plays in American history, it is instructive to comment briefly on how it first came into being. It is not enough to say that the movement was precipitated by a black woman's imprisonment for failing to give up her seat on a bus to a white, because it does not tell us why this particular incident and not others led to the formation of the SCLC. While there are a number of factors that could be considered, the most relevant for present purposes is that members of the black community responded to the Montgomery bus incident by demanding a meeting with local black church leaders to discuss the situation. During the course of this meeting, the church leaders were accused of hypocrisy for failing to act on behalf of the imprisoned woman, on the one hand, while espousing pious concerns about her welfare, on the other. This moral confrontation is said to have activated the church leaders—and, in particular, Martin Luther King—to form a protest movement that came to be known as the Southern Christian Leadership Conference, a local movement that in a few years would engulf the whole South and then the nation as a whole. We can only speculate about the extent to which the Conference leaders—and, in particular, Martin Luther King—were shaken and influenced by their own moral self-confrontation as hypocrites. What is clear is that they proceeded to employ this same strategy in their exhortative appeals to other blacks, the larger white community, and decision makers.

At the heart of the SCLC movement was its moral advocacy of nonviolence. Their first effort was a boycott of the segregated Montgomery bus system. Overcoming their enormous inertia and fear to mount and sustain this boycott, and later demonstrations, must have taken a special coalescence of moral forces, which included a leader endowed with special moral qualities,[2] compelling strategies of moral confrontation, organizational ties (Freeman, 1975; Weller & Quarantelli, 1973) between community and church, and incidents that could readily be translated into questions of values.

Many blacks must have undergone their own individual moral confrontations before they could change from a lifetime of resigned and passive acceptance of segregation to, suddenly, a shared, yet nonviolent

---

[2]Potent and effective morality plays would seem to be conducive to the attribution of "charisma" to the movement leader.

militant resistance to discrimination on buses, in restaurants and schools, and at the voting booth. SCLC's tactics for mobilizing the black members of the community included strategies of moral confrontation to make them dissatisfied with their images of themselves: How can we go on saying among ourselves that we are as good as anyone else, yet behave in public as though we are not (Hypocrisy)? How come some of us are their Uncle Toms, and how come we go on thinking of ourselves as they do (False Consciousness)? How can we maintain our dignity and self-respect when we are so polite and obedient to those who oppress us (Forced Choice)?

It was possible to couch variants of such moral confrontation strategies to appeal more specifically to whites. Two examples of the Hypocrisy strategy come readily to mind: an espousal of Christian love and brotherhood, yet indifference or discrimination against black Christian brethren; an espousal of Constitution-sanctioned principles of justice and fairness for all, yet condoning of one or another instance of discriminatory treatment of black Americans. And three examples of the Forced Choice strategy: justice and fairness versus law and order; supporting the funding of the war on poverty versus funding the war in Vietnam; equal treatment and opportunity for all versus individual freedom to exploit or profit from the labor of others.

But whereas the third strategy, False Consciousness, was more directed by SCLC to black Americans, the fourth strategy, Disaster, was probably more directed to white Americans: If you don't listen to those few of us who preach love and nonviolence, you will strengthen the hand of many others of us who preach hate and violence; if you continue to ignore our demands for equal treatment, you will have to face certain disastrous consequences—moral decay, rioting, looting, burning of our ghettos, and loss of prestige and influence abroad.

What can be said of the fifth strategy, Purity? As far as we can tell, it was not employed by SCLC, but it was employed by Black Separatists and somewhat later by Black Power advocates. Appeals to such values as "Black is beautiful," separatism, and the superiority of Afro-American culture were appeals directed solely to black Americans—to preserve their purity or their moral authority. At this stage of analysis, we can only wonder whether the Purity strategy is a strategy of despair, a dogmatic moral strategy employed as a last resort when all other moral confrontation strategies have failed.

Our case study analysis of the moral confrontation strategies of the civil rights movement must be supplemented by at least a brief analysis of the moral confrontation strategies employed by right-wing social movements opposing civil rights: the Ku Klux Klan, the White Citizens Council, the American Nazi Party, the John Birch Society, and so on. We observe, by and large, their employment of the same moral confrontation (except for False Consciousness), but with a different content. They argue that it is hypocritical to claim that America is the land of the free when there are so many laws to constrain our freedom to reside, to rent, to employ, to educate our children, to eat, and to play. They argue that advances in equality cannot be brought about without substantial reductions in individual freedom. They argue that Disaster will follow if we lose our individual freedom. And they appeal in various ways to Purity: Anglo-Saxon purity, fear of mongrelization, and a return to a fundamentalist interpretation of the Bible.

Having identified the primary strategies of moral confrontation employed to gain members, activate potential supporters, and counter the arguments of opponents, we turn now to an examination of the means used by movements to create viable morality plays capable of gaining media coverage. Again, we shall use the SCLC as our prototype.

GAINING MEDIA COVERAGE

SCLC was able to command media and audience attention by becoming a martyred, heroic victim of violence. Central to SCLC's assumption of this role was its commitment to nonviolent forms of protest, on the one hand, and to religious values, on the other. A simple, easily communicated contrast thus emerged between SCLC's approach and the approach of the opposition. The uniformed police and jeering white onlookers at demonstrations became the readily identified "bad guys" that the media could portray unambiguously to their audience. Drama and action were added when the controlled deliberateness of SCLC marchers refusing to obey the law elicited violent responses from rock-throwing onlookers and police who used dogs, hoses, and clubs in clear view of the cameras. Another factor that SCLC strategists effectively played upon was the Southern setting, which fostered a parallel between its struggle and the "let my people go" morality play of a century earlier.

The national news media entered increasingly into the emerging morality play in the role of chorus as appeal to news value became apparent. The civil rights demonstrations had all of the characteristics of newsworthy events—drama, action, conflict, violence, good guys, and bad guys. It is said that Dr. Martin Luther King deliberately selected schoolchildren for his marches to heighten the drama. Dr. King had said that the black struggle for justice and equality would be *shown* to the American people on television. An important strategic factor in maintaining media and audience interest was the SCLC's ability to focus on different incidents, avoiding repetition and boredom. SCLC thus made it easy and profitable for the media to articulate and present the larger morality play to its audience. Moreover, the clear roles of bad and good and the simplicity and intensity of the drama combined to prevent the media from blurring the morality issues conveyed.

GAINING PUBLIC ATTENTION AND SUPPORT

Now SCLC had to put it all together by creating a morality play that would touch, involve, and confront a substantial portion of the media audience. They posed their multifaceted lamentations in concrete contexts that the media could transmit to the audience through vignettes and minidramas, and viewers were able to identify with the victims. Many viewers were able to imagine for perhaps the first time what it was like to be black, not in the abstract, but in the context of a Southern bus, restaurant, motel, what it was like trying to exercise the right to vote, and so on. Making people aware of such legally sanctioned forms of discrimination would probably not have succeeded in eliciting a sympathetic audience reaction if put in the context of a speech. Success in eliciting audience identification was probably a combined product of the dramatic moral confrontation between the "good" and "bad," and the legitimation provided by continual national coverage.

The most critical audience reaction needed to bring about a genuine moral confrontation between SCLC and the audience was introspective or reflective responses that link the self to the problem posed by the movement. It is not enough to have a large, involved audience that sees the problem as merely existing "out there." Such an audience can avoid the experience of self-dissatisfaction that is needed to initiate value, attitude, and behavior change. This is where the several moral confrontation strategies discussed earlier become relevant. These strategies, singly and in combination, and employed in varying contexts over time, stimulated self-examination, self-awareness, and self-dissatisfaction. Equally important, SCLC provided a way to reduce or alleviate self-dissatisfaction; namely, support or join the movement.

Although as yet there is no direct experimental evidence, we think it is a reasonable hypothesis that the process of change initiated by the arousal of moral self-confrontation is sustained when self-dissatisfaction is reduced or removed. This is because the change is psychologically rewarding, if for no other reason than that it eliminates a source of discomfort. It is also sustained by group support. Most Americans watching the morality play portrayed in the media were probably not watching it in isolation from others. The daily media contact probably became a frequent topic for conversation. Group discussion probably mediated and sustained whatever the impact of the moral confrontation, either by supporting and sustaining belief and behavior changes that would reduce self-dissatisfaction, or by group support of individual efforts to deny the validity of the moral confrontation and thus avoid the experience of self-dissatisfaction. In brief, the SCLC morality play and its strategies of moral confrontation were probably most effective with: (1) persons considering themselves egalitarian who were confronted with a discrepancy between their espoused egalitarianism and their behavior; (2) persons considering themselves compassionate Christians who were confronted with a discrepancy between their espoused compassion and their antiegalitarianism; (3) persons experiencing self-dissatisfaction, whatever the discrepancy with which they were morally confronted; and (4) persons receiving group support for their belief or behavior change.

There is some evidence that the pain of moral self-confrontation did indeed lead to belief and behavior change amongst the American citizenry and decision makers. Many blacks underwent belief and behavior change. They created and adopted positive images of themselves (e.g., "black is beautiful"), stopped teaching their children to defer to whites and to think of themselves as inferior to whites, and began applying the organizational skills developed in the movement to acquire more individual, community, and national power (Tallman, 1976). Equally significant, research indicates that the importance of equality went up in the value hierarchy of many white Americans between 1968 and 1971 (Chapter 7). The proportion of whites who believed that blacks were inferior or deserved inferior treatment went down, while the proportion willing to vote for black candidates for political office went up (Campbell, Converse, & Rodgers, 1976). Decision makers and policy makers in and out of government passed and implemented civil rights legislation that they had previously opposed.

We do not claim that the only precipitant of all such belief and behavior change was the threat to people's conceptions of themselves as moral human beings. The legal tactics of NAACP, the militant tactics of CORE and SNCC, the threat tactics of the Panthers, and the urban riots all undoubtedly played their part. The key difference, we believe, between all these and SCLC's impact was that SCLC as a social movement succeeded in forcing a moral confrontation of right versus wrong on a large segment of Americans. Above all, President Kennedy had stated in a special national address that the issues posed by SCLC constituted a "moral issue" for the nation.

THE FALL

While many factors can probably account for the fall of SCLC and the black civil rights movement in general, one of the most relevant was surely the rise of a competing morality play concerning America's participation in the Vietnamese war. By 1968 the peace movement had become national in scope, producing an even more active citizen involvement than did the civil rights movement. Much of the media's and the audience's attention was diverted from issues of equality and freedom for blacks to issues of peace and national security.

As we all know, Dr. King felt compelled to take a public stand against the Vietnamese war, largely because he could not compartmentalize the moral issues of the civil rights movement from the peace movement: black Americans were far more often drafted, maimed, and killed in Vietnam. It is reasonable to suggest that no social movement can successfully manage more than one major morality play at a time, unless there is an almost complete overlap of players and themes. Two such powerful and divergent themes as racial equality in America and peace in Vietnam could not both be maintained despite SCLC efforts to portray them as but different aspects of a single problem—racism at home and abroad. The attempt to merge these two morality plays into one failed because it was possible for many people to support the peace movement, and thus enhance their conception of themselves as moral, regardless of their position on civil rights. Thus, the door was open to subordinate or even to ignore the push for peace. Not enough overlap between those playing the role of the good and the bad in the two movements further served to muddy the waters. The U.S. government, for example, was the number one bad guy of the peace movement, but it was one of the good guys in the civil rights movement.

Several additional factors may have effected the fall of SCLC. One of these was its growth from a regional to a national movement. As SCLC moved increasingly into the national arena, the simple moral goal of seeking equality in "the racist South," supported by law and custom, was replaced with the more complex and difficult goal of removing "institutionalized racism" in America. A second factor was the assassination of Dr. Martin Luther King in the spring of 1968. His assassination meant not only the loss of organizational and material resources, but, equally important, the loss of the central symbol of the good in the morality play. A third possible factor, about which not enough has been said, and which admittedly needs more detailed documentation, is the Nixon Administration's attempt to destroy a movement which they regarded as threatening their own political interests.

THE AFTERMATH

By the end of the Vietnamese war, the black civil rights movement had lost its momentum and vitality. While blacks have been elected to local and national office, they were not able to bring about the equalization of the economic and social conditions for which they had hoped

The importance of the value "equality" had once again slipped back to its pre-1968 position in the average American's value hierarchy (Inglehart, 1975). Affirmative Action programs had failed to equalize the distribution of blacks and whites in the occupational structure. We are now entering an era wherein the concept "reverse discrimination" is becoming more salient than the concept of discrimination. All this suggests that conventional institutional forces are not yet altogether ready to continue on the course toward racial equality set by the civil rights movement of the sixties. Thus, we may anticipate that future progress to realize the goals of SCLC will probably depend on the success of yet other civil rights movements.

One such post-SCLC movement is Jesse Jackson's People United to Save Humanity (PUSH), an innovative movement that shows promise of producing a new kind of morality play. Jackson, another young black minister, developed his skills as an SCLC lieutenant to Martin Luther King. Rather than attempting to revitalize the SCLC's morality play in which good and bad roles were assigned mainly to black and white Americans, Jackson has created a new black–black morality play that confronts blacks with the idea that *competence* is the main moral imperative, and that the main players are good blacks who are competent and bad blacks who are incompetent. The goal is to raise the importance of competence values in black value hierarchies so that blacks may ultimately help themselves rather than be helped by others to achieve the "good life."[3]

The stage, players, and content of the PUSH morality play are in the context of the black, rather than the larger, community. Center stage is the predominantly black school. The theme of "moral confrontation" is that if blacks want equality they must not rely on a racist society to give it to them, but must concentrate on raising the priority of values that underlie and culminate in work competence. The role of the good is assigned to those blacks who seek to "excel" in school and at work, while the role of the bad is assigned to those who would not.

In contrast to earlier civil rights movements, PUSH argues that to be moral one must not only be committed to moral principles of church and family, justice and fairness, but also to competence. Its appeals include several strategies of moral confrontation discussed earlier. For instance, black children are confronted with the proposition that they are doing poorly in school because they have internalized what whites believe about their inferiority and about their greater preference for more immediate hedonistic pleasures (False Consciousness). "Poor diet and ra-

---

[3]This is not to say that Jackson and his colleagues have retreated from confrontations with the white community and decision makers. Rather, the movement for black competence is embedded in continuing social and legal struggles for racial equality.

cism didn't prevent us from excelling in sport, so how come it prevents us from excelling in school" (Forced Choice)?

While the media has drawn some public attention to the PUSH movement, its chorus role in developing an effective morality play is obviously less central than it was when SCLC was at the center of the stage. Despite this and other differences between PUSH and SCLC, both movements serve to illustrate the utility of a simple morality play that is able to incorporate strategies of moral confrontation to create a state of self-dissatisfaction that can generate the belief and behavior changes sought by the social movement.

A CONCLUDING COMMENT

A task that remains for students of social movements is to test more systematically and empirically the perspective outlined here. For example, is PUSH effective in creating states of self-dissatisfaction in black students and their parents? And does this dissatisfaction lead to the desired value and behavior change? Empirical data are needed on successful and less successful movements to ascertain the extent to which they differ in creating clear morality play roles of "good" and "bad," the other key components of a morality play, and in effective and ineffective strategies of moral confrontation. Such empirical studies would not only permit evaluation of the fruitfulness of the present analysis, but would also provide knowledge that social movements could apply to design more efficient change strategies. Perhaps most important, such research would also extend our knowledge about the conditions under which value, attitude, and behavior change are brought about, not in the laboratory, but by naturally occurring collectives that deal with real world social conditions that have real consequences.

PART TWO

Some Major Determinants and Consequences of Value Organization

6

Assimilation of Values in Migrant Groups

Norman T. Feather

Our understanding of the conditions under which basic values may change depends upon a wide array of different sorts of evidence. At the one extreme are those experimental studies that manipulate selected variables under conditions of careful control and that draw upon a set of theoretical principles to predict the changes in value priorities that are expected to occur. At the other extreme are those field studies that do not involve deliberate interventions but that investigate value change under naturally occurring conditions trying, where possible, to develop a theoretical understanding of the processes that are involved and the conditions under which value systems are modified.

The studies to be described in the present chapter fall at the latter pole. They investigate the value systems of migrant groups in Adelaide, South Australia. The studies have in common an interest in comparing the value systems of migrants and/or their children with those of members of the host society. A consideration of the similarities and differences that occur throws some light on some of the factors that might lead to change in the value systems of migrants who come to settle in a new country.

A more detailed treatment of the studies described in this selection and their relationship to other studies in our program can be found in

Values in Education and Society (Feather, 1975b). The present chapter closely follows Chapter 9 of that book in describing the Ukrainian and Latvian studies but also introduces some new ideas.

MIGRANT ASSIMILATION

The study of migration has a long history in social science. It has been a topic that has engaged the interest of sociologists, economists, psychologists, anthropologists, historians, and political scientists, each looking at migration from a different point of view, but adding some component to the overall picture. Social psychologists and sociologists have been particularly interested in the question of the degree to which a minority group comes to resemble the host society it has entered. The conditions that lead to change in the direction of the host society and the nature of the changes that occur (e.g., whether they are superficial or at a deeper level) have been investigated in many different studies, especially from the 1920s onward. The interest of social scientists in the study of migrant assimilation has been felicitous in that it has to some extent satisfied both applied and theoretical concerns, providing information of undoubted value to policy makers, while at the same time generating a more sophisticated understanding of how people cope with new environments.

The situation confronted by migrants who leave their own country to settle in a new one is basically the problem of learning to adapt to an unfamiliar culture. The need to adapt to new situations is part of life. No two situations are ever identical and adjustments must continually be made to changed circumstances. Workers who change their occupations, women who marry, students who move to new schools, tourists who visit a foreign country, elderly persons who move into old-age homes, peasants who are confronted by modern technology—all are involved in the process of coping with new environments (Feather, 1975b; Taft, 1977).[1] Some changes in situation are relatively minor ones and can be adjusted to quite easily on the basis of past learning. But other changes are more dramatic and force more extreme and wide-ranging adaptations if an individual is to cope effectively with the new situation.

[1]The study of migrant assimilation is only one part of the general area of culture contact—though a very important one. The effects of more temporary sojourns on people when they become involved in a different culture—as when tourists, students, businessmen, diplomats, Peace Corps volunteers, and so on visit another country—have also been investigated. This sojourn research has been reviewed by Brein and David (1971) and by David (1972). Taft (1977) has also provided an interesting general discussion of how people cope with unfamiliar cultures, in which he classifies the different forms of coping situations that might arise, discusses how a person learns to become a member of a society, reviews his own and other contributions to the study of migrant assimilation, and explores the generality of his multifaceted model for culture-coping situations.

The kind of change faced by migrants is especially dramatic. In most cases, they have to leave behind those who have been important agents in their socialization (parents and friends) from childhood onward. The culture that they enter may be very different from the one they leave. They may have to learn a new language, and they will be exposed to some patterns of beliefs and values and forms of behavior that are quite foreign to them. The society they enter may be organized differently, with new forms of institutions and social structures. Within this unfamiliar culture, they have to proceed with the sorts of tasks that are common to most people, such as finding a home and job, making friends, extending the network of social groups, developing skills, and so on. At a more general level, they have to satisfy and express their needs, achieve some meaningful organization of the continual flow of information that comes to them, develop new responses, and establish some stable anchor points that enable them to avoid being tossed around like a cork in a moving current. In the course of the process, some of the beliefs, attitudes, and values that they brought with them may alter as they are exposed to new types of information, establish new reference groups, and are influenced by those people from the new culture whom they like and respect.

We cannot hope to capture the complexity of this process. Any general theory of how migrants come to resemble members of their host society would have to draw upon ideas and information from different areas of social science, and not only from psychology and sociology. Uncovering the psychological and sociological mechanisms involved is only part of the story. The path that migrants take is governed by many factors that have little to do with themselves as originators and actors. While some of the opportunities and restrictions provided by the new environment may be outcomes of the person's own behavior, others may be a function of economic and political forces that are outside of his or her control. One's own personal efforts may be to no avail in the face of these external realities. There are, however, some relevant theoretical approaches that deal with stages in the assimilation process. Some of these theories are psychological in nature, focusing more upon individuals and the processes involved in their assimilation; others are closer to the sociological pole, focusing more upon the structure of the society that a migrant group enters and how this group comes to be absorbed into the society. To a consideration of these stage theories we now turn.

STAGE THEORIES OF ASSIMILATION

In *Values in Education and Society* (Feather, 1975b), we summarized three stage theories of assimilation developed by Eisenstadt (1954), Gordon (1964), and Taft (1965), respectively. The first two approaches are more sociological in nature. Thus, Eisenstadt (1954) discusses the process of the absorption of a migrant group into a new society, seeing this process as including three different, though closely connected, phases: acquisition of skills, performance of various new roles, and changes in the self-concept that involve sets of values tested in relation to the new roles that are available. He believes that a certain amount of resocialization must occur, and that this develops as the primary groups to which the migrant belongs are gradually transformed and interwoven into the social structure of the receiving society. As this process proceeds, the migrant's roles become institutionalized, values and aspirations develop that are more in tune with those of the absorbing society, and previously held values and aspirations may be restructured to fit the new setting. Gradually, migrants develop new channels of communication with the wider society, extending their social participation and activities further and further beyond the initial primary groups of family and friends. The whole process is not a smooth one. Nor is it always successful. The host society sets limits to what migrants can do and how far they can go.

Eisenstadt discusses three main criteria that one might employ to gauge the degree to which migrants may have been absorbed into the host society: acculturation (or the extent to which the migrant has learned the various roles, norms, and customs of the absorbing society), personal adjustment (as evidenced by low rates of mental illness, suicide, crime, and so on), and institutional dispersion (or the degree to which migrants have become dispersed and absorbed within the various institutional spheres of the society). Full absorption is assumed to have occurred when the migrant group populates the society's institutions and ceases to have a separate identity. Institutional dispersion and the dissolution of the migrant group is seen by Eisenstadt as the principal evidence for full absorption of a migrant group, but he points out that in reality this criterion is never satisfied, and that usually a pluralistic structure arises in which different groups coexist, having some roles in common, some roles unique, and with each group maintaining some degree of separate identity.

Gordon (1964), in an examination of assimilation into American life, presents an influential analysis in which seven different but interrelated subprocesses of assimilation are distinguished. These are: (1) *cultural or behavioral assimilation* (acculturation), where cultural patterns have changed toward those of the host society; (2) *structural assimilation*, where large-scale entry of the migrants into cliques, clubs, and institutions has occurred within the host society, on a primary group level; (3) *marital assimilation*, where extensive intermarriage has taken place; (4) *identificational assimilation*, where migrants have developed a sense of peoplehood based exclusively on the host society; (5) *attitude receptional assimilation*, where social relations involve an absence of prejudice toward members of the migrant group; (6) *behavioral receptional assimilation*, where there is no discriminatory behavior toward members of the migrant group; and (7) *civic assimilation,* where conflict between migrants and the host society is absent over issues concerning values and power. For some migrants, assimilation may go no further than stage 1 (acculturation). Migrants may acquire the language of the host society and learn something about other aspects of the culture so that they can exist within the society, yet their roots may still be firmly planted within the migrant group. Gordon (1964) assigns special status to structural assimilation:

> Once structural assimilation has occurred, either simultaneously with or sub-sequent to acculturation, all of the other types of assimilation will naturally follow . . . structural assimilation, then, rather than acculturation, is seen to be the keystone of the arch of assimilation. The price of such assimilation, however, is the disappearance of the ethnic group as a separate identity and the evaporation of its distinctive values. (p. 81)

Gordon applies his analysis to three views of assimilation that have been discussed in relation to American life: the Anglo-conformity goal, the melting-pot goal, and the pluralistic society goal. He argues that the present American situation reveals a high degree of structural pluralism:

> The most salient fact . . . is the maintenance of the structurally separate sub-societies of the three major religious and the racial and quasi-racial groups, and even vestiges of the nationality groupings, along with a massive trend toward acculturation of all groups—particularly their native born—to American culture patterns. (p. 159)

Taft's approach to migrant assimilation is primarily psychological. Whereas both Eisenstadt and Gordon concentrate upon the absorption or assimilation of immigrant groups or communities into the host society, Taft claims that he is more interested in "changes in the attitudes, reference-groups, identifications, satisfactions, and personality of individual immigrants" (Taft, 1965, p. 2). His theoretical ideas have evolved from a program of studies conducted in Australia by himself and his colleagues, involving migrant groups of various nationalities. In this program he has attempted to develop a multifaceted analysis of assimilation, which he defines as "the process whereby the immigrants and the native population become more alike as a result of interaction" (p. 4). Assimilation involves a certain amount of desocialization and resocialization, as some of the old ways of adapting to society are replaced by new ones that are more appropriate to the new culture (Taft, 1977).

In a recent version of his multifaceted approach, Taft (1973) lists the following five facets, each of which may be further analyzed by considering their dynamics (motivation, conation, perceived achievement, and actual achievement): (1) *cultural knowledge and skills,* in which the new migrant learns the language, acquires other skills necessary for communication, learns about the history and culture of the new group, its ideology, values, norms, and social structure; (2) *social interaction,* in which the migrant feels accepted by the host group and where interpersonal contacts and relationships of different degrees of intimacy develop with members of the host group; (3) *membership identity and social integration,* in which the migrant gains formal membership in groups within the host society and becomes integrated into the structure of the new society, being allowed to carry out the roles and receive the privileges that go with the position (e.g., economic integration in the workplace); (4) *social and emotional identification,* in which migrants feel allegiance to the host society and accept new groups within it as their reference groups; and (5) *conformity to group norms,* in which migrants adopt the values, frames of reference, attitudes, and expectations about role behaviors that are held by the host society, behave in accordance with the norms of the new society, and conform to the norms in their behavior, in their appearance, and in the way they express themselves.

Each of these different facets of assimilation has been looked at separately in questionnaire and interview studies that elicit both subjective information from migrants themselves and objectively observable information about their assimilation status. When the relationships between different measures were investigated, using factor analysis, there was evidence for two main groupings: a factor of "primary assimilation" relating to satisfaction with life in the new country, feeling identified with it, feeling at home in it, and wanting to remain there; and a factor of "acculturation" related to knowing and using the vernacular language, adopting the values of the host society, and social mixing with the members of the host society.

Are some of the facets of assimilation noted by Taft more important than others, in the sense that some may be preconditions if complete assimilation is to occur? According to Taft (1973):

> The Australian studies suggest that the more common sequence is that a degree of satisfaction with the new country must be experienced before the immigrant can become identified with it; and some degree of identification is needed before acculturation occurs. However, for any particular immigrant there may be an individually determined sequence of assimilation. Generalizations concerning sequences, at best, can only apply to limited groupings of "types" of migrants. (p. 236)

This sequence of satisfaction–identification–acculturation has been discussed by Richardson (1974)—a major proponent of it—in a report of his studies of British immigration into Australia, and by Taft (1977), in an essay that examines how people cope with unfamiliar cultures. Both Richardson and Taft note exceptions to it.

The various theories that we have just considered span sociological and psychological perspectives, yet they have certain features in common. As we concluded in *Values in Education and Society* (Feather, 1975b):

In each case there is reference to acculturation, structural assimilation, the performance of new roles, and changes in the beliefs, attitudes, and values of the migrant. And these various aspects of assimilation are not to be thought of as independent, but as interrelated. All three approaches stress the realities of the structured nature of society.... Finally, all three approaches distinguish between changes that occur at the surface and can be easily identified (such as increased skill in employing the language idiom of the host society), and changes that are more central or basic (such as a restructuring of the attitudes and values that the migrant brought with him to the host society). (p. 236)

Finally, it is worth emphasizing that the different aspects of assimilation that we have discussed apply to other forms of assimilation as well. Children who move to a new school, for example, have to adjust to a new culture, learn its traditions, rules, and expectations, discover its attitudes and values, learn about its structure, make new friends, develop some degree of identification with the school, and perhaps take on new roles and responsibilities. In the course of this adaptation, they may become more and more like members of the receiving community, just as the migrant becomes similar in some ways to people in the host country.

Social scientists still have a long way to go before they understand the precise conditions that lead to increasing assimilation and the causal mechanisms that underlie the process. Theories about minority–majority group relations, social learning, stereotyping, social roles, attitude change, social motivation, cognitive discrepancy, and social influence are but a few of the lines of analysis that are relevant. The general approaches to migrant assimilation that we have outlined represent a useful starting point, however, for they enable us to classify some of the important aspects of the process and to explore their interrelationships.

SUBJECTIVE ASSIMILATION

The two studies from the Flinders program, now to be described, were not set within the context of an all-embracing theory of assimilation. Instead, they were concerned with a limited but very important aspect of assimilation, namely, central changes in the cognitive sphere—especially the internal or subjective changes that occur as the migrant's beliefs, attitudes, and values come to resemble those of members of the host culture. This internal or *subjective assimilation* can be distinguished from other aspects of assimilation which are more open to inspection to an outside observer. Migrants may provide external signs of assimilation in that they may have learned the language of the host culture, may use the language frequently, may have joined neighborhood groups, may have become integrated into a work situation, and so on, yet internally they may still hold onto many of the old beliefs, attitudes, and values that they brought with them to the new country. And they may still retain feelings of identification with the country that they left.

Subjective assimilation should be looked upon as one aspect of a complex chain of events that may occur over time as a migrant adapts to a new culture. For some migrants, these internal changes may never occur, even though external forms of acculturation and cultural competence may be apparent. In other cases, there may be a considerable shift toward the subjective culture of the host society, along with associated changes in behavior.

It is reasonable to expect more evidence of subjective assimilation among the children of migrant groups. These young people are being socialized within the new society, and they are learning about the new culture from an early age. They have less of a residue of past experience that might conflict with new experiences within the host culture. Older migrants have already been subject to basic forms of socialization within the primary groups (e.g., family) that most of them left behind in their native country. The effects of this primary socialization will persist, and may be extremely resistant to modification. The socialization that occurs within primary groups determines important aspects of a person's self-identity. Enculturation within the new society may disturb some of these residues, but it will not extinguish them—past events cannot be undone. On these general grounds, we expected that second-generation migrant children would display more evidence of subjective assimilation than their parents.

Strictly speaking, the two studies to be described do not provide evidence about *change* in beliefs, attitudes, and values. Instead, they map similarities and differences at the one point in time. A study of change would investigate migrants over time, obtaining measures of their value priorities, for example, before they left the old country, and measures for the same group at different periods after they had settled in the new culture. We have not attempted this formidable task. Our aims have been much more modest ones, governed by the samples and resources that were available at the time.

THE UKRAINIAN STUDY

Predictions

This first study investigated the value systems of a group of second-generation Ukrainian migrants, and their relation to those of their parents and of the wider Australian community. As we just noted, it is reasonable to assume that adult migrants will be more resistant to change in their basic values, attitudes, and ways of living. Their children are closer to a "clean slate," less set in their ways and patterns of belief. At school and in their leisure time, they have mixed with children of the host society, achieving a degree of acceptance into peer groups. We would expect their value systems to resemble more closely those of members of their host culture than would the value systems of their parents. The study also enabled comparisons to be made between the value systems of children and their parents, adding to other evidence about intergenerational similarities and differences (Feather, 1975b). Finally, it was also possible to explore differences in *ethnocentrism* between the migrant groups and their Australian counterparts.

Subjects and Procedure

Details of sampling and procedure have been provided in earlier reports (Feather, 1975b; Feather & Wasyluk, 1973). Here we outline some of the main features of the investigation. George Wasyluk, himself a second-generation Ukrainian migrant, conducted the testing in 1971. The subjects who were tested consisted of Australian male and female students from the Adelaide University Science Association and their families, and Ukrainian male and female students from the Ukrainian Students Association and their families. These student samples were recruited with the help of leaders of the two student organizations. The students completed a questionnaire under group conditions, and then took sufficient copies home for their parents and other members of the family who were more than 15 years of age. They were cautioned against prompting family members while these members were completing the questionnaire. All questionnaires were completed anonymously, and it was made clear that answers would be treated in strictest confidence.

About 80 percent of the Ukrainian students had been born in Australia, the remainder coming to Australia at a very early age. Most Ukrainian families came to Australia as refugee migrants between 1948 and 1951 under a resettlement program. They were part of the mass immigration to Australia that followed World War II (see Feather, 1975b, pp. 237–239, for a brief description of this postwar immigration).

The questionnaire that subjects completed contained a number of items designed to elicit information about the age and sex of the respondent, length of time in Australia if foreign born, education, and present employment. These were followed by Form E of the Rokeach Value Survey, with the usual instructions (Rokeach, 1973), and by the Australian Ethnocentrism Scale (Beswick & Hills, 1969). This test taps five areas of attitudes derived from Levinson's theory of ethnocentrism (Adorno, Frenkel-Brunswik, Levinson, & Sanford, 1950), namely, stereotyped positive imagery and submissive attitudes regarding ingroups, intolerance of ambiguity and inflexibility, favoring a hierarchical society and suppression of outgroups, segregation within Australia, and rejection of groups outside Australia. Ethnocentrism was defined as a general tendency to discriminate against any possible outgroup that might include aborigines, criminals, Asians, Communists, migrants, or Australians. Scores on the test could range from +64 (maximum ethnocentrism) to −64 (minimum ethnocentrism).

Analysis of Value Rankings

The median rankings of terminal and instrumental values are presented in tables 6.1 and 6.2 for students and parents from each sample. These average value systems were compared for similarity, using Spearman's rho as a similarity index, and the results of these comparisons are presented in Table 6.3.

Table 6.3 shows that the average terminal value systems for the two groups of students were highly similar (rho = .77), and so were those of their parents (rho = .70). It is interesting to note that the average value priorities of the Ukrainian students for the set of terminal values were closer to those of the Australian parents than to those of their own Ukrainian parents (rhos of .79 and .42, respectively). The Australian students also provided average value systems for the terminal values that were closer to those of the Australian parents than to those of the Ukrainian parents (rhos of .65 and .15, respectively). These data suggest that, so far as terminal values are concerned, the Ukrainian students were more similar to the host culture than to their own parents.

When one turns to the results for the instrumental values, it is again apparent that the average value systems were very similar for the Ukrainian and Australian students (rho = .89). But the parental value systems were rather dissimilar (rho = .44). The four cross-correlations were all at about the same level (rhos of .57, .54, .51, and .56).

These results support the prediction that assimilation of migrants toward the value systems of the host culture will be more apparent among the second generation. The Ukrainian students were very similar to the Australian students in their average value systems, more similar than the migrant and host parents were to one another. The Australian students saw *happiness, freedom, true friendship, a sense of accomplishment,* and *wisdom* as most important among the terminal values and *a comfortable life, social recognition, national security,* and *salvation* as least important. The four most important instrumental values for the Australian students were being *honest, broadminded, responsible,* and *loving,* and the four least important were being *polite, imaginative, clean,* and *obedient.* These average value priorities were very similar to those obtained with other

TABLE 6.1. Median Rankings and Composite Rank Orders of Terminal Values for Ukrainian Students, Australian Students, Ukrainian Parents, and Australian Parents

	MEDIAN RANKINGS				SIGNIFICANT EFFECTS
	Students		Parents		
TERMINAL VALUE	Ukrainian	Australian	Ukrainian	Australian	
N	48	53	36	39	
A comfortable life	11.50 (13)	13.83 (15)	7.00 (5.5)	13.31 (14)	A,B
An exciting life	11.00 (12)	7.63 (10)	14.50 (18)	14.07 (16)	B
A sense of accomplishment	6.83 (6)	6.25 (4.5)	11.50 (13)	7.88 (9)	—
A world at peace	8.20 (10.5)	7.13 (8)	5.33 (3)	5.88 (4)	—
A world of beauty	12.80 (16)	10.30 (13)	11.75 (14)	13.38 (15)	—
Equality	7.60 (9)	7.30 (9)	10.00 (11.5)	9.50 (11)	—
Family security	6.40 (3)	9.06 (12)	1.78 (1)	2.75 (1)	A,B
Freedom	6.50 (4.5)	5.93 (2)	6.00 (4)	6.75 (5)	—
Happiness	4.33 (1)	5.50 (1)	5.00 (2)	5.75 (3)	—
Inner harmony	7.00 (7.5)	6.92 (7)	7.83 (7)	7.83 (8)	B,AB
Mature love	8.20 (10.5)	6.50 (6)	12.50 (16)	8.70 (10)	B
National security	15.00 (17)	14.69 (17)	7.00 (5.5)	11.50 (12)	B
Pleasure	12.17 (14)	13.50 (14)	14.25 (17)	14.10 (17)	—
Salvation	15.67 (18)	15.92 (18)	8.75 (9)	12.50 (13)	B
Self-respect	6.00 (2)	7.70 (11)	8.33 (8)	6.88 (6)	—
Social recognition	12.50 (15)	14.30 (16)	12.00 (15)	15.28 (18)	A
True friendship	6.50 (4.5)	5.94 (3)	10.00 (11.5)	7.10 (7)	A,B
Wisdom	7.00 (7.5)	6.25 (4.5)	9.40 (10)	5.25 (2)	A

Note: The lower the median, the higher the relative value. The rank order of each median (low to high) is shown in parentheses. "A" effects refer to Ukrainian versus Australian. "B" effects refer to students versus parents. Ns are for error-free rankings. Alpha level is $p < .01$.

Source: Data are from Feather & Wasyluk, 1973.

TABLE 6.2. Median Rankings and Composite Rank Orders of Instrumental Values for Ukrainian Students, Australian Students, Ukrainian Parents, and Australian Parents

	MEDIAN RANKINGS				SIGNIFICANT EFFECTS
	Students		Parents		
INSTRUMENTAL VALUE	Ukrainian	Australian	Ukrainian	Australian	
N	46	52	34	38	
Ambitious	10.71 (14)	11.40 (14)	9.00 (7.5)	12.67 (15)	B
Broadminded	5.71 (3)	5.33 (2.5)	9.00 (7.5)	9.50 (10.5)	—
Capable	9.20 (10)	9.35 (11)	7.33 (4)	8.20 (5)	A
Cheerful	9.50 (11)	7.67 (7)	12.00 (16)	8.50 (7.5)	B
Clean	13.67 (17)	14.38 (17)	8.00 (5)	9.67 (12)	—
Courageous	9.00 (8)	8.40 (8)	9.00 (7.5)	9.50 (10.5)	—
Forgiving	8.00 (5.5)	6.75 (6)	6.50 (3)	9.33 (9)	—
Helpful	8.00 (5.5)	8.67 (9)	9.00 (7.5)	10.17 (13)	—
Honest	3.50 (1)	2.33 (1)	1.67 (1)	2.20 (1)	B
Imaginative	10.00 (13)	13.00 (16)	15.44 (18)	15.29 (18)	B
Independent	9.00 (8)	6.40 (5)	9.33 (10)	11.50 (14)	—
Intellectual	9.67 (12)	10.33 (13)	10.00 (13.5)	13.20 (16)	—
Logical	11.33 (16)	9.00 (10)	10.00 (13.5)	8.50 (7.5)	—
Loving	5.50 (2)	5.75 (4)	9.40 (11)	5.50 (3)	—
Obedient	14.67 (18)	15.00 (18)	13.00 (17)	13.50 (17)	—
Polite	11.00 (15)	12.40 (15)	10.40 (15)	8.00 (4)	—
Responsible	7.80 (4)	5.33 (2.5)	6.00 (2)	4.00 (2)	A
Self-controlled	9.00 (8)	9.29 (12)	9.50 (12)	8.33 (6)	—

Note: The lower the median, the higher the relative value. The rank order of each median (low to high) is shown in parentheses. "A" effects refer to Ukrainian versus Australian. "B" effects refer to students versus parents. Ns are for error-free rankings. Alpha level is $p < .01$.

Source: Data are from Feather & Wasyluk, 1973.

TABLE 6.3.   Similarity Indexes Comparing Median Rankings Across Groups

	STUDENTS		PARENTS	
	Ukrainian	*Australian*	*Ukrainian*	*Australian*
Students				
Ukrainian		.77	.42	.79
Australian	.89		.15	.65
Parents				
Ukrainian	.57	.54		.70
Australian	.51	.56	.44	

Note: Similarity indexes for average terminal value systems are above the diagonal; similarity indexes for average instrumental value systems are below the diagonal. Higher similarity indexes indicate greater similarity between the average value systems involved in the comparison.

Source: Data are from Feather & Wasyluk, 1973.

Australian adolescent student groups in studies reported in *Values in Education and Society* (Feather, 1975b), and the average order of priorities of the Ukrainian students overlapped with them.

But some interesting differences emerged when two-by-two analyses of variance were applied to the transformed ranks for each value (Feather, 1975b, pp. 23–24), with country of origin (Ukrainian versus Australian) as the first factor (A) in the analysis and generation (parent versus student) as the second factor. The statistically significant effects are presented in tables 6.1 and 6.2. When the rankings of Ukrainian respondents were compared with those of Australian respondents (irrespective of whether they were parents or students), several significant ($p < .01$) effects of country of origin occurred (A effects). Ukrainian respondents ranked the following values as more important when compared with Australian respondents: *a comfortable life, family security,* and *social recognition.* The Australian respondents ranked the following values as more important: *true friendship, wisdom, cheerful,* and *responsible.* When the rankings of parents were compared with the rankings of their children (regardless of country of origin), several significant ($p < .01$) effects of generation occurred (B effects). The following values were ranked as more important by the students: *an exciting life, mature love, true friendship, broadminded, imaginative,* and *independent.* Their parents ranked these values as relatively more important: *a comfortable life, family security, national security, salvation,* and *clean.* One significant interaction (AB effect) emerged, due to the fact that Ukrainian parents ranked *mature love* especially low in importance relative to the other groups. These various differences can be observed when the medians are compared.

In summary, both parents and children from the Ukrainian families assigned more importance than their Australian counterparts to values that related to various forms of security and recognition, whereas parents and children from the Australian families gave more emphasis to affiliative values, a mature understanding of life, and being responsible and cheerful. The greater stress placed by the Ukrainians on security can be understood in terms of the experience of the parents as refugees, and the fears and insecurities that this experience would provoke. No doubt the parents communicated these concerns to their children. In a new and somewhat alien culture it is not surprising that these families would value national security, not wanting a repetition of past events, and that they would look to the family unit as an especially significant source of psychological comfort.

The parent–child or generational differences in value priorities were similar to other results reported and discussed in *Values in Education and Society* (Feather, 1975b), to which the reader is referred. They were strong enough to emerge despite differences in national backgrounds and suggest that some intergenerational differences in value priorities may have considerable cross-national applicability.

Analysis of Ethnocentrism Scores

Let us now turn to the evidence about subjective assimilation that comes from the analysis of the ethnocentrism scores. Table 6.4 presents the mean scores on the Australian Ethnocentrism Scale and Table 6.5 summarizes results for three groups of items concerning aborigines, Communists, and Asians.

The total ethnocentrism scores were analyzed, using a two-by-two-by-two analysis of variance with sex of respondent, country of origin, and generation as factors in the analysis. The following statistically significant effects emerged: Total ethnocentrism scores were higher for parents than for children ($p < .001$), irrespective of whether respondents came from Ukrainian or Australian families. Parents and children from Ukrainian families had higher total ethnocentrism scores than

TABLE 6.4.   Mean Total Ethnocentrism Scores for Ukrainian Students, Australian Students, Ukrainian Parents, and Australian Parents

	MALE	FEMALE
Ukrainian students	−17.34	−22.84
Australian students	−27.25	−20.42
Ukrainian parents	.75	1.59
Australian parents	− 4.50	− 6.90

Source: Data are from Feather & Wasyluk, 1973.

their Australian counterparts ($p < .05$). Males and females did not differ in their total ethnocentrism scores at a statistically significant level, nor were any of the interaction terms from the analysis statistically significant.

Analyses of the individual items contained in Table 6.5 reinforce the general differences just reported. In nearly all cases, the parents were significantly more ethnocentric than their children. The Ukrainians were particularly ethnocentric toward Communists, with Ukrainian parents showing the greatest antagonism toward this particular group. Their attitudes had a basis in reality, when one considers that they were refugee migrants who had fled their homeland. Quite apart from this difference, however, it is possible that older migrants may be rather suspicious of outgroups in general, being particularly sensitive to the possibility of threats to their security. As we noted, these migrants also placed a higher premium on security values than did their Australian counterparts. Thus, the attitude differences were consistent with some of the value differences already reported.

We do not intend to dwell on the generational differences in ethnocentrism evident in tables 6.4 and 6.5 except to say that they are consistent with differences in conservatism described in Chapter 9 of *Values in Education and Society* (Feather, 1975b), and in later reports where parents were significantly more conservative than their children (Feather, 1977a, 1977b). The measure of conservatism used in the related study was the Conservatism Scale developed by Wilson and Patterson (1968; see also Wilson, 1973). A number of the items in this scale relate to outgroups (for example, mixed marriage, apartheid, white superiority, colored immigration). Factor-analytic studies of the items in the Conservatism Scale have also provided evidence for a factor involving ethnocentric attitudes (Feather, 1975a; Wilson, 1973).

Generational differences have to be interpreted with great care, especially when they are based upon cross-sectional evidence. The more pronounced ethnocentrism and general conservatism among the parents could reflect genuine ontogenetic or life-cycle changes as people grow older and take on new roles and responsibilities. They could also reflect historical events and other effects that occur because different generations belong to different age cohorts and are subject to different influences (e.g., differences in education, war and its aftermath, economic frustrations); for a discussion of this point, see Feather (1975b, 1977a) and Jennings and Niemi (1975). The same argument applies to generational differences in value priorities. The causal influences are difficult to disentangle and quite sophisticated investigations are required involving a mixture of cross-sectional and longitudinal designs, in which different age cohorts are followed up from different starting points in the flow of historical time.

TABLE 6.5. Items from Australian Ethnocentrism Scale Concerning Aborigines, Communists, and Asians

	MEANS				
	Students		Parents		SIGNIFICANT EFFECTS
ITEM	Australian	Ukrainian	Australian	Ukrainian	
Aborigines					
1. It is far better for all concerned to keep aborigines on reserves and mission stations.	1.68	1.93	2.12	2.69	A*, B***
2. If we let aborigines live in our communities the standards of hygiene might be lowered.	2.10	2.65	2.72	3.11	A*, B**
3. Given equal pay aborigines will work as hard as a white man.	3.85	3.86	2.90	3.87	A*, B*, AB*
4. I wouldn't like any member of my family to marry an aborigine.	2.06	3.13	3.89	4.00	A**, B***, AB*
5. Aborigines should be helped to settle in the cities and given the same advantages as white people.	4.48	4.27	3.93	3.75	B***
6. I would not like an aborigine to be my boss.	1.66	2.07	2.83	2.72	B***
7. When he is given a fair chance the aborigine can live as decently as any white man.	4.53	4.32	3.91	3.87	B***
Communists					
1. Australia should aim at closer contact with Communist China	4.04	3.10	3.30	1.59	A***, B***

2. People who hold Communist beliefs should not be allowed to hold high positions in the public service.	2.77	3.27	3.75	4.52	A**, B***
3. The Australian government should prevent the forming of groups such as Nazis and Communists in Australia.	2.45	3.33	4.18	4.44	A**, B***
Asians					
1. Allowing educated Asians to immigrate benefits Australian society.	4.11	3.71	4.06	2.90	A***, B*, AB*
2. The White Australia policy is a good policy because it helps to keep Australia white.	1.70	2.15	2.86	3.35	A*, B***
3. It is wrong to say that Asians, in general, are not to be trusted.	4.13	4.00	3.51	3.80	B*
4. We must be careful not to let too many Asians into the country or they'll take over the place.	2.46	2.65	3.31	4.08	A*, B***
5. Asians should be allowed to migrate to Australia.	3.71	3.51	3.06	2.48	B***
6. The Japanese are very productive people and should be allowed to settle in Australia.	3.87	3.18	2.55	2.51	B***

Note: Possible responses to each item were "strongly agree," "agree," "disagree," or "strongly disagree," keyed to scores of 5, 4, 2, and 1, respectively. A total score for the scale was obtained by summing scores on the 16 positive items expressing an ethnocentric position, and then subtracting the sum of scores on the 16 negative items expressing the opposite position. Hence, scores could range from +64 (maximum ethnocentrism) to −64 (minimum ethnocentrism). In the two-by-two analysis of variance for each item, Factor A = Ukrainian versus Australian, Factor B = students versus parents.

*p < .05.
**p < .01.
***p < .001.

By way of summary, we can conclude that there was evidence from the Ukrainian study that the migrant children were more assimilated to the values of the host culture than were their parents. But within each group there were pronounced generational differences in social attitudes and value priorities that were consistent with those found in other studies.

THE LATVIAN STUDY

Predictions

The Ukrainian study was the very first attempt to look at subjective assimilation within the context of the Flinders program. As such, it was a relatively straightforward and simple study that tried to make the most of the opportunities available for testing Ukrainian and Australian groups without pretending to involve any great theoretical or methodological sophistication. But it opened up new territory and pointed the direction for further research.

The Latvian study went further, including measures of different aspects of assimilation, such as acculturation, ethnic identity and identification, structural assimilation, and subjective assimilation. Its main concern was to explore the effects of attending an ethnic school on value priorities and to discover how accurate the Latvian and Australian groups were in perceiving the value priorities of the other. Parent–child differences were not investigated.

Like the Ukrainians, the Latvians represent a refugee migrant group. Most of them arrived in Australia in 1949 and 1950 as displaced persons, and since then there have been few additions to their number. They have a strong national identification; many of them see themselves as keepers of a national heritage that they believe is being destroyed in their homelands. Taft (1965, p. 67) noted that migrants from the Baltic States who were tested in the Perth study had very low identification with Australia when compared with other migrant groups, and Kukurs (1968) found that Latvians in Canberra had strong ethnic identification. The ethnic schools that some young Latvians attend represent an attempt to inculcate and preserve ethnic consciousness. These schools, which are outside of the Australian educational system, meet in Latvian community centers and sometimes in private homes, usually on a weekly basis. Pupils are taught about the Latvian language and literature, and learn aspects of Latvian history and geography, the main aim being to preserve Latvian literacy and ethnic consciousness. In the report of her study on Eastern European minorities in Adelaide, Martin (1972) estimates that approximately 33 percent of Latvian children were attending these ethnic schools.

It is reasonable to expect that the Latvian children who attend these ethnic schools will be less assimilated to Australian life than the Latvian children who do not attend. In its emphasis on identity and Latvian traditions and heritage, the ethnic school would tend to counter assimilation toward Australian mores. Also, children attending the ethnic school would probably tend to come from families that are less assimilated than those of the nonattenders. These families may have less group contacts within the Australian community, less motivation to move toward Australian ways, and a stronger desire to preserve their Latvian identity and identification and the language and cultural heritage of their homeland. These concerns would be communicated to their children. The study to be described could not disentangle the relative importance of ethnic school and family as influences on the path of assimilation. Both influences would be expected to work in the same direction, however, for the ethnic school attenders in such a way as to slow down their movement toward greater similarity with their Australian peers.

Subjects and Procedure

Again, details of sampling and procedure can be found in previous reports (Feather, 1975b; Feather & Rudzitis, 1974), and only the main features will be abstracted here. Two groups of male and female Latvian adolescents were involved in the study: one consisted of those who had attended the Latvian Saturday or ethnic school (the "attenders"); the other comprised those who had never attended the ethnic school (the "nonattenders"). These two groups of respondents were contacted at high schools widely dispersed in Adelaide. All were second-generation immigrants with Latvian parents. Those who attended the Saturday school had done so for about six years, on the average. The Australian sample consisted of adolescents of about the same age as the Latvians (mean age between 15 and 16 years) who were obtained from various youth organizations covering a wide area of Adelaide. All of the testing was organized by Arnold Rudzitis, a second-generation Latvian migrant, and respondents were tested in group settings with the help of high school teachers and supervisors in 1972. All respondents completed the questionnaires anonymously, with the usual request to read the instructions carefully, to work quietly, and to give their own answers.

There were two versions of the questionnaire, one for the Latvian respondents and one for the Australian respondents. Both versions began with Form E of the Rokeach Value Survey in its usual form, respondents being asked to rank the sets of terminal and instrumental values in their order of importance in regard to self—that is, to give their own priorities. The Latvian respondents were then asked to rank the two sets of values according to how they thought Australians of their own age would rank them. Similarly, the Australian respondents were then asked to rank the two sets according to how they thought new Australians of their own age would answer them. In each case, therefore, rankings for self were obtained before rankings for the other group. This procedure was followed because it was thought that the rankings for self would provide a meaningful reference frame for judgments of the value systems of the other. The Australian respondents were not asked to rank the values for Latvians because we considered that this task would be too specialized, given the relatively small number of Latvians in Australia. Instead, they ranked for new Australian migrants in general.

Following the Value Survey, respondents completed the Australianism Scale, developed by Taft (1962, 1965; see also Putnins & Taft, 1976) to measure degree of assimilation to Australian society, the Conservatism Scale (Wilson, 1973; Wilson & Patterson, 1968), and a specially constructed set of items. These three sections of the questionnaire were presented in counterbalanced order to control for possible order effects. Because there were no statistically significant differences in the mean scores on the Australianism and Conservatism scales when the two Latvian groups and the Australian group were compared, this part of the study will not be discussed further (but see Feather, 1975b, pp. 261–263). Differences did emerge, however, for the specially tailored items. Hence, these items will be described in more detail.

There were 10 special items for the Latvians; for seven of these items, the respondent had to choose one of five possible answers that were scored from 1 to 5 in the direction of increasing assimilation to Australian society. Three items were concerned with *ethnic identity* as perceived by self, by parents, and by friends. In the case of own identity, for example, the question was: "Generally, do you think you are: Completely Latvian (1)? More Latvian than Australian (2)? Half Latvian–Half Australian (3)? More Australian than Latvian (4)? Completely Australian (5)?" (Note that the way answers were scored in degree of assimilation is indicated after each possible response, though, of course, these scores were not included in the items as presented to respondents.) *Ethnic identification* was investigated by the question: "Generally, would you prefer to be Completely Latvian (1) . . . ?" and so on, the alternative responses being the same as those for the three identity items. One item was concerned with *ethnic origins of friends:* "Would you say that you have: All Latvian friends (1)? More Latvian than Australian friends (2)? Half Latvian–half Australian (3)? More Australian than Latvian (4)? All Australian friends (5)?" Another related to the ability to speak the *ethnic language,* and still another to the preferred use of this language: "Can you speak Latvian: Very Well (1)? Well (2)? Reasonably Well (3)? Badly (4)? Not at all (5)?" and "When you have a choice do you: Speak Latvian only (1)? Speak more Latvian than English (2)? Speak Latvian and English equally (3)? Speak more English than Latvian (4)? Speak English only (5)?" Finally, two items asked the Latvian respondents to list the Latvian and Australian groups and organizations to which they belonged. And one item asked them if there were any preferred countries in which they would like to live more than Australia. The 10 items were presented in mixed order.

There were also five specially tailored items for the Australian respondents. Three of these items corresponded to those in the Latvian questionnaire that were concerned with memberships in Australian groups, memberships in new Australian groups, and countries of residence in preference to Australia. The remaining two items have been described in the original report (Feather & Rudzitis, 1974). These five items were also presented in mixed order.

All respondents completed the questionnaire by providing biographical information concerning place of birth, date of birth, sex, religious affiliation, suburb of residence, school attended, father's occupation, and nationality of parents. They were also asked whether (and, if so, when) they had ever attended the Latvian ethnic school.

Analysis of Value Rankings

The median rankings by the Australian and Latvian respondents, for themselves (own priority) and for the other (perceived priority), are presented in tables 6.6 and 6.7. Table 6.8 presents the similarity coefficients (Spearman rho) when these sets of median rankings (or average value systems) were compared with each other. Higher values of these coefficients imply increasing degrees of similarity between average value systems.

There are a number of interesting findings in Table 6.8 (Feather, 1975b, pp. 254–256), but we will focus upon two of them only. First, the *own* average value systems of Latvians and Australians were very similar, and this similarity was rather more pronounced for the set of terminal values than for the set of instrumental values (compare the triads of similarity coefficients for own priorities above and below the diagonal). All three groups ranked *a world at peace, freedom, happiness,* and *true friendship* as among their most important terminal values, and *national security, pleasure,* and *salvation* as among their least important terminal values (see Table 6.6). All three groups ranked being *honest, broadminded, responsible,* and *loving* as among their most important instrumental values, and being *obedient* and *imaginative* as among their least important ones (see Table 6.7). These highest and lowest priorities are similar to

TABLE 6.6. Median Rankings and Composite Rank Orders of Terminal Values for Latvian and Australian Groups, in Relation to Own Priorities and Perceived Priorities of Other Group

| | LATVIAN GROUPS | | | | AUSTRALIAN GROUPS | |
| | School Attenders | | School Nonattenders | | | |
TERMINAL VALUE	Own	Perceived Australian	Own	Perceived Australian	Own	Perceived New Australian
N	59	51	28	28	51	48
A comfortable life	9.50 (8.5)	5.58 (3)	11.00 (12.5)	5.67 (4)	13.50 (17.5)	9.50 (10)
An exciting life	8.13 (6)	3.93 (1)	8.00 (8)	6.00 (5.5)	10.50 (12)	12.67 (17)
A sense of accomplishment	9.30 (7)	6.63 (5)	8.25 (9)	10.33 (10)	8.21 (8)	9.00 (8.5)
A world at peace	5.25 (3)	5.88 (4)	4.33 (2)	4.67 (2)	3.93 (1)	5.50 (1)
A world of beauty	10.83 (14)	11.63 (14)	11.00 (12.5)	10.67 (11)	10.88 (13)	11.67 (16)
Equality	9.50 (8.5)	8.63 (10)	5.67 (3)	6.50 (7.5)	6.93 (6)	6.20 (5)
Family security	10.06 (12)	12.10 (15.5)	7.00 (6)	13.00 (16)	8.38 (9)	5.75 (3)
Freedom	5.50 (4)	4.30 (2)	4.00 (1)	4.00 (1)	6.17 (4)	6.00 (4)
Happiness	4.79 (2)	7.75 (9)	6.33 (4)	6.50 (7.5)	5.63 (3)	7.00 (6)
Inner harmony	9.70 (11)	11.10 (13)	10.33 (11)	12.00 (13.5)	7.50 (7)	10.00 (11.5)
Mature love	9.56 (10)	6.88 (6)	9.50 (10)	11.00 (12)	8.50 (10)	11.50 (15)
National security	12.70 (16)	14.25 (17)	13.00 (15)	14.00 (17)	13.25 (16)	10.33 (13)
Pleasure	10.75 (13)	7.25 (7)	13.33 (16)	6.00 (5.5)	13.13 (15)	10.60 (14)
Salvation	16.25 (18)	16.19 (18)	13.80 (17)	16.67 (18)	13.50 (17.5)	13.25 (18)
Self-respect	11.70 (15)	12.10 (15.5)	12.33 (14)	12.33 (15)	10.21 (11)	9.00 (8.5)
Social recognition	14.17 (17)	9.08 (11)	14.67 (18)	9.00 (9)	12.50 (14)	8.00 (7)
True friendship	4.75 (1)	7.70 (8)	6.60 (5)	4.80 (3)	4.30 (2)	5.57 (2)
Wisdom	6.75 (5)	9.79 (12)	7.50 (7)	12.00 (13.5)	6.83 (5)	10.00 (11.5)

Note: The lower the median, the higher the relative importance of the value. In each column the rank order of each median (low to high) is denoted in parentheses after the median. Ns are for error-free rankings.

Source: Data are from Feather & Rudzitis, 1974.

TABLE 6.7. Median Rankings and Composite Rank Orders of Instrumental Values for Latvian and Australian Groups, in Relation to Own Priorities and Perceived Priorities of Other Group

INSTRUMENTAL VALUE	LATVIAN GROUP				AUSTRALIAN GROUP	
	School Attenders		School Nonattenders			
	Own	Perceived Australian	Own	Perceived Australian	Own	Perceived New Australian
N	59	53	28	28	52	50
Ambitious	8.38 (7)	6.08 (4)	6.00 (3)	6.00 (3.5)	9.25 (9)	4.25 (1)
Broadminded	4.13 (1)	4.79 (2)	7.50 (4)	5.00 (2)	7.33 (5.5)	6.50 (4)
Capable	8.75 (9)	7.42 (6)	8.00 (5.5)	7.67 (8.5)	10.00 (11)	7.00 (6)
Cheerful	8.50 (8)	6.38 (5)	9.25 (9)	4.83 (1)	8.00 (8)	10.75 (15)
Clean	10.50 (14)	11.38 (16)	11.00 (15.5)	12.00 (16.5)	11.63 (15)	10.50 (13.5)
Courageous	12.10 (15)	5.75 (3)	11.00 (15.5)	7.67 (8.5)	10.33 (13)	8.50 (7)
Forgiving	7.50 (6)	11.30 (15)	11.00 (15.5)	11.00 (15)	7.33 (5.5)	11.00 (16)
Helpful	9.50 (10)	10.58 (14)	9.50 (10)	9.00 (11)	7.75 (7)	8.75 (8.5)
Honest	5.42 (2)	10.50 (12.5)	5.60 (2)	7.00 (6.5)	5.80 (2)	6.75 (5)
Imaginative	12.50 (16)	9.75 (10)	15.00 (18)	8.33 (10)	13.00 (16.5)	10.50 (13.5)
Independent	9.83 (11)	4.38 (1)	9.00 (8)	6.00 (3.5)	9.40 (10)	6.33 (3)
Intellectual	13.06 (17)	9.83 (11)	10.00 (11.5)	10.00 (12.5)	13.20 (18)	9.75 (11)
Logical	9.93 (12)	10.50 (12.5)	11.00 (15.5)	10.00 (12.5)	11.50 (14)	9.83 (12)
Loving	6.21 (5)	9.30 (9)	8.00 (5.5)	7.00 (6.5)	5.00 (1)	9.33 (10)
Obedient	13.90 (18)	14.50 (18)	10.50 (13)	14.75 (18)	13.00 (16.5)	12.40 (18)
Polite	10.10 (13)	13.56 (17)	8.67 (7)	12.00 (16.5)	10.25 (12)	12.20 (17)
Responsible	5.79 (3)	8.17 (8)	5.00 (1)	6.50 (5)	6.00 (3)	6.00 (2)
Self-controlled	5.92 (4)	7.88 (7)	10.00 (11.5)	10.60 (14)	7.25 (4)	8.75 (8.5)

Note: The lower the median, the higher the relative importance of the value. In each column the rank order of each median (low to high) is denoted in parentheses after the median. Ns are for error-free rankings.

Source: Data are from Feather & Rudzitis, 1974.

TABLE 6.8. Similarity Indexes Comparing Median Rankings Across Conditions

	OWN PRIORITIES			PERCEIVED PRIORITIES OF OTHER GROUP		
	1	2	3	4	5	6
Own Priorities						
1. Latvian school attenders		.86	.81	.67	.69	.52
2. Latvian school nonattenders	.68		.87	.46	.52	.65
3. Australians	.93	.63		.30	.41	.70
Perceived Priorities of Other						
4. Perceived Australian by (1)	.36	.34	.25		.86	.20
5. Perceived Australian by (2)	.54	.60	.46	.82		.45
6. Perceived new Australian by (3)	.54	.65	.44	.71	.69	

Note: Similarity indexes for average terminal value systems are above the diagonal; similarity indexes for average instrumental value systems are below the diagonal. Higher similarity indexes indicate greater similarity between the average value systems involved in the comparison. In the columns, 1 = Average own value priorities of Latvian school attenders, 2 = Average own value priorities of Latvian school nonattenders, 3 = Average own value priorities of Australians, 4 = Average perceived value priorities of Australians by Latvian school attenders, 5 = Average perceived value priorities of Australians by Latvian school nonattenders, 6 = Average perceived value priorities of New Australians by Australians.

Source: Data are from Feather & Rudzitis, 1974.

those obtained in other studies involving Australian adolescents (Feather, 1975b). Thus, as was the case in the Ukrainian study, there was evidence that a considerable degree of subjective assimilation had occurred among the second-generation immigrants, as indicated by the similarity in average value systems and also by the similar mean scores for Australianism and Conservatism noted previously. But there was no evidence from these comparisons that the Latvian school attenders were any less assimilated than the Latvian school nonattenders. In fact, not only were the average value systems similar across all three groups, but there was a complete absence of significant differences (setting a conservative level of .01 for significance) when the transformed ranks for each of the terminal and instrumental values (in regard to *own* priorities) were compared across the three groups using simple one-way analyses of variance.

This takes us to the second point. The difference in degree of value assimilation between the two Latvian groups emerged in a very subtle way. Table 6.8 shows that the Australians more accurately perceived the own value priorities of the Latvian school nonattenders than those of the Latvian school attenders. The relevant comparisons are rhos of .65 and .65 for the terminal and instrumental values, respectively, compared with rhos of .52 and .54. Correspondingly, the Latvian school nonattenders more accurately perceived the own priorities of the Australians than did the Latvian school attenders. The relevant comparisons are rhos of .41 and .46 for the terminal and instrumental values, respectively, compared with rhos of .30 and .25. Both of these comparisons suggest greater assimilation of the Latvian school nonattenders if one uses *accuracy of perception of the other's values* as an index of degree of assimilation.

Analysis of Questionnaire Items

Table 6.9 compares the Latvian school attenders with the Latvian school nonattenders on several of the items from the Latvian version of the questionnaire. The results of simple one-way analyses of variance of the item scores are included in Table 6.9. It will be recalled that item scores could range from 1 to 5, a higher score representing increased assimilation in the Australian direction.

Table 6.9 shows that, on all of the items, the Latvian school nonattenders showed more evidence of assimilation. They were more likely to see themselves as toward the Australian pole as far as their *ethnic identity* was concerned, and thought that their parents and friends would see them that way too. They were more likely to express a preference for being Australian *(ethnic identification)*, and to indicate that more of their friends were Australian than Latvian *(ethnic origins of friends)*. They were also more likely to state that they had low ability in speaking Latvian *(language ability)* and to prefer to speak English rather than Latvian *(language preference)*.

Among the Latvian school nonattenders, 82 percent of the group memberships reported were Australian, compared with 38 percent by the Latvian school attenders. All of the Australian respondents reported memberships with Australian groups. Among the Latvian school nonattenders, 36 percent said that they would prefer to live in countries other than Australia. The corresponding percentages for the Latvian school attenders and the Australian respondents were 56 percent and 35 percent, respectively. All of these differences supported the expectation that the Latvian school nonattenders would be more assimilated in the Australian direction.

Discussion

These results indicate that the group of Latvians who did not attend the ethnic school were further along the path of assimilation than the group of Latvians who did. This greater degree of assimilation was particularly evident when responses to the tailored items on the question-

TABLE 6.9. Percentage of Respondents for Different Categories of Assimilation and Mean Item Scores of Latvian Saturday School Attenders and Nonattenders on Items from Questionnaire

		PERCENTAGE OF RESPONDENTS FOR DIFFERENT ITEM CATEGORIES						
ITEM	Assimilation	1 Low	2	3	4	5 High	Mean Item Score	Significance Level (p)
Ethnic Identity								
Perceived by Self								
School attenders		1.6	44.0	35.5	16.9	1.6	2.73	< .001
School nonattenders		0.0	10.7	21.4	50.0	17.8	3.75	
Perceived by Parents								
School attenders		28.8	42.3	15.2	11.8	1.6	2.15	< .001
School nonattenders		10.7	14.2	21.4	32.1	21.4	3.39	
Perceived by Friends								
School attenders		1.6	22.0	30.5	33.8	11.8	3.32	< .001
School nonattenders		0.0	3.5	10.7	35.7	50.0	4.32	
Ethnic Identification								
School attenders		10.3	31.0	41.4	13.8	3.4	2.69	< .01
School nonattenders		3.5	14.2	42.8	7.1	32.1	3.50	
Ethnic Origins of Friends								
School attenders		0.0	15.5	46.6	31.0	6.9	3.29	< .001
School nonattenders		0.0	3.5	7.1	67.8	21.4	4.07	
Ethnic Language								
Ability								
School attenders		28.8	44.0	22.0	5.0	0.0	2.03	< .001
School nonattenders		0.0	10.7	28.5	10.7	50.0	4.00	
Preference								
School attenders		3.3	8.4	30.5	52.5	5.0	3.47	< .001
School nonattenders		0.0	0.0	3.5	32.1	64.2	4.61	

Note: For details of the low-to-high, 1-to-5 columns, see Feather, 1975b, p. 253.

Source: Data are from Feather & Rudzitis, 1974.

naire were compared, and it appeared both in visible forms (such as membership in groups, country of preference, ethnic origins of friends, language ability and preference) and in more subtle and private aspects (such as perception of ethnic identity and identification). These Latvian school nonattenders, therefore, showed more acculturation, more identificational assimilation, and more evidence of structural assimilation than did the Latvian school attenders. The ethnic school attenders were more likely to possess bilingual skills and to prefer using the Latvian language, more likely to belong to Latvian groups and organizations and to have Latvian friends, more likely to perceive themselves as Latvian and to see their parents (especially) and their friends (less firmly) as perceiving them that way, and more likely to prefer being Latvian.

We cannot disentangle the chains of causation involved in the assimilation process from these results, although it seems likely that moving out into the new community in various ways, making friends with Australian peers, and becoming absorbed into informal and formal structures within the host society were all important aspects, intertwined with developing feelings of identification and with deepening acculturation.

At the level of values, the Latvian second-generation immigrants were quite similar to their Australian peers. In the Ukrainian study, we also found that the average value systems of the young second-generation immigrants were similar to those of a group of Australians of similar age. Hence, both studies supported the prediction that second-generation immigrants would be close to their peers in the host culture as far as value assimilation was concerned—at least when average value systems were compared.

The subtle result emerging from the Latvian study was that the ethnic school nonattenders were more *accurate* judges of Australian values than were the Latvian school attenders. Why? The answer probably lies in the greater social interaction of the Latvian school nonattenders within the host community, as evidenced by the greater frequency of Australian friends they reported, the more Australian group memberships they indicated, and so on. The Latvian school attenders were relatively more removed from Australian society and, with decreased opportunity for testing beliefs against reality, they might have been less accurate in their views and more willing to fall back on stereotypes about Australians that were not the product of their own experience in social interaction. It is interesting to note that this difference in accuracy of perception between the Latvian attenders and nonattenders occurred even though the segregation involved (attendance at an ethnic school once a week) was relatively mild. One can speculate about the consequences had the segregation been severe, with the migrant families insulated in ghettos or enclaves with little or no contact with the host community. The effects of a mild degree of segregation may be reinforced, however, by the attitudes and behavior of the child's parents. As noted, it is likely that the parents of the Latvian school attenders, with strong commitments to preserving Latvian culture and traditions, would influence their children in their choice of friends and in terms of the other groups to which they chose to belong. Thus, one can speculate about a consistent set of forces that would operate to inhibit full assimilation to Australian ways among the ethnic school attenders.

ASSIMILATION AND DISCREPANCY THEORY

The Ukrainian and Latvian studies of assimilation highlight some of the major aspects involved in the assimilation process and some of the differences that may occur (for example, between migrant parents and their children, ethnic school attenders and nonattenders, and so on). The analysis of these differences helps to deepen our understanding of a multifaceted, complex process. In this final section, we will look at migrant assimilation more generally within the context of discrepancy theory (Feather, 1971a, 1975b), giving special attention to the subjective assimilation of values.

As we remarked, the two studies that have been reported do not provide evidence about change in value systems over time as a consequence of migration from one country to another. But they do show that second-generation immigrants had value systems that were relatively similar to those of their Australian peers. In other studies involving adult migrants in Australia, evidence has been adduced for shifts toward increasing similarity with the host culture, with some individuals showing greater degrees of assimilation than others (Richardson, 1974; Taft, 1965).

We believe that the modification of value systems among migrants is a very complex process, intimately connected with the nature and extent of the social interaction in which the migrant engages within the host culture and with the degree to which the basic value priorities that migrants bring with them from their homeland are discrepant with those of the new culture. Large discrepancies in value systems are more difficult to resolve than small ones, and there may be minimum changes if the migrant does not have the opportunity to interact with members of the host culture. Without social interaction, the discrepancy might not even be noticed because conflicting information does not come to light.

In a general sense, therefore, we can view the changes that may occur in migrant value systems as ways of coping with the sorts of cognitive discrepancies that implicate values and that develop as the migrants expose themselves to more and more information about the host culture, especially during social interaction with the host members. The adult migrant starts with value systems already established, and these may be difficult to change. Migrant children born into the new culture have not been preset, however. Their values are formed and modified within the new society. Their parents may pass on to them a legacy of national traditions and heritage, but this indirect experience of their parents' native culture has to compete with the overwhelming strength and immediacy of the children's own direct experience of life within the new culture. It is not surprising that in so many ways the young second-generation immigrants become similar to their host peers.

But the situation is different for the adult migrants. When they leave their own country to settle in a new culture, they will be subject to a wide range of experiences that are discrepant from what they have been used to previously. The physical environment itself (e.g., its light, color, vegetation, landscape, climate, and so on) may be strange and unfamiliar. They may find that the new society involves a different language, different economic opportunities, different social and political institutions, different forms of social stratification, different norms and values—indeed, a host of differences, some obvious, some subtle. They have to learn to adapt to these discrepancies, and in the course of doing so may have to modify existing responses or develop completely new ones.

The degree to which they feel comfortable in the new environment will relate to the nature and extent of the discrepancies that they encounter. When the environment satisfies their basic needs and abilities and is congruent with their already developed systems of beliefs, attitudes, and values they should feel more satisfied and adjusted than when the person–environment fit is imperfect, involving serious discrepancies that demand resolution. As they learn more and more about the new environment, some discrepancies (e.g., those involving beliefs, attitudes, and values) may be found to be based upon false perceptions of reality, and these discrepancies may then be modified in the light of more accurate information. In this way, the migrants may build up a veridical perception of the new environment. If this is to happen, obviously, a considerable amount of interaction with both the physical and social aspects of the new environment will be necessary. In the case of values, for example, the adult migrants might start with rather vague and undifferentiated perceptions of the dominant values of the host society. These perceptions may become more refined and more accurate as they expand their network of social interaction within the host community. The initial pattern of value discrepancies may be modified in the light of this experience, giving rise to new satisfactions, or perhaps to new dissatisfactions, with the environment.

Some person–environment discrepancies that develop as the migrant interacts with the new culture are more important than others. For example, if persons cannot satisfy their basic needs because they cannot find outlets for their skills and abilities in a work situation, they are obviously confronted with a dramatic discrepancy that demands quick resolution—in the short term, by obtaining forms of social support and temporary relief where they are available, and in the long term, by learning new skills that enable them to cope. At the level of higher-order concepts such as values, some discrepancies that occur between migrants' value systems and those that they attribute to particular social environments are more important than others, involving more pressure for resolution. What makes these discrepancies more important? To answer this question would take us far afield into the psychology of social influence (Abelson, Aronson, McGuire, Newcomb, Rosenberg, & Tannenbaum, 1968; Feather, 1967; Jones & Gerard, 1967; Katz, 1960; Kelman, 1961, 1974; McGuire, 1969; Rokeach, 1973). But we can provide a summary answer based upon that literature (Feather, 1975b):

> The discrepancies between value systems that turn out to be important are those that arise when the discrepant information comes from a highly attractive, legitimate, and credible source—especially if this source belongs to a reference group . . . when that source is seen as acting voluntarily and without coercion, when the receiver of the communication is also exposing himself to the discrepant information of his own free will and accord, when the discrepant information is clear and unequivocal and cannot be distorted, when the extent of the discrepancy is within reasonable bounds and not so great as to evoke outright rejection, and when the discrepant information concerns some issue that is important to the receiver of the communication—especially when it implicates central aspects of the self-concept, such as one's important values. (p. 108)

These kinds of discrepancies may be resolved by modification in underlying value systems in the direction of increased congruence with the discrepant information, particularly if these important discrepancies continually recur as the migrant mixes with the host community and enters its various structures. The change may not be entirely one-way. In the course of their social interactions, the migrants may themselves be sources of information that produce important cognitive discrepancies among members of the host society with whom they interact, leading to some changes in their value structures. So some degree of mutual social influence may take place in a social field of interacting and interdependent members.

Discrepancies that involve value systems may be resolved in other ways apart from value change, depending upon which modes of resolution are available and which are blocked off. Migrants might misperceive or distort the value priorities of the social environment so that they are seen as closer to their own, if such distortion is possible. They might also denigrate the social environment that promotes the discrepant values, diminishing its credibility and legitimacy; seek more information about the social environment in the hope that they can bolster their own value commitments; attempt to change the social environment in an active way by trying to influence important agents within it by persuasion or confrontation; or move to an alternative and more congenial environment that is viewed as promoting value priorities more consonant with their own, becoming more protective of existing cognitive structures. Some of these solutions might be more available to the migrant than others. Older migrants whose value systems are firmly set, and whose opportunities to act on the new environment so as to produce change are limited, might find it very difficult to cope with large and important value discrepancies in an alien culture. They might preserve their own value systems and find peace of mind by living and interacting with others from their homeland who have similar views to themselves, limiting their interaction with the host society to essential settings such as the workplace, where they have to earn the means of support. Other migrants who find that they cannot adjust to the new environment at all may return to their homeland, where the territory is familiar and where cognitive discrepancies between present reality and normative cognitive structures are diminished. These returning migrants, however, may not have been unaffected by their experience as settlers in a new land. Their underlying belief systems may have undergone some change, so that on returning to their homeland they will have to cope with new kinds of discrepancies involving perceived and abstract structures (Feather, 1971a, 1975b).

The preceding discussion needs to be qualified by recognizing that there are individual differences in the degree to which people can tolerate cognitive discrepancies, and also differences in the degree to which environments demand consistency (Feather, 1971a). Some migrants, because of their personality makeup, may be able to live in a bicultural or multicultural world without a great deal of strain, especially if the environment is tolerant of differences. In general, Australian society has shown a fair degree of tolerance toward its new settlers. As Martin (1972) puts it:

> Most modern large-scale societies contain people of diverse ethnic origins and have accordingly developed plural ethnically based foci of cultural, social, economic, or political organization. In the past twenty years Australia's population has been substantially increased by immigration from different countries. Had we emerged from this period as a homogeneous society, we would be the exception in the modern world. The distinction would be nothing to be proud of, for it would mean that we had succeeded in imposing on our ethnic populations a rigid conformism that is increasingly unacceptable in our own lives and alien to the spirit of the times. (p. 133)

There is stagnation in sameness and richness in diversity.

CONCLUSIONS

Throughout the preceding discussion, we have seen that one of the major problems that confronts migrants settling in a new country is that of coping with the cognitive discrepancies that emerge as new information from the environment is related to existing cognitive structures. If discrepancies between personal characteristics and the new environment cannot be resolved, migrants will suffer some degree of cognitive strain because they cannot easily achieve a meaningful and consistent view of themselves and their new world. Furthermore, reduced discrepancies probably imply that some valued reinforcements in the environment will be more readily available (Feather, 1975b, pp. 61–62). So there will be considerable pressure on migrants to adapt to their new surroundings. This adaptation will typically involve some assimilation and accommodation at the cognitive level, which is paralleled by assimilation at the social and national levels. And these cognitive adaptations will be accompanied by many necessary behavioral adjustments.

The unraveling of cause and effect in this process is extremely difficult. As far as subjective assimilation is concerned, we have argued that social interaction with members of the host community is an essential requirement. Otherwise, migrants will be protected from many of the potential cognitive discrepancies that may occur in beliefs, attitudes, and values, and movement toward subjective assimilation with the host culture will be impeded. Obviously, if people in the host culture are hostile to the new settlers, the possibilities of social interaction are limited and significant change toward greater similarity with the host members will be unlikely. But, in an accepting environment that is conducive to social interaction, change will be facilitated and migrants will gradually develop new coping repertoires, along with cognitive structures that are more in tune with the new environment.

But are the values that migrants learned in the course of their socialization in their homeland ever completely extinguished as a result of their contact with the new culture? Probably not. What happens is a rearrangement of priorities, just as the importance of particular values alters over the course of the life span, with some values that are dominant during adolescence losing their relative importance as a person grows older, yet continuing to remain as significant values within the hierarchy (Feather, 1975b; Rokeach, 1973). So the impact of a new culture may act over time to shift the priorities, providing that the migrants move outside of the protective bubble of their own initial national membership and reference groups and sample the diversity of new information that flows from their adopted land.

7

Change and Stability in American Value Systems, 1968-1971

Milton Rokeach

The main purpose of this chapter is to report the value stabilities and changes that have been observed in American society over a three-year period, 1968-1971. A second purpose is to report on the underlying factorial structure of American values over the same three-year period.

In the spring of 1968 and again in the spring of 1971, value measurements were obtained from a national area probability sample of Americans over 21. The test employed was the Rokeach Value Survey (Rokeach, 1967), on both occasions administered by the National Opinion Research Center (NORC).

The Rokeach Value Survey consists of 18 terminal values—ideal end-states of existence—and 18 instrumental values—ideal modes of behavior. Respondents were instructed "to arrange them in order of their importance to YOU, as guiding principles in YOUR life."

The average adult requires about 15 to 20 minutes to complete the rankings. Form D of the Value Survey, which employs pressure-sensitive

gummed labels, has been successfully employed with respondents ranging in age from 11 to 90. The 18 labels are presented alphabetically on
the right-hand side of the page; the respondent's task is merely to rear-
range them in order of importance into boxes 1 to 18 printed down the
left-hand side of the page. The gummed label technique gives the Value
Survey a highly motivating, game-like quality that is distinctly superior to
the more usual paper-and-pencil tests.

Reliability and validity data obtained in previous research are reported in considerable detail elsewhere (Rokeach, 1973). Test–retest reliabilities for each of the 18 terminal values considered separately, employing time intervals ranging from three to seven weeks, range
from .51 for *a sense of accomplishment* to .88 for *salvation;* comparable
instrumental value test–retest reliabilities range from .45 for *responsible*
to .70 for *ambitious.*

Reliability of the total value system has moreover been ascertained by
correlating for each respondent the overall rankings obtained for test
and retest. Employing a 14- to 16-month test interval, the median reliability is .69 for terminal values and .61 for instrumental values. For
shorter time intervals the test–retest reliabilities are, of course, higher.
Using south Australian college students, Feather has reported reliability
data highly similar to those that we have obtained in the United States,
both with respect to the reliability of individual values and with respect
to the reliability of value systems considered as a whole (Feather, 1971b).

In previous research, various subsets of the 18 terminal and 18 instrumental values have been found to distinguish significantly between
men and women, rich and poor, educated and uneducated, and among
persons varying in age, occupation, and life style (Rokeach, 1973). Various terminal and instrumental values are significantly correlated with
logically related attitudes and, far more important, with logically related
behavior. On the average, approximately one-third of the 36 values have
been found to distinguish at statistically significant levels (a) among persons varying in attitude (for example, toward blacks, American presence
in Vietnam, religion); and (b) among persons varying in behavior (for
example, joining or not joining a civil rights organization, cheating or
not cheating on an examination).

Consistent with a theory of cognitive and behavioral change proposed elsewhere, previous experimental research has demonstrated that
long-range changes in values, attitudes, and behavior are possible as a
result of objective feedback of information about one's own and others'
values and attitudes (Rokeach, 1973). Such feedback made many of the
experimental subjects conscious of certain contradictions existing within
their own value–attitude system, resulting in long-term cognitive and
behavioral changes. There is also evidence that the basic psychological

mechanism that initiates or generates such a process of change is the arousal of an affective state of self-dissatisfaction, the source of which is highly specific and identifiable.

Feedback of information led many of the experimental subjects to become aware that they held certain values and attitudes or had engaged in certain behavior that was contradictory to self-conceptions, thus arousing an affective state of self-dissatisfaction. To reduce such self-dissatisfaction, the subjects reorganized their values, attitudes, and behavior to make them all more mutually compatible and, even more important, to make them all more compatible with self-conceptions.

There is no reason to think that long-term changes in values, attitudes, or behavior that might occur naturally in one's everyday life would occur by processes any different from those that we have observed in more controlled experimental settings. During the particular period under consideration, 1968-1971, a number of specific issues were at the forefront of attention in the minds of many Americans: the continuing American involvement in Vietnam, institutional racism, an emerging awareness of institutional sexism, and the problem of pollution. To be sure, not all Americans were willing to recognize all these as genuine problems requiring solution. Many, no doubt, felt that these issues were overblown or exaggerated, that they did not really require any special attention, action, or solution. But the more these issues were in the news, the more salient they became for more people, and the greater the receptivity to consider solutions. It is within such an everyday context of issue salience that certain values, attitudes, and behavior— those most logically related to these issues—are especially vulnerable to change, either in American society as a whole or in those segments of American society that perceive themselves to be the most affected by these issues.

Moreover, it is reasonable to expect certain values to undergo change in an opposite direction: a social problem or issue that has been previously salient may become less salient, perhaps because it has been alleviated in whole or in part. For instance, if, as a result of legislation, social security or medical care benefits became routinely extended to all, we would expect this to be reflected in a lowered concern over certain values, such as economic security. Less concern over security-related values should, in turn, pave the way for the emergence of an increased concern with higher-order values (Maslow, 1954).

However, not all of a society's values are expected to undergo change. Values not related to the emergence or alleviation of major societal problems should remain relatively stable. Thus, we may expect that only those values directly related to the particular economic, political, and social issues confronting American society during the relatively brief time interval under consideration will have undergone measurable change.

RESULTS

Value Change in American Society as a Whole

Table 7.1 shows the changes and stabilities in the 18 terminal and 18 instrumental values obtained for the national sample during the period from 1968 to 1971. This table, like all the others presented in this chapter, shows the median ranking for each value and, in parentheses, its composite ranking. For instance, Table 7.1 shows that *a world at peace* had a median ranking of 3.3 in 1968 and 2.9 in 1971. This terminal value had the highest median rankings for both years, indicated by a composite ranking of 1, which is shown in parentheses. Conversely, *an exciting life* had the lowest median rankings on both occasions, indicated by a composite ranking of 18.

Significance of difference was determined separately for each value by the median test, a nonparametric chi square test based upon the number of persons scoring above and below the median in 1971 as compared with 1968 (Siegel, 1956). The probability level for each value, which is based on the chi square test, is shown in the last column of Table 7.1.

Before proceeding to a consideration of the specific value changes that took place, it is perhaps worth noticing that the value hierarchies found for the whole American sample were remarkably stable between 1968 and 1971. The composite ranking of the terminal value *a world at peace* was first in 1968 and first again in 1971; *family security* was second and *freedom* third on both occasions; *an exciting life, pleasure, social recognition,* and *a world of beauty* were at the bottom of the national sample's terminal value hierarchy in both 1968 and 1971. For both years, the most important instrumental values were *honest, ambitious,* and *responsible;* the least important were *imaginative, logical, obedient,* and *intellectual.*

These findings may be summarized somewhat as follows: More than anything else, adult Americans perceived themselves as peace loving, freedom loving, family oriented, honest, hardworking, and responsible; they perceived themselves as neither hedonistically, aesthetically, nor intellectually oriented; nor, at least consciously, as status oriented. To what extent would these self-reported value patterns coincide with those reported by objective observers? More important, to what extent would these value patterns turn out to be similar to and different from those that might be obtained from other major cultural or national groups (Rokeach, 1973, 1974b).

TABLE 7.1.   Changes in Terminal and Instrumental Values for Entire Adult American Sample, 1968–1971*

Values	1968 (N = 1,409)	1971 (N = 1,430)	p
Terminal Values			
A comfortable life			
(A prosperous life)	9.0(9)	10.6(13)	.01
An exciting life			
(A stimulating, active life)	15.3(18)	15.2(18)	—
A sense of accomplishment			
(Lasting contribution)	9.0(10)	9.6(11)	.01
A world at peace			
(Free of war and conflict)	3.3(1)	2.9(1)	.05
A world of beauty			
(Beauty of nature and the arts)	13.6(15)	12.5(15)	.01
Equality			
(Brotherhood, equal opportunity for all)	8.5(7)	7.6(4)	.01
Family security			
(Taking care of loved ones)	3.8(2)	4.2(2)	.05
Freedom			
(Independence, free choice)	5.5(3)	5.3(3)	—
Happiness			
(Contentedness)	7.6(4)	7.7(6)	—
Inner harmony			
(Freedom from inner conflict)	10.5(13)	10.2(12)	—
Mature love			
(Sexual and spiritual intimacy)	12.5(14)	11.9(14)	.05
National security			
(Protection from attack)	9.5(12)	9.0(8)	—
Pleasure			
(An enjoyable, leisurely life)	14.6(17)	14.7(16)	—
Salvation			
(Saved, eternal life)	8.8(8)	9.2(9)	—
Self-respect			
(Self-esteem)	7.7(5)	7.7(5)	—
Social recognition			
(Respect, admiration)	14.4(16)	14.9(17)	.05
True friendship			
(Close companionship)	9.3(11)	9.4(10)	—
Wisdom			
(A mature understanding of life)	8.0(6)	8.2(7)	
Instrumental Values			
Ambitious			
(Hard-working, aspiring)	6.5(2)	6.9(3)	—
Broadminded			
(Open-minded)	7.5(5)	7.5(5)	—
Capable			
(Competent, effective)	9.5(9)	9.4(9)	—

(continued)

TABLE 7.1.   *Continued*

Values	1968 (N = 1,409)	1971 (N = 1,430)	p
Cheerful (Lighthearted, joyful)	9.9(12)	10.4(13)	—
Clean (Neat, tidy)	8.7(8)	9.5(10)	.05
Courageous (Standing up for your beliefs)	7.8(6)	8.1(6)	—
Forgiving (Willing to pardon others)	7.2(4)	7.2(4)	—
Helpful (Working for the welfare of others)	8.2(7)	8.7(7)	—
Honest (Sincere, truthful)	3.3(1)	3.3(1)	—
Imaginative (Daring, creative)	15.4(18)	15.2(18)	—
Independent (Self-reliant, self-sufficient)	10.5(13)	10.2(12)	—
Intellectual (Intelligent, reflective)	13.0(15)	12.7(15)	—
Logical (Consistent, rational)	14.2(17)	13.4(17)	.01
Loving (Affectionate, tender)	9.7(11)	8.7(8)	.01
Obedient (Dutiful, respectful)	13.3(16)	13.3(16)	—
Polite (Courteous, well-mannered)	10.8(14)	11.0(14)	—
Responsible (Dependable, reliable)	6.7(3)	6.5(2)	—
Self-controlled (Restrained, self-disciplined)	9.6(10)	9.6(11)	—

*Figures shown are median rankings and, in parentheses, composite rank orders.

Let us now consider the changes found between 1968 and 1971, as reported in Table 7.1. Twenty-five of the 36 values show no statistically significant changes for the national sample as a whole, while 11 of them do show significant changes. Significantly more important in the American value hierarchy in 1971 compared with 1968 were *a world at peace, a world of beauty, equality, mature love,* being *logical,* and *loving;* significantly less important were *a comfortable life, a sense of accomplishment, family security, social recognition,* and being *clean.*

A major question is whether these changes were manifested in all segments of American society or occurred only in certain segments. To answer this question the value rankings obtained in 1968 and 1971 were further analyzed for Americans varying in sex, race, race and sex, income, education, and age.

Value Changes in American Men and Women

Over the three-year period, seven values changed significantly for men, and six changed significantly for women (Table 7.2).[1] Comparing these two sets of changes, it becomes apparent that the results are the same for only two values: American men and women both placed significantly more importance on *a world of beauty* and significantly less importance on *a comfortable life* in 1971 than they did in 1968.

The remaining changes are different for the two sexes. *A world at peace*, although ranked as the most important terminal value by American men in 1968, became even more important for them in 1971; *mature love* was also ranked higher by American men in 1971. Three other values—*a sense of accomplishment, social recognition,* and being *helpful*—turned out to be significantly less important for them in 1971. For American women, *family security* became significantly less important in 1971, and *equality,* being *logical,* and *loving* became significantly more important.

Value Changes for White and Black Americans

Table 7.3 shows the comparable changes found for white and black Americans. Ten of the 36 values changed significantly among whites, and six changed significantly among blacks. The fact that more values changed significantly for white Americans is not particularly surprising; it was probably due to the fact that there were many more whites than blacks in the total sample—about 85 percent compared with 15 percent in both years. More noteworthy is the fact that white and black Americans changed significantly on completely different values; not a single one of the changes were the same for the two races.

White Americans attached significantly more importance in 1971 to *a world at peace, a world of beauty, equality,* and being *intellectual;* they attached significantly less importance to *a comfortable life, a sense of accomplishment, family security, social recognition,* being *clean,* and being *helpful.* Black Americans apparently had other preoccupations: *mature love,* being *loving* and *imaginative* became significantly more important; *inner harmony,* being *ambitious* and *honest* became significantly less important.

Value Changes in Americans Varying in Sex and Race

We also analyzed the value changes from 1968 to 1971 separately for white men and women and for black men and women. White men and

[1]Table 7.2 also shows that there are many sex differences in values. Since the main focus of this chapter is value change over time rather than demographic differences, sex and other value differences (e.g., race, age, income, education) are not considered here. For a discussion of such demographic differences, see Rokeach (1973).

TABLE 7.2. Changes in Terminal and Instrumental Values for American Men and Women, 1968–1971*

	American Men			American Women		
Values	1968 (N = 665)	1971 (N = 687)	p	1968 (N = 744)	1971 (N = 743)	p
Terminal Values						
A comfortable life	7.8(4)	9.2(9)	.01	10.0(13)	11.7(13)	.01
An exciting life	14.6(18)	14.6(17)	—	15.8(18)	15.6(18)	—
A sense of accomplishment	8.3(7)	9.3(10)	.01	9.4(10)	9.8(12)	—
A world at peace	3.8(1)	3.2(1)	.05	3.0(1)	2.6(1)	.01
A world of beauty	13.6(15)	12.8(15)	.05	13.5(15)	12.4(14)	.05
Equality	8.9(9)	8.0(6)	—	8.3(8)	7.4(4)	.05
Family security	3.9(2)	4.0(2)	—	3.8(2)	4.4(2)	.01
Freedom	4.9(3)	5.1(3)	—	6.0(3)	5.5(3)	—
Happiness	7.9(5)	7.6(4)	—	7.3(5)	7.8(8)	—
Inner harmony	11.1(13)	11.0(13)	—	9.8(12)	9.5(11)	—
Mature love	12.6(14)	11.4(14)	.01	12.3(14)	12.4(15)	—
National security	9.2(10)	9.0(8)	—	9.8(11)	8.9(9)	—
Pleasure	14.1(17)	14.3(16)	—	15.0(16)	15.1(17)	—
Salvation	9.9(12)	10.9(12)	—	7.3(4)	7.6(6)	—
Self-respect	8.2(6)	7.9(5)	—	7.4(6)	7.4(5)	—

Social recognition	13.8(16)	14.6(18)	.01	15.0(17)	15.1(16)	—
True friendship	9.6(11)	9.4(11)	—	9.1(9)	9.5(10)	—
Wisdom	8.5(8)	8.9(7)	—	7.7(7)	7.7(7)	—
Instrumental Values						
Ambitious	5.6(2)	5.4(2)	—	7.3(4)	8.0(6)	—
Broadminded	7.2(4)	7.1(4)	—	7.6(5)	7.8(5)	—
Capable	8.9(8)	8.7(6)	—	10.1(12)	10.3(12)	—
Cheerful	10.4(12)	11.0(13)	—	9.4(10)	9.8(10)	—
Clean	9.4(9)	10.2(11)	—	8.1(8)	9.0(9)	—
Courageous	7.5(5)	8.0(5)	—	8.1(6)	8.2(8)	—
Forgiving	8.2(6)	8.8(7)	—	6.4(2)	5.9(2)	—
Helpful	8.4(7)	9.2(9)	.05	8.1(7)	8.0(7)	—
Honest	3.4(1)	3.3(1)	—	3.2(1)	3.2(1)	—
Imaginative	14.3(18)	14.5(18)	—	16.1(18)	15.8(18)	—
Independent	10.2(11)	9.9(10)	—	10.7(14)	10.4(13)	—
Intellectual	12.8(15)	12.5(15)	—	13.2(16)	12.9(15)	—
Logical	13.5(16)	12.8(16)	—	14.6(17)	13.9(17)	.05
Loving	10.9(14)	10.6(12)	—	8.6(9)	7.3(4)	.01
Obedient	13.5(17)	13.4(17)	—	13.1(15)	13.2(16)	—
Polite	10.8(13)	11.2(14)	—	10.7(13)	10.8(14)	—
Responsible	6.6(3)	6.2(3)	—	6.8(3)	6.7(3)	—
Self-controlled	9.6(10)	9.2(8)	—	9.6(11)	10.0(11)	—

*Figures shown are median rankings and, in parentheses, composite rank orders.

137

TABLE 7.3. Changes in Terminal and Instrumental Values for White and Black Americans, 1968–1971*

Values	White Americans				Black Americans		
	1968 (N = 1,195)	1971 (N = 1,205)	p		1968 (N = 202)	1971 (N = 213)	p
Terminal Values							
A comfortable life	9.6(12)	11.2(13)	.01		6.6(5)	7.1(5)	—
An exciting life	15.3(18)	15.3(18)	—		15.3(18)	14.8(18)	—
A sense of accomplishment	8.8(8)	9.4(10)	.05		10.2(11)	11.3(12)	—
A world at peace	3.2(1)	2.8(1)	.05		3.5(1)	3.3(1)	—
A world of beauty	13.4(15)	12.4(15)	.01		14.1(16)	13.5(16)	—
Equality	9.5(11)	8.1(6)	.01		4.6(2)	5.0(4)	—
Family security	3.6(2)	4.1(2)	.05		5.1(4)	4.8(3)	—
Freedom	5.6(3)	5.5(3)	—		5.0(3)	4.7(2)	—
Happiness	7.5(4)	7.8(5)	—		7.6(7)	7.2(6)	—
Inner harmony	10.3(13)	9.9(12)	—		10.9(12)	12.1(13)	.05
Mature love	12.0(14)	11.8(16)	—		13.7(14)	12.4(14)	.05
National security	9.1(9)	8.7(8)	—		11.4(13)	10.2(11)	—
Pleasure	14.6(17)	14.9(16)	—		14.3(17)	13.7(17)	—
Salvation	8.5(7)	9.1(9)	—		9.4(9)	9.4(10)	—
Self-respect	7.7(5)	7.5(4)	—		7.5(6)	8.3(7)	—
Social recognition	14.5(16)	15.0(17)	.05		13.7(15)	13.5(15)	—

True friendship	9.2(10)	9.5(11)	—	9.8(10)	9.2(8)	—
Wisdom	7.9(6)	8.1(7)	—	8.5(8)	9.3(9)	—
Instrumental Values						
Ambitious	6.7(3)	6.8(3)	—	5.2(2)	7.9(6)	.01
Broadminded	7.3(5)	7.2(4)	—	8.0(8)	8.8(8)	—
Capable	9.4(10)	9.3(9)	—	10.4(13)	10.6(13)	—
Cheerful	9.8(12)	10.4(13)	—	10.2(12)	10.1(11)	—
Clean	9.2(8)	10.1(12)	.01	5.2(3)	6.3(2)	—
Courageous	7.8(6)	8.1(6)	—	7.8(7)	8.6(7)	—
Forgiving	7.0(4)	7.4(5)	—	7.6(5)	6.7(3)	—
Helpful	8.3(7)	9.0(8)	.05	7.8(6)	7.3(4)	—
Honest	3.1(1)	3.1(1)	—	3.8(1)	4.8(1)	.05
Imaginative	15.3(18)	15.4(18)	—	15.8(18)	14.6(17)	.01
Independent	10.6(13)	10.3(12)	—	10.2(10)	9.6(10)	—
Intellectual	13.1(15)	12.8(15)	—	12.6(16)	12.4(16)	—
Logical	13.9(17)	13.1(16)	.01	15.1(17)	15.0(18)	.01
Loving	9.3(9)	8.5(7)	—	11.9(15)	9.2(9)	—
Obedient	13.4(16)	13.6(17)	—	11.5(14)	11.8(15)	—
Polite	10.8(14)	11.2(14)	—	10.2(11)	10.2(12)	.01
Responsible	6.5(2)	6.3(2)	—	7.6(4)	7.6(5)	—
Self-controlled	9.4(11)	9.4(10)	—	10.1(9)	10.9(14)	—

*Figures shown are median rankings and, in parentheses, composite rank orders.

women both significantly increased their regard for *a world of beauty* and *equality;* both significantly decreased their regard for *a comfortable life.* They manifested other changes, however, that they did not share with each other: white men regarded *mature love* as more important in 1971 and *a sense of accomplishment, social recognition,* and being *helpful* as less important; white women regarded being *logical* and *loving* as more important in 1971 and *family security* as less important.

Whereas white men and women had both increased their ranking of *equality* in 1971, black men and women both decreased their *equality* rankings, although not significantly so. Black men changed significantly with respect to only one value: *inner harmony* became less important. And black women changed significantly by increasing their rankings of *mature love* and *loving* and by decreasing their rankings of *ambitious.*

Education, Income, and Age as Determinants of Value Change

The extent to which the observed changes were a function of socioeconomic level or age may also be questioned. Further analysis revealed that neither education nor income were determinants of value change. The values that changed from 1968 to 1971 were just as likely to occur among the poor or uneducated as among the affluent and educated.

The findings did differ with respect to age, however. These data, which are not presented here to conserve space, show that younger adults within the national sample underwent more extensive value changes than older adults. Respondents in their twenties, thirties, forties, fifties, sixties, and those over seventy manifested, respectively, 10, 4, 2, 0, 2, and 0 significant value changes over the three-year period. Americans in their twenties attached significantly greater importance in 1971 to *a world at peace, a world of beauty, equality, inner harmony,* and being *logical;* they attached less importance to *a comfortable life, salvation,* and being *clean, obedient,* and *polite.* Those in their thirties showed considerably fewer significant changes: *a world at peace, a world of beauty,* and *national security* had increased and *family security* had decreased in importance. The significant value changes found for persons beyond the thirties are few in number and could easily have arisen by chance.

Additional analyses, again too complex to present here, revealed that these age-related changes were found primarily among white men and women and not among black men and women. Moreover, as previously stated, they were not related to differences in socioeconomic status.

Factorial Structure of Values, 1968 and 1971

The significant value changes found between 1968 and 1971 should not obscure the fact that most of the 36 values did not change, as even a cursory inspection of tables 7.1 through 7.3 will reveal. As already stated, the overall value patterns in 1968 and 1971 look very similar. Are the underlying factorial structures also similar?

To answer this question, we carried out identical factor analyses (principal factor solution with iteration using the varimax rotation technique) for the total samples obtained in 1968 and 1971. Moreover, separate factor analyses were carried out for subsamples of American men and women and for white and black Americans.

Table 7.4 shows the range of correlations obtained in 1968 and 1971 for the total national sample and, separately, for the four subsamples.[2] In reading this table the reader should be mindful of the fact that each correlation matrix was based on 36 values, thus generating 630 correlations. Thus, Table 7.4 shows the range of 630 correlations obtained for each of ten separate matrices. Five of these pertain to the 1968 samples, and five pertain to the 1971 samples.

The highest positive correlation found in all ten matrices was .41, between *a comfortable life* and *pleasure;* the highest negative correlation was −.38, between *an exciting life* and *salvation.* Since these are the largest positive and negative correlations found in ten matrices consisting of 6,300 correlations and since the average correlation between values was close to zero both in 1968 and in 1971 a conclusion reached earlier on the basis of the 1968 sample alone is now doubly reinforced: "The ranking of any one of the 36 values is for all practical purposes unrelated to the ranking of any other value, and it is therefore unlikely that the 36 values can be effectively reduced to some smaller number of factors" (Rokeach, 1973, p. 44).

Nonetheless, factor analyses of these ten matrices provide us with some additional insights into the underlying structure of American values. Previously reported factor analyses of the 1968 data yielded six bipolar factors accounting for approximately 37 percent of the total variance, with no single factor accounting for more than 8 percent (Rokeach, 1973). These six factors have previously been identified as follows: immediate versus delayed gratification, competence versus religious morality, self-constriction versus self-expansion, social versus personal orientation, societal versus family security, and respect versus love. These factors described not only the total 1968 national sample but also the male and female, white and black subsamples considered separately.

The comparable factor analyses carried out with the 1971 data yielded results that are essentially the same as those found for 1968: the first six bipolar factors accounted for 36.9 percent of the total variance in 1971 compared with 37 percent in 1968. In 1968, the immediate versus delayed gratification factor accounted for more variance than any other

---

[2]The 1968 data have already been reported (Rokeach, 1973). In the present chapter the main focus is on a comparison of the results obtained in 1971 with those obtained in 1968.

TABLE 7.4. Highest and Lowest Correlations Found within 36-Value Matrix for Total National Samples, American Whites and Blacks, and American Men and Women, 1968 and 1971

Group	N	Highest Correlation (Between)		Lowest Correlation (Between)	
Total NORC sample, 1968	1,409	.35	(A comfortable life—Pleasure)	−.32	(A comfortable life—Wisdom)
Whites, 1968	1,195	.38	(A comfortable life—Pleasure)	−.32	(An exciting life—Salvation)
Blacks, 1968	202	.31	(Obedient—Polite)	−.35	(A comfortable life—Wisdom)
Men, 1968	665	.30	(Cheerful—Clean)	−.38	(An exciting life—Salvation)
Women, 1968	744	.41	(A comfortable life—Pleasure)	−.32	(A comfortable life—Wisdom)
Total NORC sample, 1971	1,429	.32	(A comfortable life—Pleasure)	−.34	(An exciting life—Salvation)
Whites, 1971	1,204	.37	(A comfortable life—Pleasure)	−.34	(An exciting life—Salvation)
Blacks, 1971	213	.32	(Happiness—Cheerful)	−.35	(Broadminded—Obedient)
Men, 1971	687	.33	(A comfortable life—Pleasure)	−.36	(An exciting life—Salvation)
Women, 1971	743	.35	(A world at peace—National security)	−.34	(Clean—Logical)

factor—8.2 percent; in 1971, this same factor also accounted for the most variance—9.4 percent. Moreover, the findings are essentially the same in 1971 for the four subsamples of men and women, whites and blacks as they were for the total national sample. And all these findings for the total sample and for the four subsamples are, in turn, highly similar to those already reported for 1968 (Rokeach, 1973). Thus, no useful purpose would be served by reporting them in detail here.

DISCUSSION

Survey research has long been concerned with the assessment of attitude changes over time but not with the assessment of value changes, perhaps because simple methods for measuring values have previously not been available. This chapter represents, as far as is known to the present writer, a first quantitative attempt to measure value change and stability in American society.

Moreover, the data reported here may reasonably be regarded as social indicators of the quality of life in American society (Bauer, 1966; Gross & Springer, 1970). For instance, decreases in the perceived importance of having a *comfortable life* and being *clean* could be interpreted as social indicators of an improved socioeconomic status; increases in the importance of *a sense of accomplishment* and being *capable* could be interpreted as indicators of increased strivings for achievement or self-actualization; increases in the importance of *equality* could be interpreted as an indicator of an increased egalitarianism; increases in the importance of *a world of beauty* could be interpreted as an indicator of an increased willingness to sacrifice material comforts in return for a less polluted environment.

It perhaps goes without saying that the statistically significant differences in values reported in this chapter are not large. It is not reasonable to expect large value changes over so short an interval as three years of a society's history. Nonetheless, the fact that we did find statistically significant changes in several values during this period suggests, at least, that: (1) the value measure employed is sufficiently sensitive to register short-term changes, (2) certain values had in fact undergone change in American society between 1968 and 1971, and (3) more clear-cut trends are likely to become discernible with measurements over longer time intervals.

The significant value changes between 1968 and 1971 reported for the total adult American sample are, for the most part, reflections of selective, rather than ubiquitous, changes that had taken place in various strata of American society. They are attributable mainly to differential changes occurring among Americans varying in race, sex, or age.

Consider first the changes that were found for the terminal value *equality*. *Equality* had increased significantly between 1968 and 1971 for white Americans but had decreased for black Americans. This suggests that the civil rights movement had a significant impact on white Americans during this period. In contrast, the decreases in *equality* among black Americans, although nonsignificant, reflect a change in the direction of separatism, perhaps as a result of the impact of the black power and black nationalist movements, and perhaps also because of a growing despair or impatience over a loss of momentum during the Nixon years.

The fact that the terminal value *equality* increased significantly for white Americans between 1968 and 1971 is consistent with the long-term increases between 1942 and 1970 in pro-integration attitudes that have been reported by Greeley and Sheatsley (1971). Placing their findings alongside those reported here, it now becomes possible to assert that not only are racist attitudes in American society undergoing change, at least for the time intervals under consideration, but so, too, is the main value known to underlie such attitudes (Rokeach, 1973).

Moreover, white, but not black, Americans exhibited statistically significant increases in the importance they attached to *a world of beauty*. This finding suggests that concern about ecology between 1968 and 1971 was a preoccupation mainly of white Americans, and was not especially salient for black Americans. This finding becomes more understandable perhaps in the context of Maslow's theory of self-actualization (Maslow, 1954). Pollution of the environment is not likely to become a salient issue or to affect values when there are more pressing needs and values concerning safety and security.

Consistent with these findings are the comparable changes for white, but not for black, Americans concerning having *a comfortable life* and being *clean*. Previous research has shown that rankings of these two values are the two best predictors of socioeconomic status: the higher one's socioeconomic status the lower the rankings of these two values (not so much because these are no longer important but because they are taken for granted) (Rokeach, 1973). This suggests that socioeconomic level may have improved more for white than for black Americans. Partial evidence that this may have been the case comes from a 1972 Census Bureau report to the effect that the number of poor blacks had increased in the preceding year while the number of poor whites had decreased (*Lewiston Morning Tribune*, July 23, 1973).[3] In any event, we have found that the two main economic values had become significantly less important in 1971 for white, but not for black, Americans.

[3]Other data on income, obtained directly from the 1968 and 1971 NORC samples, are more equivocal since they are imprecise: responses about income were made in terms of seven categories rather than in actual amounts; in addition, the seven categories were uneven.

What are we to make of these and other findings showing that white and black Americans had changed for the most part in different ways, implicating different values? Did the values of black and white Americans converge or diverge from one another between 1968 and 1971? The findings are ambiguous on this point because the terminal values of black and white Americans became more similar from 1968 to 1971 (the rho correlations between the composite rankings of white and black Americans increased from .815 to .88), and the instrumental values became more dissimilar (the rho correlations decreased from .88 to .78). Thus, it is not possible to answer this question in any definite way until more extensive data become available.

Other significant value changes found in the total national sample can be traced mainly to changes occurring only among white women or white men. White women downgraded the importance of *family security* and upgraded the importance of being *logical,* a change that can reasonably be attributed to an increasing awareness between 1968 and 1971 of institutional sexism as a national problem and to the concomitant rise of the women's liberation movement—a movement that was probably more salient for American women than men, and perhaps more salient for white women than for black women.

On the other hand, white men exhibited a nearly significant increase in their ranking of *a world at peace* and significant decreases in *a sense of accomplishment* and *social recognition.* This suggests that white American men were more preoccupied with problems of war and peace and devoted less attention to their traditional pursuits of education, career, and social status. These value changes can possibly be attributed to the Vietnam war, the Cambodian invasion, the antiwar protests, the Kent and Jackson shootings, and, perhaps, to a fear of being drafted. It will be interesting to see if these particular changes persist now that the Vietnam war and the draft have ended.

Other significant value changes are more difficult to interpret: white men and black women both increased their rankings of *mature love;* white and black women both increased their ranking of *loving;* black Americans decreased their rankings of *honest* and increased their rankings of *imaginative;* black women decreased their rankings of *ambitious.* It is hard to say what these findings mean. Most were not statistically significant for the total sample. Various *post hoc* interpretations are possible but would not be intuitively appealing; they may or may not represent chance differences. Further research should enable us to sort out which of these significant value changes are replicable and thus to be taken seriously.

Finally, attention should be drawn to the fact that most of the significant changes found between 1968 and 1971 for the national sample are traceable to changes occurring among white Americans in their twenties and, to a lesser extent, in their thirties. The findings suggest that this subgroup of adult Americans may be undergoing more extensive value changes than any other segment: toward a lesser emphasis on tradition and religion; toward greater concerns with racial and sexual egalitarianism, ecology, peace, and peace of mind.

It is not clear from these latter data, however, whether the changes between 1968 and 1971 actually occurred among adults in their twenties or, alternatively, whether they were a result of the movement of persons between 18 and 21 in 1968 into the 21–30 age category in 1971, or both. Future research with respondents under 21 years of age should help us answer this question.

Turning to the factor analytic findings, two interrelated conclusions seem warranted. First, the fact that the intercorrelations among the 36 values were uniformly negligible for both years suggests that the way a respondent ranks any one value is a rather poor predictor of the way he or she will rank any other value. Even logically related values are negligibly related to one another. For instance, the average correlation between rankings of *salvation* and *forgiving* is only about .25; the average correlation between rankings of *freedom* and *equality* is only about .11. Second, the same half-dozen factors obtained for 1968 and 1971 seem to possess little "explanatory power" since taken together they account for well under half of the total variance, with no one factor accounting for more than 10 percent. Thus, the findings suggest that the 36 values cannot safely be reduced to some smaller number of values.

Returning to the main findings, it should perhaps be reiterated that what has been reported thus far about value changes and stabilities in American society is based only on two points in time, obtained three years apart. But, even within such a short interval, we found that certain values underwent significant change. These changes seem to be a result of economic factors and the emergence of various issues concerning war and peace, racism, sexism, and ecology, all of which become salient and thus a source of dissatisfaction for various subgroups of adult Americans.

It would be helpful to see these data supplemented at regular intervals in the future. This would provide a more continuous monitoring of values in American society and, it is hoped, would guide social policy and help set national priorities.

In conclusion, it might be appropriate to mention some logical next steps in our ongoing research program on values as social indicators of the quality of life. First, there is no compelling reason why we should not also monitor the stabilities and changes of those who are well below the age at which they become eligible to vote. As previously stated, the Rokeach Value Survey has been successfully employed with persons ranging in age from 11 to 90.

Second, there is no reason why social indicator research should focus only, or mainly, on stabilities and changes within a single country. If values are indeed meaningful indicators of the quality of life, then attempts should be made to determine to what extent they might also turn out to be useful as international social indicators. It would, for instance, be interesting to compare the relative importance of certain political, religious, or self-actualization values across various national samples and, moreover, to plot their stabilities and changes over time. Ultimately, we might seek to develop global social indicators that would allow us to assess stabilities and changes in quality of life across cultural space as well as across historical time.

8

Value Transition and Adult Development in Women: The Instrumentality-Terminality Sequence Hypothesis

Carol D. Ryff

Theoretical and empirical research on adult personality development is undergoing a widespread phase of differentiation, as illustrated, in part, by various conceptual positions reviewed by Baltes and Schaie (1973), Neugarten (1973), and Schaie and Gribbon (1975). Reviewers (Baltes & Willis, 1976) are impressed (1) with the overwhelming evidence for large interindividual differences and multidirectionality of adult development, and (2) with the lack of measurement frameworks appropriate for the study of behaviors salient to adulthood and aging. These are, however, not necessarily independent, since the current emphasis on diversity and complexity with regard to adult development may indicate little more than failure to identify relevant behavioral domains. As a good part of the initial work in adulthood involved extrapolations from research conducted in early life (Emmerich, 1973; Flavell, 1970; Hartup & Lempers, 1973; Kohlberg, 1973), it seems reasonable to suspect that many of the key issues of adulthood may have been overlooked. If these more meaningful domains could be established, they would most assuredly provide rich, new opportunities for developmental investigations in the second half of life.

The resurgence of interest in phenomenological, self-acknowledged change (Brim, 1976; Nardi, 1973; Riegel, 1972; Thomae, 1970) represents one approach toward improving the relevance of research on adult development. Within this realm, the clues to developmental changes are sought in the adult's own perspective—the way in which he or she sees and interprets both change in self as well as in the surrounding world. The present study was conceived within such a framework. It is phenomenological in the sense of focusing on self-perceived values, and it is developmental in its focus on possible value change—from a strong interest in instrumentality during middle age to a predominant interest in terminality during old age.

The distinction between instrumental values and terminal values has been made by Rokeach (1973). Although this distinction has not been applied to the field of adult development and aging, various theoretical positions suggest its relevance. Erikson (1950), for example, formulated a life-span framework of psychosocial tasks which implies a sequence from instrumentality (e.g., initiative, industry) to terminality (e.g., generativity, integrity). Gutmann (1964), focusing on men only, posits an adult sequence from control of outer world affairs (e.g., alloplastic mastery) to a more internal, self-oriented emphasis (e.g., autoplastic mastery, omniplastic mastery). Neugarten (1973) suggests an active-to-passive mastery sequence, wherein middle age reflects boldness and risk taking while old age reflects conformity and accommodation.

Working within a phenomenological framework, therefore, it appears justified to explore the possible existence of an instrumentality–terminality sequence in adult value systems. Moreover, since Maas and Kuypers (1974) suggest that women more than men show change in life style or personality from middle to old age, this initial study focused attention solely on women. The main hypothesis tested is that value assessments pertaining to middle age will reveal a greater emphasis on instrumentality, while those pertaining to old age will indicate a preference for terminality.

METHOD

As the present study was interested in subjectively perceived change, a cross-sectional method was employed. Measures of change were obtained by comparing present value assessments (concurrent) with those held in the past (retrospection) or those predicted to occur in the future (prospection). This strategy of age simulation (Baltes & Goulet, 1971) is similar to those employed in earlier work on phenomenological aspects of personality development (Ahammer & Baltes, 1972; Nardi, 1973).

Design. Value hierarchies were investigated by asking middle- and old-aged women to respond, under varying instructional conditions, to a modified form of the Rokeach Value Survey. The study called for a 2 (Actual Age) x 2 (Target Age) x 2 (Desirability Condition) x 2 (Class of Values) design with repeated measures over class of values. *Actual age* referred to the participants' chronological age and consisted of two age ranges: 40–50 years of age (middle-aged) and 65 years of age and older (old-aged). *Target age* referred to the criterion age level (middle age versus old age) that the participants were instructed to use when ranking values. One group of middle-aged persons was asked to rank their current values, and another group of middle-aged persons was asked to prospect their value assessment to when they would be 65 years old and over; similarly, one group of old-aged persons was asked to provide their current value rankings, and another group to retrospect a value assessment to when they had been in the 40–50-year age range. *Desirability condition* referred to a difference in instructional set. Under personal desirability conditions, respondents ranked the values according to their own individual priority preferences, while under social desirability conditions, they ranked according to their view of society's preference. Social desirability was construed as a control condition, since social desirability ratings are highly similar across a wide range of subject populations. *Class of values* referred to the distinction made by Rokeach (1973). Instrumental values pertain to "desirable modes of conduct" (p. 7), such as "ambitious," "capable," "courageous." Terminal values refer to "desirable end-states of existence" (p. 7), such as "a sense of accomplishment," "freedom," "happiness." Variation of all conditions resulted in a total of eight instructions, each presented to a different group of participants.

Measurement variables. The Rokeach Value Survey requires ranking according to preference separate lists of 18 terminal and instrumental values. In order to obtain comparative judgments involving both terminal and instrumental values, the two scales were randomly mixed, producing two new scales, each having nine terminal and nine instrumental values. Participants ranked two such mixed lists from highest to lowest priority. Each respondent received two separate scores, one for terminal and one for instrumental values, both consisting of the two-form cumulation of the rankings. High scores indicated high terminal or instrumental value preferences.

Participants. A total of 119 women comprised the research sample. Middle-aged women (N= 57; average age = 43.1 years; SD = 6.3) were contacted through Pace University of Westchester. Old-aged women (N = 62; average age = 70.4 years; SD = 6.3) were contacted through the New York Institute for Retired Professionals. Except for three individuals, participants had all attended college.

Data analysis. Analysis of variance was employed with the following variables: actual age (middle age, old age), target age (middle age, old age), desirability condition (personal versus social), and class of values (instrumental versus terminal). The key prediction was that for the target "middle age," participants of both age groups would assign comparatively higher priority to instrumental than terminal values and, correspondingly, both age cohorts would assign higher priority to terminal than instrumental values for the target "old age." Since the social desirability condition was conceptualized as a control treatment, it was predicted that this prediction would hold only under personal desirability. Therefore, the critical test for the core hypothesis of this study is a triple interaction involving classes of values, target age, and desirability condition.

RESULTS

In addition to a main effect of class of values, $F (1,112) = 37.94$, $p < .01$, the predicted Target Age x Desirability Condition x Class of Values triple interaction was obtained, $F (1,112) = 6.64$, $p < .01$. The main effect of class of values (a by-product of this study) reveals an overall preference for terminal over instrumental values.

The triple interaction is presented in Figure 8.1. Under social desirability, no differences due to target age and class of values result, which is an expected finding, since social desirability was construed as a control condition. Under personal desirability, however, the rankings given for instrumentality and terminality vis-à-vis the target middle age (but not vis-à-vis the target old age) are identical. Since the overall finding is one of preference for terminal values, this can be interpreted as a relative increase for instrumental values for the target middle age. The outcome of equal preference for terminal and instrumental values for the target middle age applies both to the concurrent rankings of middle-aged persons and the retrospective rankings of old-aged persons (both under personal desirability). That is, not only do middle-aged women describe themselves as being relatively more instrumentally oriented, but also old-aged women indicate that they *were* more instrumentally oriented when they were middle aged. The counterpart findings for the target old age is that middle-aged women state (under personal desirability) that they *will be* more terminally oriented when they become old aged.

DISCUSSION

In general, the outcomes are remarkably clear and consistent with the hypothesis that middle age would reveal a relatively stronger emphasis on instrumentality while old age would reveal a similar preference for terminality. This finding, though cross-sectional in nature, is strengthened by the consistency of prospective, retrospective, and concurrent assessments.

The results of the present study support and expand previous work on the restructuring process as one moves from middle to old age. In fact, it is one of the very few studies which provides a clear empirical base for some of the theoretical propositions espoused in the literature, especially regarding their applicability to women. First, the data seem to confirm the reality of self-acknowledged transitional or reorganizational phases, what Erikson (1950) called "necessary turning points." Transitional shifts in values are evident despite the existence of a generally greater preference for terminal over instrumental values.

Figure 8.1

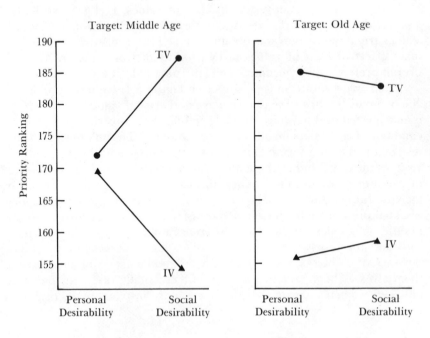

Middle age evokes a heightened personal emphasis on being instrumental. This finding holds for those individuals who were actually middle aged as well as for older persons as they retrospect back to midlife. Neugarten's (1968) theoretical list of the executive processes of middle age, including manipulation, control of the environment, mastery, and competence, are consonant with these results, as is Gutmann's (1964) work on the ego psychology of the aging process.

Old age, correspondingly, is characterized by an equally distinct personal emphasis on terminal or end-state values. And, as before, this preference is manifested both among those who are actually old aged and for middle-aged individuals asked to imagine what they will be like in old age. These findings are consistent with other studies showing an inward turn of ego functions in old age (Gutmann, 1964; Neugarten, 1968).

The social desirability measures incorporated into the design, in addition to being an important control arrangement, provide a useful amplification to previous value studies. Regardless of age, respondents generally give a higher social desirability ranking to terminal than to instrumental values. More revealing than the clear societal mandate (as reflected in the social desirability rankings), however, is the fact that personal desirability measures for the middle age period gave comparatively higher priority to being instrumental. That is, external ambition and achievement are personally espoused in middle age, even though society and the surrounding cultural influence places a greater emphasis on a terminal orientation. This finding suggests that the occupational and social contradictions facing those approaching retirement are no more, perhaps even less, problematic than for the middle-aged person striving and competing within a context that disclaims being instrumental. Contrary to the traditional concern for stressful adaptation in aging, it is perhaps the middle-aged adult who has to face a major discrepancy between his or her personal and societal value systems (Neugarten, 1968).

In sum, the evidence for a value transition from middle age to old age is clearly established. In so doing, the usefulness of a phenomenological orientation in identifying issues relevant to the study of adult development is reinforced. This instrumentality–terminality sequence, therefore, represents a significant finding both for the adults themselves who revealed the process, and for the developmentalist who searches for time-related regularities in behavioral processes.

9

A Study of Values in the British House of Commons

Donald D. Searing

Members of Parliament, journalists, and historians would be hard put to describe politicians without mentioning their values. But rarely have these matters been pursued in quantitative research. It is puzzling that this should be so. From the viewpoint of those involved, political conflict is about values, ends, and means protagonists believe desirable; to them it appears obvious that politicians are evaluating animals whose outlooks and behaviors are shaped by organizing principles. This chapter reports an effort to measure politicians' values as part of a broader inquiry into their socialization and belief systems.

Compared with policy opinions and personality drives, values have suffered perfunctory consideration. Often by habit, sometimes by design, survey research overlooks values to ask politicians about their policy views, a research strategy which insures obvious relevance and agreeable interviews. Other studies more self-consciously avoid values, drawing attention instead to drives defined as internal stimuli which push or propel political behavior. Hobbes' power drives, Marx's materialistic motives, and Freud's Eros and Thanatos have all had greater influence than value analysis upon contemporary elite studies (Schlesinger, 1966; Downes, 1957; Lasswell & Lerner, 1965; George & George, 1956). An attractive feature of drive theories is their economy: they explain politicians' actions by a few independent variables, rescuing us at a stroke from the labors of unraveling their complicated value systems. Yet, drives have not convincingly explained much variance in specific political beliefs and behavior. Nor is it clear that they perform unique motivational functions unknown to the values which politicians themselves regard as important (McGuire, 1969; Greenstein, 1969; Lane, 1969). On both counts it seems appropriate to rehabilitate the values concept and reconsider relationships between goals and actions.

This requires an instrument which gathers a broad range of value data and, at the same time, satisfies two practical constraints for interviewing national politicians. One is that it must be acceptable to intelligent people of high status; the other, that it cannot consume too much of the limited time they make available for academic interviews. The value-ranking technique passes these tests and generates data appropriate for analyzing representation, agenda setting, consensus, and similar topics involving relationships between values and other beliefs and behavior. The present chapter proposes to develop a methodological foundation for such investigations. After reviewing the values concept and the instrument's development, it describes difficulties in the form's administration and assesses its performance as a satisfactory measure of political ideals.

THE INSTRUMENT'S DEVELOPMENT

Concepts and Sample

Attempts to measure values began with Thurstone's work in 1927 and today include many different scales used in psychology, sociology, and anthropology (Thurstone, 1927; Dukes, 1955; Pittel & Mendelsohn, 1966). Although political science has not developed a comparable literature, there have been several innovative explorations of politicians' values, most notably the International Study of Values in Politics project and an application of Lasswell's value inventory to content analyze Democratic and Republican Party platforms spanning a century (Jacob, Flink, & Schuchman, 1962; Jacob, Teune, & Watts, 1968; Namenwirth & Lasswell, 1970). Still other studies have used values terminology in reporting data, albeit with less attention to definitions and theoretical discussion (Hargrove, 1969; Zaninovich, 1973).

The values concept covers phenomena ranging from whatever interests an individual to that which he regards as good or bad. Among diverse definitions, two themes stand out: values are more general than other sorts of beliefs, and they shape the individual's evaluative experience (Williams, 1968). Both themes are reflected in M. Brewster Smith's characterization of values (1949) as "highly generalized attitudes that define a person's orientation to life in terms of the things he deems most important." Behind most definitions is the idea that people seek to give order and meaning to their lives through basic principles which, when combined with assumptions about human nature, have been referred to as a personal philosophy (Newcomb, Turner, & Converse, 1965; Kluckhohn, 1951). A British politician put it this way: "I'm talking about my political philosophy; I'm not talking, you know, about a realistic assessment of the world in the next 10 years." Individuals often depict the essential features of their political beliefs in a few compact images or personal anecdotes. For example:

> I remember quite distinctly: my governess asked me to paint certain historical characters and I instantly and instinctively disliked Oliver Cromwell and was instantly attracted by Charles I. And those feeling are still with me! Quite irrational but later on, of course, backed up by argument.

Most politicians can carry on with the subject for hours; some write books about it. Obviously, the complexity and nuance of their views cannot be captured in standardized forms requiring all of 15 minutes to complete. But survey instruments can, I believe, identify satisfactorily some of the more important values involved. At the outset, we must be clear about what to look for, an undertaking complicated by the fact that value definitions come in many more varieties than actual measures used in research. Distinctions having substantial measurement consequences concern goals, awareness, and generality.

Lasswell and Kaplan's often cited definition (1950) describes values as goals, such as wealth or security, which individuals aim at and act to promote. Goals can include either immediate *wants* or *ideals,* depending on the project's theoretical focus: where affect is of primary interest, any want may count as a goal; if evaluation is emphasized, measures seek only those goals which subjects regard as good or as ideals.[1] A related problem is goal awareness: the distinction between *implicit* and *explicit* values. Because people may not be self-conscious about all their wants, research in this vein proposes to measure implicit values through inference from an individual's actions and activities. The ideals side of the argument, by contrast, tends to restrict its attention to explicit values, ideals the individual is aware he holds and whose importance to him can be discussed with an interviewer (Kluckhohn, 1951). Regardless of how the wants–ideals and implicit–explicit choices are resolved, nearly all

---

[1]This seems to be the point of Clyde Kluckhohn's distinction between "the desired" and "the desirable" (1951). In constructing measures of criteria people apply in their evaluations, some studies operationalize values not as goals but rather as assumptions about human nature (e.g., "Man is trustworthy and perfectable") which are believed to be influential determinants of behavior (Kluckhohn & Strodtbeck, 1961).

commentators introduce a generality criterion to distinguish values from other evaluative beliefs such as norms, attitudes, and opinions. Thus, values are said to be "extremely inclusive goals," few in number, and not bound to particular contexts (Newcomb, Turner, & Converse, 1965; Williams, 1968; McGuire, 1969; Rokeach, 1968). The present inquiry will treat values as political ideals, abstract conceptions of ends and means that are explicitly held by individuals and serve as standards for interpreting and evaluating their political experience.

The value-ranking instrument was developed for interviews with Members of the British House of Commons. To satisfy broader project purposes, the research design sought a dense sample, a compromise between thinly spread random samples and saturation samples which include all organization members (Coleman, 1961). Of the 630 Members of Parliament, 83 percent (521) were interviewed. And, 84 percent of these respondents (438) returned value-ranking data. Reasons for refusing interviews were quite diverse and do not seem to have compromised the sample whose population response rate is closely approximated among Ministers, Opposition Front Bench Spokesmen, and all other subgroups examined thus far. Respondents were contacted between January, 1972, and July, 1973, the Conservative Heath government being in power throughout this period. Five interviewers worked on the project, including the principal investigator who did one-quarter of the interviews and supervised other personnel. Meetings arranged in the House of Commons, Ministers' offices, and Members' homes produced, on average, an hour and a half of tape-recorded conversation structured by projective, open-ended, and closed-ended questions. During these sessions several written forms were completed, including a value-ranking instrument. The tapes have been transcribed and, supplementing the value form, provide a basis for the analysis at hand.

Measuring Politicians' Values

The value-ranking exercise, adapted from Rokeach's work (1968, 1973), requires subjects to rank order a total of 36 values presented in four separate lists of nine values each. In constructing the instrument, it is necessary to decide which values shall be included. One strategy is to select values the investigator considers theoretically or normatively significant.[2] So long as these items are not meaningless to respondents, useful data can be produced for specific research purposes. But, if the

[2]There have been several attempts to identify value categories relevant to all cultures (Rokeach, 1968, 1973; Lasswell & Kaplan, 1950; Kluckhohn & Strodtbeck, 1961). This approach runs the risk of constructing items which are so diffuse that they encompass everything, but, by the same token, may be related to few other beliefs and behaviors in any particular culture or subset of political systems.

research goal includes mapping a population's belief system, as in the present study, it is necessary to seek values which ,subjects *themselves* think central to their concerns. While such value lists can be compiled through exploratory discussions with interviewees, this procedure may prejudice results in small organizations when the developed instrument is later applied to the same population (Denitch, 1972). Fortunately, a great deal has been written, though not without ambiguities and contradictions, about British political culture and its politicians' values, often by politicians themselves. An inventory was constructed from values found in MPs' speeches and writings and in academic studies of British political life. Sources for this inventory included parliamentary debates, commentaries by parliamentary correspondents, recent political memoirs such as those by Lord Butler and Prime Minister Wilson, and academic attempts at synthesis (Beer, 1965; Blondel, 1965; Mackintosh, 1968; McKenzie, 1963; Richards, 1959; Finer, Berrington, & Bartholomew, 1961; Rose, 1964; Pulzer, 1972; Christoph, 1965; Potter, 1966). Efforts were made to include value distinctions which might seem minor to outsiders, but important to politicians.

After eliminating overlapping items, the list was revised through student pretests which identified confusing labels and helped sharpen definitions. Next, British scholars specializing in the study of politics and Parliament reviewed the revised instrument, making further suggestions about overlaps, definitions, and possible additions and deletions. Final changes followed tape-recorded sessions with former Members of Parliament who were not returned in the 1970 General Election and could not therefore appear in the study's sample. These pretest respondents filled in the value-ranking form's penultimate version and suggested how it might best be presented to Members of the House. The final version proved quite satisfactory. During project interviews, Honesty was the only value MPs mentioned as missing from the lists. Yet, Honesty, probably the value most highly regarded by Members of all parties, would likely have been ranked at the top of nearly everyone's list and would not, therefore, have provided much differentiation for data analysis.

In developing the value-ranking technique, Rokeach (1973) produced one version which requires subjects to write ranks on a printed form and another using printed gummed labels respondents could move about till satisfied with the resulting ranks. Since it was not feasible to confront MPs with gummed labels, the project's form requested written ranks, as illustrated in Figure 9.1. Values were grouped in lists of 9, rather than 18, as Rokeach had done, because shorter lists seem likely to yield more complete responses and satisfactory reliabilities. After a brief introduction to the notion of values and ideals, the form was presented with this instruction: "It would help us a great deal if you could rank the ideals in each group in the order of their importance to you. For each list, could you write the number '1' alongside the ideal which is most important to you? Then write '2' alongside the ideal which is second most important to you, and so on. In each group, the ideal which is least important should be given the number '9.'" Completing the value sheet required from 6 to 20 minutes, a period very similar to the 10 to 20 minutes taken by most of Rokeach's respondents.

FIGURE 9.1.   Example of a Completed Values Form

List A	List B
AUTHORITY	CAPITALISM
the right to command	competition, private ownership
COMMUNITY	FELLOWSHIP
harmonious social relations	companionship among equals
ECONOMIC EQUALITY	MERITOCRACY
equal wealth for all	advancement by merit
FREEDOM	PARTICIPATORY DEMOCRACY
independence, free choice	maximum political participation
FREE ENTERPRISE	PRIVACY
absence of government control	avoidance of intrusion and publicity
PROPERTY	PUBLIC ORDER
private ownership	maintenance of law and order
SOCIAL EQUALITY	SOCIALISM
equality in dignity and privileges	public ownership and equality
SOCIAL HIERARCHY	SOCIAL PROGRESS
integrated social strata	continuous social improvement
UNITY	STRONG GOVERNMENT
solidarity	decisive government

List C	List D
CAUTION	COOPERATION
prudence and circumspection	teamwork
COMPASSION	DISCIPLINE
concern for human welfare	obedience to the rules
DEFERENCE	EFFICIENCY
respect for superior judgment	skill and effectiveness
DUTY	EMPIRICAL APPROACH
fulfillment of obligations	being guided by experience
INTELLIGENCE	GRADUALISM
intellect and awareness	wariness of sweeping change
LOYALTY	RATIONALISM
adherence to persons and promises	a rigorously reasoned approach
PATRIOTISM	SECURITY
devotion to country	freedom from uncertainty about the
SELF-DISCIPLINE	future
self-control	SOCIAL PLANNING
SELF-RELIANCE	application of practical principles
self-help, individual enterprise	STRONG LEADERSHIP
	initiative, direction

For interviewing national elites there are not as many alternatives to the value-ranking technique as would be desirable. Respondents' reactions made it quite plain that even this format, handled as politely and pleasantly as possible, was pushing against the limits of acceptability. Its major source of legitimacy was that most values listed were common coin of Members' own political conversations; arranging them in the order of their importance to the individual did not seem utterly absurd on the face of it. Less familiar items, Rokeach's "salvation" and "loving," for example, would have met disdain and resistance. Likewise, semantic differentials, or a series of items of the sort included in standard value scales (e.g., "Which do you expect ultimately will prove more important for mankind—mathematics or theology?"), would be regarded by many as bald insults to their intelligence and status. Some such items might be tolerated in a mail questionnaire, provided they are watered down with more familiar and straightforward questions; but they simply "are not on" for face-to-face interviews in the House.

One feasible alternative is contextual coding of conversational interviews that have been tape recorded (Putnam, 1973). This has the important advantage of utilizing dimensions of meaning in value statements which are missed altogether by ranking instruments or conventional scales. On the other hand, its potential for sensitive measurement must be weighed against difficulties with missing data and problems of reliability and validity (Aberbach, Chesney, and Rockman, 1974; Dexter, 1970). The two approaches need not be mutually exclusive: by combining a ranking instrument with contextual analysis of taped discussions there is something to be learned from both worlds. Thus, interview transcripts have already provided circumstantial evidence that the ranking form was interpreted much as intended and measured values in a manner meaningful to respondents. For example:

> Now, List B. Well, number 1 undoubtedly is Socialism, no question, although it means more than public ownership. And, I would think that Participatory Democracy must come number 2. . . . Capitalism, competition, private ownership I would almost put last—I'm just trying to see if there's anything which I regard as even worse.

The measurement technique is based on an assumption that people order their priorities so that some values take precedence over others in situations requiring choice (Woodruff & DiVesta, 1948; Kluckhohn & Strodbeck, 1961; Rokeach, 1968). The fact that values are wrapped in terminology such as "better than" or "more appropriate than" suggests rank orders of importance which can be roughly represented on the value form. This assumption, which sometimes poses as a definition, must remain open to further investigation; even should it prove basically sound, value hierarchies may be neither well crystallized nor inflexible. The point was made by MPs who, while accepting the plausibility of a rank order model, noted that the exercise imposed more structure than was actually present in their usual thinking about the subject. In particular, they emphasized that: (1) the values form forced them to choose between pairs of values they had never before considered competitors; (2) people differ a great deal in the range of situations to which they apply a given ordering; and (3) the stability of value hierarchies varies considerably among their colleagues in the House.

Although the exercise provoked discussion and doubt entered in the taped record, on balance it generally seemed reasonable to most respondents. If we assume that individuals arrange their values in a rough order of importance, how might this come about? Pairs of values like Capitalism and Socialism may be learned together as political antipodes; others may be deduced from a few core beliefs: "I am a Socialist and therefore value Social Planning"; while the majority probably become ordered through everyday situations requiring that one value be placed above another. Comprehensive school reorganization policies, for instance, can catalyze conflict between Social Equality and Freedom. Or, taking an example from the transcripts: "If I find that British troops are mistreating even a few people in Northern Ireland, I'm moved more by Compassion, concern for human welfare, than I ever would be by any ideas of Patriotism." Experience with a series of such choices leads people to develop rules of thumb for making judgments and taking action; they define hierarchical criteria which concern the relative importance of their values. The value-ranking instrument presents them with yet another situation in which priorities must be assessed and some values chosen over others.

Value items were printed alphabetically within lists. Deciding which values shall be placed in which lists is more difficult. A convenient criterion is the ends–means distinction which, as explicated by Aristotle, includes a middle category between the usual two: (1) values desired only for their own sake (Social Equality); (2) values which are desired for their own sake, but also because they have further consequences (Loyalty); and (3) values desired entirely as means and very rarely for their own sake (Social Planning). In measuring ends and means, Rokeach (1973) postulates two distinct and *separate* value systems, terminal (ends) and instrumental (means). Lasswell and Kaplan (1950) make a similar distinction between intrinsic and instrumental values. The interview tapes suggest serious operationalization problems: ends–means classifications are not uniform across individuals, for one person's end is often another's means. Indeed, sensitivity to this fact is a common resource used by politicians to manipulate one another's behavior. The Opposition may seek to convince a Minister, for instance, that the end his bill proposes to promote is really a means to other ends he himself believes undesirable. Moreover, it is not obvious that ends and means values are compartmentalized or held separately; MPs are often asked to give Loyalty, a means value, priority over their ends values when these conflict with party policy. They usually do so because they realize that, without loyalty and unity, their party will be unable to sustain a government or achieve any ends at all.

Despite disagreement over individual interpretations of ends and means, the range of variation may be restricted within particular populations. From this perspective, a former Member of Parliament suggested, in project pretests, regrouping the initial value items into lists which he thought British politicians might generally regard as ends and means. This was done, lists A and B in Figure 9.1 representing ends and lists C and D means. During the interviews, many MPs recognized ends and means as the implicit principle by which values had been sorted, even noting anomalies in the means lists, such as Patriotism and Security, which are frequently considered ends. In the same vein, Rokeach (1973) reports greater reliability for his terminal than for his instrumental values, indicating that respondents may care more about values he calls "terminal"—which is as it should be if they are understood as ends rather than means.[3] Similarly, MPs found it easier to rank values in ends lists A and B than in means lists C and D where distinctions seemed difficult to draw. In sum, there is reason to believe that many respondents interpreted A and B as ends and C and D as means, though these are certainly neither firm nor universally held classifications throughout the sample.

Considering value systems and means–ends distinctions in this way highlights the instrument's stark abstraction and lack of context. Rokeach argues that these characteristics allow the measure to function as a semiprojective test: unaware they are revealing something about themselves, subjects have little incentive to disguise their values.[4] Lack of context seems to have had something of this effect with MPs who, moreover, knew they could never be held to account politically, or publicly embarrassed, by ranks they assigned items like Public Order in such an obtuse academic exercise. Several respondents did, in fact, comment on the self-examination implications of what they were doing. Some re-

[3]Kluckhohn (1951) argues, by contrast, that means values, including ways of acting, are regarded as just as important as ends.

[4]It could be claimed that the value-ranking form taps implicit as well as explicit values. A more cautious assessment would be that, in addition to measuring highly salient values, the instrument directs the subject's attention to others which, though prevalent in his subculture, he himself does not usually discuss.

quested copies of the sheets; and one insisted on repeating the process after a fortnight to assess the stability of his rankings. But even these interviewees had little reason to hide their values. Indeed, Members of Parliament work hard at publicizing their values rather than disguising them; not doing so would be deviant behavior in the House, generally counterproductive and, in some circumstances, stigmatized as dishonest. While I do not think it wholly accurate to claim the exercise was projective for the politicians, I believe they tried their best to give us an accurate picture of their values within the instrument's limitations.

ADMINISTERING THE INSTRUMENT

Completions and Interpretations

Measuring values was easily the interviewer's most delicate task. Members were invariably courteous and helpful; most completed the value-ranking exercise without serious objection, seeking only to clarify instructions and offer a few observations on the instrument's validity and probable results. The rest were more reluctant: "I don't know, this is very difficult, isn't it? . . . How much more of this have you got, by the way?" Despite considerable discussion and persuasion, 16 percent refused to touch the form.[5] Some said they did not have time for what they perceived as a lengthy task; in several cases the interviewer made this decision for them in order to avoid spending the remainder of a rushed interview discussing the methodology behind this curious request. Such situations were relatively few, as were those where respondents objected to the exercise as an invasion of privacy. A larger minority declined on the basis of vigorous intellectual objections to the instrument's assumptions. Several of their reservations have already been stated; others will be considered later.

But the majority among those who refused (always politely, albeit firmly) did not seem motivated by any of these reasons. Members granted the interview as a kindness to a professor, proposing to help him with his research by discussing their outlooks on political matters, views of Parliament, and careers. What they found in this particular exercise was a "test," administered by overly clever university people, which put them in the position of pupils rather than statesmen or even expert informants: "What a load of jargon. It's like an intelligence test in an exam. I'm just reading my way through all the lists first to see which

[5]Social scientists' forms—whether checklists, ranking exercises, or Likert scales—have never been the highlights of a tired politician's week.

one's the easiest—I do that in exams too." This reaction usually came from respondents of long service and high status.[6] In retrospect, it is quite understandable that the exercise, and indeed any printed attitude scale or checklist, might be interpreted as an imposition on their generosity. It made even amenable respondents noticeably uncomfortable: few middle-aged or older people relish the thought of being tested in this way. Satisfactory rapport was easily reestablished, but 16 percent of the value sheets remained blank.

Interview transcripts provide data relevant to Larson's reservations (1969) about how respondents decode abstract values. Often subjects did request the contexts and sentences Larson regards as essential for thinking meaningfully about values; and, when cues were not forthcoming from interviewers, some respondents provided their own, stating these for the tape. By and large, however, MPs appear to have treated the items more as abstract symbols than might have been anticipated. Here is an example of a typical request for context: "The most important to me, as what?" Our standard answer was: "For you personally, as an MP." It is my impression that rankings would have been substantially the same regardless of the type of ambiguous response we offered, so long as the "personally" was emphasized. Beyond a minimal context given by abbreviated dictionary definitions printed beneath each value item, respondents were left to their own interpretations.

MPs are well aware that their value profiles differ: one gave his personal rankings and then wrote alongside the different ranks he believed would be awarded by most of his party colleagues; another recorded his impressions of ranks which might be forthcoming from the other side. Part of these differences, it was claimed, are attributable to the fact that value items do not mean the same thing to all respondents. Judging by the transcripts there is evidence for this view, though it is difficult to say how widely interpretations actually differ. A few cases are unmistakable. For instance, Tories who rank Socialism 9 put forward definitions ranging from totalitarian controls to a cumbersome economic system. Likewise, Social Planning receives high marks from both left- and right-wing Labour Members, the one seeing it as a road to equality, the other as a tool for managing the welfare state. Although transcripts alert us to variations in connotative meaning, the value-ranking technique itself is ill equipped to capture them. At the same time, it should be stressed that for several decades respondents have been rubbing elbows

[6]According to Lewis Anthony Dexter (1970), one of the few satisfactions interviews offer elite respondents is the opportunity to teach someone, to explain matters about which interviewers know little and interviewees have the wisdom of experience. The value-ranking exercise, in the perception of some MPs, apparently reversed these anticipated roles. An extreme example of the interviewee-as-teacher role is described by Harriet Zuckerman (1972), whose Nobel laureates peppered her with a stream of competence tests throughout their interviews.

and exchanging ideas in the small world of British politics. This experience might be expected at least to narrow the range of interpretations for familiar values in their environment.

Methods by which values sheets were filled in can also inform us about how the instrument was interpreted. Everybody proceeded one list at a time, generally following the A, B, C, D order. Within lists, MPs would read all nine items before assigning the number 1, reread the remaining eight, and write in the number 2 and so on. This was the predominant pattern, upset only by one eccentric Member who insisted on doing the exercise upside down. After assigning their top two or three ranks, more than a third of the MPs skipped on to identify the list's values they disliked most, rating these 9, 8, and 7, respectively. The remainder of the values were then distributed among middle ranks. Ranking from the bottom as well as from the top has been observed in other studies and reinforces the point that the technique produces ordinal rather than interval data (Rokeach, 1973). It is clear that intervals separating ranks for different people may vary widely, as may intervals between different ranks recorded by a single individual. While Conservatives, for instance, generally ranked Socialism low, some were not satisfied with a mere 9, but insisted on writing 99 instead; and, a few resolutely refused to allow Socialism a place even on the lowliest rung of their hierarchy: "There are some of these I don't agree with at all. I don't even rate them as worthy of listing." Several Labour Members reciprocated: "I mean, could I strike out Free Enterprise, Property, and Authority?" In the same vein, while many respondents easily ranked means values in lists C and D, others were reluctant to order what they found more or less agreeable: "Hm. It's rather like asking what's one's favorite sunshine." Since values are ranked in relation to one another within lists, the technique measures only their relative importance. Unless his transcript provides the information, it is impossible to tell whether an interviewee regards a few values as having great importance and others none at all, or whether he sees all values in a list as generally desirable.

It has been pointed out that applications of value-ranking instruments force rank orders despite the possibility that individuals may regard several values as equally worthy (Gorsuch, 1969). Interview tapes confirm that this is a difficulty. The following comment was not unusual:

> I tend to put some at the front and some lower down ... but there are some here I find it very difficult to distinguish between ... they're concepts which shade into one another ... I'm sure (were I to do this again later) my ones and twos would be very similar. But those between number six and number four would be all jumbled up.

Unlike undergraduates, Members of Parliament cannot readily be dragooned into accepting rules of the exercise which exclude ties: approximately one out of four began by awarding several values the same rank. For some respondents this was primarily a strategy to avoid tedious distinctions and hasten return to the discussion format. With others it was plain that the ties accurately reflected a considered judgment. Interviewers were instructed, therefore, to argue firmly against equal ranking and persist until it was clear that Members did not in fact prefer one value over another. Some MPs, when pressed, eventually assigned ranks which seemed to us to reflect meaningful though difficult distinctions. Sixteen percent stuck to their guns and insisted on recording two or more ties. On the basis of this experience, it appears necessary strongly to discourage ties, while remaining prepared to accept them in the end when they apparently reflect genuine equivalencies.

Order Effects and Social Desirability Effects

Although values were arranged alphabetically within lists, it is possible that order effects occurred such that items at the top artificially received higher ranks than those at the bottom (Rokeach, 1973). This was investigated by using Spearman's rho to correlate alphabetical order with the median value rankings MPs assigned each list's values. Rho equals $+1.0$ when rankings are in perfect agreement, 0.0 when there is no relationship at all, and -1.0 in circumstances of perfect disagreement. Order effects would be reflected in positive correlations between the two sets of ranks. There is no evidence of order effects for lists A, B, or C, whose rho correlations are -0.33, -0.31, and $+0.02$, none of which attains statistical significance at the .05 level. List D, however, does produce a positive correlation of $+0.60$ ($p = .05$).

While this may indicate a genuine order effect, an alternative account merits consideration: the alphabetical arrangement of values in List D could roughly match many Members' preferences. If the result is primarily due to order effects, these should operate throughout the list, in both its upper and lower sections. Partitioning the items into the top five and lower four entries reduces rho to $+0.40$ (n.s.) in the upper portion and to -0.80 (n.s.) in the lower portion, suggesting that an order effect explanation is not fully convincing. Still, despite these results for the sample as a whole, I am confident that some order effects were at work among a minority of individuals who, in ranking List C and especially List D, showed signs of fatigue, boredom, and a desire to return to more rewarding discussion as quickly as possible. This also reinforces the suspicion that reliabilities for lists C and D are lower than those for lists A and B.

Another possible source of error is the social desirability effect where respondents arrange values to enhance their image in the interviewer's eyes. This has been examined by an experiment which first presented a value ranking survey under standard instructions; later the instrument was readministered with a new requirement that values be ranked in an order which would make subjects appear admirable to the experimenter (Kelly, Silverman, & Cochrane, 1972). Absence of correlations between the two sets of rankings suggests that social desirability effects do not occur under normal conditions.

Social desirability effects are less likely with Members of Parliament than with populations drawn from the general public, a difference due to relative status between interviewee and interviewer. University students might be anxious that instructors think well of them; middle-class citizens may feel the same way about well-dressed survey interviewers. But MPs unabashedly characterize themselves as one of the most egocentric groups of people in Britain: very rarely did project staff suspect respondents of seeking to rub up their image for our benefit. In the House of Commons these days academics are almost as numerous as constituents; they are treated with the same politeness and generosity shown other visitors, but not with deference. Among all the interviews done by the principal investigator, only one respondent appeared to rank a value in a way obviously affected by my presence. This was a country squire from the Tory party who, upon reaching Intelligence in List C, said peculiarly, "Intelligence, of course, is nothing but a nuisance—no doubt it deserves a 9."

Besides social desirability effects, the researcher's presence may have other unanticipated consequences. In most cases interviewers watched respondents rank the values and were available to answer questions, albeit they were instructed to use prepared answers wherever possible and avoid giving direction and structure. Rokeach and Cochrane (1972) found no difference between rankings carried out privately and others done with experimenters in the room. Again, there is reason to believe that Members of Parliament, compared with undergraduates or the general public, are less disposed to react to an academic interviewer by altering responses that might have been recorded privately.

INVESTIGATIONS OF RELIABILITY AND VALIDITY

Reliability and Unreliable Pragmatists

Reliability refers to consistency, to whether the values measure can produce the same results in repeated trials. Some pragmatists claim they are committed to unreliability as a matter of principle and refuse to pledge themselves to a stable set of values. This was the major intellectual objection put forward by MPs who declined to fill in the form.

Confident of not having as stable a value hierarchy as some of their more ideological colleagues, they reject the exercise as meaningless for themselves. Assigning ranks as requested would, they believe, convey a misleading impression of their views. The argument has two versions, both concerned to embed values in contexts and situations. One holds that the respondent does have a nascent hierarchy, but that it is very sensitive to political events and changes a good deal from week to week. Another position is that true pragmatists will only choose among values in specific situations; so much so that the practice proscribes developing anything like the hierarchical value system defined by the ranking instrument. A pure pragmatist, it is claimed, simply does not have value orderings that exist apart from specific situations or apply across them:

> If, for instance, I was beating you up in my house, my right to Privacy would be less than the public's right to Public Order. But, if you had policemen knocking on your door at every hour of the night, then you would say that Privacy was dominant over Public Order. I cannot arrange these in any static order because I believe that the order would change depending on the conditions.

The argument is that true pragmatists do not adopt value orderings which rise above particular and usually complex situations. Although it is difficult, in practice, to be so abstemious about the abstractions of everyday speech (many did apply values across situations during the conversational interview), their objection is informative: it suggests that some individuals have substantially less stable values than others, a consideration which should be taken into account when examining a value instrument's reliability. It also suggests that the hierarchical value system assumption bears investigation regarding proportions of individuals to whom it applies in varying degrees.

Test–retest reliabilities with Rokeach's value survey are quite good. Form D, the movable label version of terminal and instrumental values, yields reliabilities in the .70s, with ranges between .65 and .80, over periods of three to 12 weeks (Rokeach, 1968, 1973). His Form E, which requests written ranks, as does the instrument used in the present study, produced less impressive but still satisfactory reliabilities ranging from .65 to .74. It was not possible to administer reliability tests to Members of Parliament. There was, nonetheless, one volunteer: skeptical of suggestions that the instrument could produce similar results after a fortnight, a Labour MP offered a retest. Spearman rho correlations between his value sheets, done two weeks apart, were +1.0 for List A, +0.93 for List B, and +0.97 with both lists C and D. In short, the rankings were nearly identical. Not surprisingly, Rokeach found that different values have different reliabilities, probably due to variations in their salience or comprehensibility for respondents. Several terms on the political ranking instrument were not universally well understood either.

Most troublesome were Unity and Social Hierarchy, labels academic commentators attach to politicians' values which, transcripts show, are regarded as rather odd and foreign. In the same vein, Rokeach notes that values ranked in the middle of lists change most from test to retest. Likewise, it was the impression of project staff that Members were least confident about these middle rankings: "I'm sure (were I to do this again later) those between number six and number four would be all jumbled up."

Validity: Pretests with British Students

Value scales usually employ a series of items to measure a single value. The ranking technique uses only one item which functions by comparison with others. This format is the basis of its plausibility and practicality for interviewing politicians and similar groups with little time and less tolerance for standard scales. But lacking multiple indicators, the technique must be examined with circumspection to insure it adequately assesses respondents' outlooks.

A series of studies have demonstrated that ranked values produce substantial and meaningful contrasts among groups differentiated by age, occupation, education, race, income, and religion. Similarly, values measured by Rokeach's instrument in the United States have been related to a variety of beliefs, including attitudes toward Vietnam and civil rights demonstrations, and to behaviors such as church attendance and joining civil rights organizations. In developing a British version of the value instrument it was desirable to explore similar validations for British subjects by correlating their ranking data with scores on better known value scales. Since few politicians would willingly serve social science in this capacity, validations were pursued with 61 undergraduates at Oxford and the London School of Economics who, under supervision of project staff, completed both the value ranking form and Allport–Vernon–Lindzey value scales.

The Allport–Vernon–Lindzey Study of Values (A–V–L) characterizes people by their dominant interests which include political, social, and economic types (1960). Combining responses to 120 statements, the A–V–L produces scores for each type and is one of the best regarded and most frequently used value measures. Administered to thousands of subjects over several decades, it has demonstrated substantial test–retest reliability and external validity. Since it measures values defined as dominant interests rather than the ideals sought in ranking instruments, this should work against the proposed validation by depressing correlations between the two scales.

Among all possible relationships between value ranks and A–V–L political, social, and economic scores, 37 percent proved significant at the .05 level or better; Pearson product-moment correlations ranged between .21 and .51. This seems an impressive outcome, particularly since the value-ranking items were not originally selected with a view to their relevance for A–V–L categories. Most importantly, nearly every relationship represents a meaningful result when interpreted in the British context. For example, Allport–Vernon–Lindzey define their political type as a person interested primarily in power; and Strong Leadership and Authority are the outstanding value-ranking correlates of political scores. Likewise, social types, characterized by a love of people, give top marks to Cooperation, Consultation, and Community. They are also said to reject the outlooks of economic types, finding them cold and inhuman. Consistent with this expectation, social and economic types take up opposite positions in the ranking data: every value related to the scores of both displays a positive sign in one case and a negative sign in the other.

The ranking instrument appears to measure values captured by a well known scale, doing so according to interpretable patterns. Its validity was further explored by correlating value ranks with policy opinions which values, as organizing principles, are said to structure. Student subjects responded to items on curbing strikes, increasing pensions, and extending nationalization. These views were related to their values at the .05 level or better in 41 out of 108 cells, with correlations ranging from .21 to .72. Again, the relationships might easily have been anticipated: those in favor of curbing strikes were well disposed toward Property; support for increasing pensions was related to Equality ranks; and pro-nationalization respondents were in the vanguard with Socialism.

Thus far we have reviewed the value instrument's development and administration, as well as studies of its reliability and validity using students and other members of the public. Now I should like to see whether or not it works for politicians.

CANDIDATES, MEMBERS OF PARLIAMENT, AND CONTENT ANALYSIS

To pursue their political goals, politicians join forces in like-minded groups. This section probes the value-ranking techniques's validity with a straightforward criterion: its capacity to segregate politicians from opposing political camps. Investigating the instrument's sensitivity to these matters necessitates a cursory review of large bodies of data; the question before us is whether or not broad patterns in the results make sense. Does the instrument measure what are regarded as major value cleavages between members of different political parties?; and, does it capture values reflected in their discussions of institutions and public policy?

Tories and Socialists

Tories and Socialists disagree over appropriate methods for discovering the public interest: Conservatives rely upon their leaders' independent deliberations; Labour politicians look toward working-class needs. Applying different criteria, they reach quite different conclusions. Their political battles are seen by many participants and voters alike as a clash between two sets of values, between two understandings of what is politically desirable and how it might best be achieved (Beer, 1965; Potter, 1966). We wish to know whether the ranking technique is attuned to these value differences, or, whether, as one MP put it, "Yes, well it's not much more than pinpricking. There you are."

Before contrasting Conservative and Labour MPs, it will be instructive to set each alongside their party's candidates who were defeated in the 1970 General Election. For theoretical purposes unrelated to this validity analysis, candidates fighting losing causes as a service to their party were isolated from the population. The same considerations excluded former Members of Parliament, thus reducing the sampling frame to candidates who had never been MPs and who came closest to entering Parliament in 1970. From their ranks was drawn a random sample of 120 individuals, 89 percent of whom were interviewed and filled in the same value form as did MPs. If the instrument is measuring political values satisfactorily, we should expect to find much closer resemblance between each party's candidates and MPs than between MPs on different sides of the political fence.

A party's candidates and MPs can be compared by the percentage within each group which awarded a value top ranks, scoring it either first, second, or third in its list. Table 9.1 summarizes these comparisons. Its first two columns report mean differences, for each value list, between candidates and MPs. These gaps are quite small, as are the ranges involved: out of all 72 individual value comparisons (36 Conservative and 36 Labour), only 6 distinguish candidates and MPs by more than 10 percent. In most of these, MPs lean toward Members on the other side, leaving their candidates to slightly more extreme stances. But what is remarkable is the consistent similarity between each party's candidates and its Members of Parliament: at the .05 level there are virtually no significant value differences between them. Even raising the significance level to a more generous .10 would only produce a total of 13 significant differences, and modest ones at that. Candidates are the mirror image of MPs from their own political camp.

By contrast, Conservative and Labour Members of Parliament are poles apart. Within the House, they refer to one another as "the other side." So they are; unlike the family resemblance between candidates and MPs, every value comparison save one produces differences which

TABLE 9.1. Summary Comparison of Value Ranking by Candidates and Members of Parliament*

	Difference Between Conservative Candidates and Conservative MPs ($\bar{X}\%$)	Difference Between Labour Candidates and Labour MPs ($\bar{X}\%$)	Difference Between Conservative MPs and Labour MPs ($\bar{X}\%$)
Value List A	6.0	3.9	28.9
Value List B	7.2	4.2	34.4
Value List C	5.6	4.6	13.8
Value List D	6.0	4.6	26.0

*Compares groups by the percentage of respondents who rank each value first, second, or third. Entries for the lists (nine values per list) are mean differences between the groups being compared.

are statistically significant, usually at the .001 level. The percentage gaps involved are summarized for each value list in the third column of Table 9.1. Individual values separating Tories and Socialists most sharply are the familiar ones found in journalistic accounts (Johnson, 1972; Raison, 1972): Social Equality, Economic Equality, Freedom, Socialism, Social Planning, and Public Order. For each, party differences in assigning the top three ranks exceeded 40 percent. The Labour movement's goals, which define its continuing socialist essence, are deeply concerned with equality; this is the value said to mark best the divide between Labour and Conservative Members of Parliament. Equality is also the key value ordering Americans along a left–right dimension (Bottomore, 1964; Beer, 1965; Rokeach, 1973). That divide is very broad indeed; with Social Equality it was the largest in the analysis. While 93 percent of Labour MPs ranked this value first, second, or third, only 37 percent of their Conservative colleagues did so. Tory ambivalence toward Social Equality was expressed this way:

> I don't like Social Equality ... that's not being fair, I do like Social Equality. I am a great believer that when the Lord made us he made us equal in his sight. But I believe each of us has different qualities.

During the age of democratic revolutions equality and freedom were allies in a struggle for political rights. More recently, issues have shifted to social and economic ground where Socialists push hard for equality while freedom becomes increasingly identified with defending the status quo; contemporary conflicts often pit the one against the other. Many Socialists still have a high regard for Freedom, particularly as it applies to conscience issues of censorship and morality. But, when forced to choose, they opt for Social Equality as relatively more desirable because, "Freedom, free choice, well yes... but not the choices of a private capitalist society which I believe are unreal and conditioned." Table 9.2 compares Conservative and Labour MPs by their relative rankings for Freedom and Social Equality.

Four out of five Tories in Table 9.2 prefer Freedom to Social Equality. This proportion is reversed among Socialists who suspect Freedom as a goal with unintended consequences which may harm the weak and as a symbol they see Tories dressing out in free enterprise and laissez-faire: "Freedom of the individual is what I want; freedom to say what I want, freedom to start a business if I wanted, freedom to have property ... they are all part of the same thing." Equality and Freedom are closely associated with Meritocracy, an ideal no longer as popular among Socialists as it once was. Despite efforts of left-wing critics to drape this albatross around Labour MPs' shoulders, only 7 percent of them ranked it first, second, or third, as compared to 40 percent on the Tory side. Meritocracy became tarnished in Socialist eyes through scuf-

TABLE 9.2. Relative Ranks for Freedom and Social Equality by Party Membership

	PARTY MEMBERSHIP	
RELATIVE VALUE RANKS	% Conservative MPs (N = 209)	% Labour MPs (N = 213)
Percent ranking Freedom over Social Equality	85	21
Percent ranking Social Equality over Freedom	15	79
	100	100

fles between opportunity for the underprivileged versus opportunity for the able (Crosland, 1963). Inequality based on merit is still inequality: "You know, I get worried about who decides what's merit," or, as another Labour Member said: "Meritocracy, advancement by merit, yes, although it's going to mean a very unequal society . . . I'm not terribly in favour."

The point is less to explicate Tory and Socialist belief systems than to determine whether the value instrument measures meaningful distinctions between them. One additional example, then, should suffice. The road to Social and Economic Equality is built by Social Planning, a means value on which Labour Members lead Conservatives by 53 percent. Linked to Social Planning are preferences for Rationalism and Intelligence, values pushed to the background by Tories in favor of what they characterize as an Empirical Approach.[7] These are all well known value differences between Britain's political parties; they are the litmus test most commentators apply to distinguish red and blue political interests. To this extent, the value-ranking technique turns in an adequate performance: it generates data congruent with impressionistic accounts of political allegiance.

The instrument is also sensitive to factionalism within political parties. Conservative MPs are active in the right-wing Monday Club and in Pressure for Economic and Social Toryism (P.E.S.T.), a ginger group on the party's progressive wing. Sharp and interpretable differences separate the proportion of each group ranking values at the top of their lists. Seven items divide them by 30 percent or more: Authority, Free Enterprise, Compassion, Patriotism, Public Order, Community, and Intelligence; each with distributions that fit characterizations of "New Tory"

[7]The Conservative perspective is: "I think God in his infinite wisdom gave it to no man to know how to solve every problem . . . different groups of people warring with one another over different ideas is a much more efficient system than somebody who plans from above and says, 'Well boys, here are the tablets; now you can do it this way.' "

outlooks as humane and compassionate, intellectual and favorable to reform and social change (Sampson, 1966). In the same way, Social Democrats, who stand on Labour's right, can be contrasted with members of the Tribune Group, keepers of the left-wing conscience. Consistent with conventional observations, the Tribune Group is far more sympathetic to Socialism, Economic Equality, Participatory Democracy, and Security than are Social Democrats who stand out by their support for Freedom, Fellowship, and Empirical Approaches to political affairs (Blondel, 1965; Rose, 1964). Taken together, the four factions represent successive steps on an ideological continuum extending from the Monday Club to the Tribune Group. And, 15 of the 36 values distribute their members' scores in stepwise progressions from right to left.

Content Analysis

Another approach to assessing the instrument's validity is to determine whether values measured by its paper-and-pencil technique are reflected in respondents' verbal behavior, in themes which they bring forward when discussing institutions and policy problems.

Interviewees were asked to tell us what they regard as the essential features of a real democracy. Encouraged to develop this in whatever direction seemed most important to them personally, they described a catalogue of characteristics which often included participation and freedom. Transcripts were examined for the presence of these themes by two coders whose intercoder reliability score was 77 percent on participation and 87 percent with freedom. The remaining cases were reviewed and either recoded by agreement or discarded from the analysis. Table 9.3 describes the relationship between individual propensities to mention each theme and value ranks for Participatory Democracy and Freedom.

Many MPs are wary of participatory democracy's crowded corridors of power. Some brought up the subject only to criticize its populist implications; others stressed the need to listen to constituents' grievances, a theme not counted as participation for present purposes. But those who did mention participation in a favorable light were, by and large, the same politicians who ranked Participatory Democracy high on the value instrument: two-thirds of them placed this ideal among the top three in its list, in contrast to only 30 percent of their colleagues (Kendall's Q = .66). They talked about the desirability of greater participation in local constituencies and communities, in national politics and, moving left across the political spectrum, in industry and other institutions as well: "And I want massive participation in democratic institutions. ... I think our schools should involve the children and their parents; factories should involve the workers and the technicians. ... I want to democ-

TABLE 9.3.   Rank for Participatory Democracy, Freedom, and Compassion by Discussion of Value Themes

	FAVORABLE MENTION OF PARTICIPATION THEME	
VALUE RANK FOR PARTICIPATORY DEMOCRACY	Participation Theme Present % (N = 145)	Participation Theme Not Present % (N = 230)
High (1–3)	67	29
Low (4–9)	33	71
	100	100

	MENTION OF FREEDOM THEME	
VALUE RANK FOR FREEDOM	Freedom Theme Present % (N = 152)	Freedom Theme Not Present % (N = 223)
High (1–3)	73	58
Low (4–9)	27	42
	100	100

	MENTION OF COMPASSION THEME	
VALUE RANK FOR COMPASSION*	Compassion Theme Present % (N = 205)	Compassion Theme Not Present % (N = 202)
First in list	63	30
Not first in list	37	70
	100	100

*Since half the respondents scored Compassion number one in its list, this rank alone is set out as the high score.

ratize all institutions and make them what I call publicly accountable." Similarly, 73 percent of the respondents who mentioned freedom as an essential feature of democracy had ranked Freedom first, second, or third, while only 58 percent of those to whom it was less salient did likewise (Kendall's Q = .32). Reference was often made to freedom of religion, freedom of political activity, and, above all, freedom of speech:

> Government by consent, that's democracy. Now that to me is very valuable largely because of its by-products and the most important of its by-products being freedom of speech, freedom to write, freedom to argue. Democracy to me is great because it generates freedom.

Always pleased to discuss policy problems, Members of Parliament spoke at considerable length about unemployment, a topic we introduced by asking them how critical a problem unemployment actually is. Almost everyone said unemployment was undesirable, but some saw it exclusively as an electoral issue: "Well, party politically it is crucial. Second to prices, and very nearly equal top, unemployment is a factor which does affect elections, will affect the next election." Others analyzed it abstractly as a waste of resources or consequence of automation. Still others found it difficult to think beyond "the layabouts and unemployables in my constituency." Coders searched for something else, a compassion theme which referred to personal suffering of the unemployed. These themes were identified with an intercoder reliability of 74 percent. For example: "As one who knows what unemployment is, and I saw plenty of it in the thirties, I know how it can rot a man's will to even want to live. He loses his self-respect and everything." Table 9.3 shows that respondents who introduced compassion themes were also disposed to rank Compassion in first place, considerably more so than Members who did not mention the human costs involved (Kendall's Q = .55).

SUMMARY AND CONCLUSIONS

This chapter provides groundwork for quantitative studies of political values. It describes the development, administration, and assessment of a ranking technique used in interviews with Members of the British House of Commons. Despite their salience in political life, values have received relatively little notice from survey research. They are widely suspected of being rationalizations for more immediate wants; but it is equally obvious that politicians often restrict impulse satisfaction in order to pursue long-range goals. There are, in fact, no convincing reasons to dismiss values *a priori* as symbolic flags with little relevance for behavior. They deserve serious investigation as potentially significant components of political belief systems.

Working from an inventory of principal values in British politics, 36 items were selected for rank ordering in lists of 9 values each. Tape recordings indicate that MPs interpreted the exercise much as intended and offer material illuminating nuance and structure in their value systems. Likewise, the transcripts identify difficulties with assumptions upon which the measure is based and also suggest improvements in its administration. Reducing the number of value items, for instance, would help minimize fatigue and dissatisfaction with the technique; two lists rather than four should, I believe, prove considerably easier to administer.

Ranked values do not appear to suffer unduly from social desirability and order effects. And, Rokeach's versions of the value survey have established unusually strong test–retest reliabilities over periods of up to

12 weeks. Validity investigations, pursued through pretests with British university students, produced interpretable relationships between value ranking data and the Allport–Vernon–Lindzey Study of Values as well as subjects' policy opinions. These results were followed up by further validity assessments which found that value data parallel known cleavages between politicians from different political camps: with few exceptions, all items separated Tories from Socialists at the .001 significance level; scores for candidates and MPs from the same party were virtually identical, a sharp contrast to vivid differences between the two sides in the House. Ranked values also demonstrated a capacity for capturing more subtle conflict dimensions by distinguishing ideological factions on the right and left of each parliamentary party. Finally, values measured by the instrument's paper-and-pencil technique were successfully related to verbal behavior in themes respondents put forward when discussing democratic institutions and public policy.

The inquiry has examined the phenomenology of values as intelligible components of politicians' belief systems and the extent to which they can be adequately studied through quantitative techniques. Thus far, evidence is generally positive on both points. The ranking instrument seems an efficient tool for describing values and analyzing their role in guiding political attitudes and behavior.

10

British Politics and the Two-Value Model

Raymond Cochrane, Michael Billig, and Michael Hogg

In this chapter the link between values and political orientations will be explored. Using groups with varying degrees of attachment to political parties in Britain, a particular hypothesis about the specific systems which underlie political orientation is tested, and this is followed by an examination of a broader hypothesis relating values in general to political beliefs.

There has been much research in the psychology of politics devoted to the question of what predisposes people to support different political orientations. Most formulations deal primarily with extremist politics and assume that there is a motivational state which pushes the individual toward this kind of belief system.

A good example is *The Authoritarian Personality*, which posits the existence of motivational states which characterize, in this case, the potential fascist (Adorno, Frenkel-Brunswik, Levinson, & Sanford, 1950). It is inner psychological weaknesses which are presumed to mark out the individual as the potential fascist. This assumption is contained in

The authors would like to thank the following for their assistance with various aspects of the work reported here: Nicole Bates, Margaret Oates, Susan Hough, Helen Windley, John Hewitt, and Susan Roelants.

modern extensions of *The Authoritarian Personality* and in attempts to extend the formulations to all forms of extremism. In all such formulations, political orientations are assumed to serve a psychological function for the individual subscribing to them.

An alternative approach to the study of potential extremism is based upon examining political values and "symbolic-attachments." Edelman (1964) hypothesized that the symbolic elements are more important in extremist politics than in centrist politics; groups far removed from the center of power must present their messages in symbolic rather than pragmatic form. Thus, potential supporters will be won over more by the symbolic nature of extreme messages than by detailed statements of intended practical actions. Cobb and Elder (1976) were able to classify a sample of American respondents in terms of their responses to a range of political symbols.

There is evidence that the concept of "symbol," as used by Cobb and Elder, and the concept of "value," as used, for instance, by Rokeach, might be theoretically linked. Both concepts cut across the customary division of attitudes into externalization, normative, and informational functions. Cobb and Elder include amongst their list of symbols such abstract terms as "Law and Order," "Freedom," and "Equality." Some of the same terms are described by Rokeach as values.

There are further reasons for thinking that symbols and values are conceptually similar. The relation between an abstract value and specific attitudes is complex. Rokeach assumes that attitudes can be derived unambiguously from a knowledge of the basic value system. However, research has indicated that the relationship is more problematic; for instance, consensus about basic political values does not imply consensus about specific issues relating to these values (McClosky, 1964). Moreover, one abstract value might contain contradictory interpretations, as in the case, for example, of Western and communist concepts of "democracy." Similarly, symbols are capable of containing contradictory meanings, and Rokeach's values, when used in political discourse, could be said to be an instance of what Edelman called the "passing parade of abstract symbols."

Rokeach (1973) has formulated a model of political belief based upon two orthogonal values. He hypothesizes that political ideologies can be categorized in terms of positive or negative values for *freedom* and *equality*. His two-value model states that socialists will value both *freedom* and *equality* highly, conservatives will value *freedom* highly but not *equality*, communists will value *equality* positively and *freedom* negatively, while fascists will devalue both *freedom* and *equality*. A content analysis of political tracts, drawn from each of the four political quadrants conducted by Rokeach, strongly supported this model.

Rokeach has used the Rokeach Value Survey (RVS) to test his model of political belief in samples of the American population. Chapters 6 and 7 of his *The Nature of Human Values* describe the results of several studies in which respondents' valuations of *freedom* and *equality* are correlated with their political orientations. Although certain aspects of Rokeach's model are confirmed by these studies, particularly that concerning the left–right split on the value *equality*, a full test was not possible with his samples. Rokeach found too few subjects with either the "fascist" or "communist" orientations described in his model to perform a proper test; such subjects together accounted for only 6 percent of his national and college samples. Similarly, he found very few people who did not value *freedom* highly, whichever presidential candidate they supported. Rokeach concluded: "What seems to be missing from the American scene are political groupings large enough to support viable political candidates for the presidency who place a low value on *freedom*" (1973, p. 181).

The most adequate test of this model would involve comparing the values of supporters of conservative, socialist, communist, and fascist parties. To date, the model has not been tested for supporters of either communist or fascist parties. In fact, generally, the American political scene may not be the most adequate testing ground for such a model. Whereas it is possible to see the Republican Party as being conservative, the Democratic Party does not proclaim itself to be socialist. Moreover, the two main American political parties are both politically and ideologi- cally highly flexible (Duverger, 1972). On the other hand, the current British political scene does provide political parties which fit better the four quadrants of Rokeach's model. The Labour Party is avowedly so- cialist and the Conservative Party can be considered eponymous. The remaining two quadrants are represented by the Communist Party, which historically is more established than its American counterpart, and by the National Front, now reckoned to be the fourth largest party in English politics (Le Lohé, 1976; Walker, 1977). Detailed analysis of the ideology of the National Front has shown it to be classically fascist in its outlook and aims (Billig, 1978).

There has not been a thorough comparison of the value systems of fascists and communists, as compared with supporters of the more "mainstream" political beliefs. The present study aimed to look not only at the different value orientations of supporters of the four main ideological orientations, but also to compare possible differences be- tween centrist (conservative and socialist) and extremist (communist and fascist) values, and also left wing (communist and socialist) as against right wing (conservative and fascist), using Rokeach's two-value model as a starting point.

METHOD

The procedures we employed are described in more detail elsewhere (Cochrane, Billig, & Hogg, 1979; Billig & Cochrane, 1978), and are summarized here.

The questionnaire consisted of three parts. Respondents provided information about demographic variables, their political persuasion, and their value systems, which was measured by the Terminal Value Scale of the Rokeach Value Survey.

Political orientation was assessed by two questions. The first asked respondents to rank order the four political parties "Communist," "Conservative," "National Front," and "Socialist," in order of their personal preference. The party ranked first was considered to be the respondent's political orientation. A second question asked how politically active respondents were, with the following options provided: *Inactive* (not interested, don't vote); *Slightly Active* (no entrenched views in any direction; vote as a habit); *Moderately Active* (moderately allied to a particular ideology; vote in the sincere hope of furthering your party); *Active* (feel very strongly that your party is right; actively participate in some form of politics).

Two methods were used to obtain a sample of people supporting each political orientation. Two local offices of each of the Conservative, Labour, Communist, and National Front political parties were contacted, and they agreed to supply lists of party workers or to distribute questionnaires at party meetings.

In addition, randomly selected homes in working- and middle-class districts of Birmingham and Bristol were contacted and one occupant was interviewed. Potential respondents were informed of the nature of the study and invited to cooperate. Of those actually contacted by this method, between 50 percent and 70 percent, depending upon area, completed the questionnaire.

RESULTS

A total of 306 completed questionnaires were thus available (see Table 10.1). Activists were defined as those who had described themselves as being "active." The proportion of activists varied from party to party, with much higher proportions of the total of the minority party supporters being activists. Although this is reasonable and to be expected because Communist and National Front supporters are few and far between, subsequent analyses are presented separately for total supporters and activists. The breakdown of sex by political party revealed a significant difference ($\chi^2 = 11.39$, $p < .01$), with a higher proportion of

TABLE 10.1. Characteristics of Respondents by Political Orientation*

	SOCIALIST	CONSERVATIVE	COMMUNIST	NATIONAL FRONT
Total number	96	148	34	28
Total number of activists	30	44	29	19
Number of respondents contacted through political parties†	27	39	27	24
Male	47	54	19	19
Female	41	79	14	7
Under 40 years	41	51	20	17
Over 40 years	38	67	14	8

*Numbers may not add to totals because of missing data.
†Not all respondents contacted in this way considered themselves as activists.

women supporting the Conservative orientation and a higher proportion of males supporting the others. This is probably an accurate reflection of the sex distribution of voting preferences (Opinion Research
Center, 1974). There were no significant age differences between supporters.

Table 10.2 contains the value medians for *freedom* and *equality* for the
supporters of each of the four orientations. The difference between
orientations for the value *equality*, with medians ranging from 1.77 for
the Communists to 16.79 for the National Front supporters, was extremely significant. *Freedom* showed no significant difference between
groups at all.

When this analysis was repeated for activists, only a somewhat different pattern emerged. Again, *equality* is the chief discriminator between the groups, and to an even greater extent than when all supporters are considered. *Freedom,* one of the critical values in Rokeach's
model, did achieve significant discrimination between groups, but not in
the manner predicted. The National Front and Conservative activists
value *freedom* more highly than do Labour and Communist activists. In
addition, there were 12 other terminal values which varied significantly
between the groups.

Rokeach's model posits that on the value dimensions of *equality*, political orientations will group according to their left- or right-wing ideology, and on *freedom,* according to degree of extremism. The value
analysis was therefore repeated, comparing first the left (Socialists and
Communists) with the right (Conservatives and National Front), and
second, comparing the extremists (National Front and Communists)
with the moderates (Socialists and Conservatives). Values indicating significant differences for these analyses are shown in tables 10.3 and 10.4.
Equality was valued much more highly by the left wing than by the
right-wing composite group, but *freedom* did not even come close to
discriminating between the extremist and centrist groupings. However,
for both sets of comparisons several other values, not included in
Rokeach's two-value model, did discriminate between the composite
orientations.

A more general hypothesis was also tested using the same data.
Whether or not Rokeach's two-value model of politics was supported by
those findings, it is still possible that values are good predictors of political orientations.

The technique used to test this hypothesis was "discriminant
analysis." Discriminant analysis is a way of generating linear combinations of independent variables that best separate (or discriminate) two or
more groups of individuals. The combinations of weighted variables
used to achieve this maximal separation are called "discriminant
functions." Discriminant analysis obviously bears a close relationship to

TABLE 10.2. Equality-Freedom Rankings for Four Political Orientation Groups

	Communists		Socialists		Conservatives		National Front		χ^2	p
	Mdn	(Rnk)	Mdn	(Rnk)	Mdn	(Rnk)	Mdn	(Rnk)		
A. *All supporters*										
N =	34		96		148		28			
Equality	1.77	(2)	6.50	(3)	11.10	(12)	16.79	(18)	37.95	.0001
Freedom	5.50	(3)	6.50	(3)	4.06	(1)	3.50	(1)	5.31	n.s.
B. *Activists only*										
N =	29		30		44		19			
Equality	1.68	(2)	3.00	(2)	11.00	(11)	17.14	(18)	62.22	.0001
Freedom	4.88	(3)	7.50	(5)	3.21	(1)	3.34	(2)	11.74	.01

185

TABLE 10.3.   Significant Value Differences Between Supporters of Left and Right Political Orientations

VALUES	SOCIALISTS + COMMUNISTS		CONSERVATIVES + NATIONAL FRONT		p
	Mdn	(Rnk)	Mdn	(Rnk)	
N =	130		176		
A world at peace	2.56	(1)	5.17	(3)	.001
Equality	4.60	(2)	11.86	(14)	.001
Family security	6.83	(4)	4.25	(2)	.05
Freedom	6.21	(3)	3.92	(1)	.05
Happiness	7.33	(7)	5.32	(4)	.05

multiple regression, where the dependent variable to be predicted is, in fact, group membership. Three related sets of information are available from a discriminant analysis:

1. Information about the extent to which individuals known to belong to certain groups can have their group membership accurately predicted on the basis of the independent variables included in the analysis. In other words, the accuracy of the prediction based on the independent variables can be measured.
2. Individuals whose actual group membership is not known can be classified as group members according to their pattern of scores on the independent variables.
3. The relative discriminatory power of the independent variables can be assessed, so that the exact nature of the differences between the groups can be explored.

Where a stepwise procedure is used to arrive at the discriminant functions, the independent variables are added to the equation at one

TABLE 10.4.   Significant Value Differences Between "Moderates" and "Extremists"

VALUES	SOCIALISTS + CONSERVATIVES		COMMUNISTS + NATIONAL FRONT		p
	Mdn	(Rnk)	Mdn	(Rnk)	
N =	244		62		
A sense of accomplishment	9.27	(8)	7.28	(5)	.01
Family security	4.50	(2)	7.17	(4)	.05
Happiness	5.96	(4)	8.25	(7)	.05
True friendship	6.58	(5)	8.75	(8)	.05

time. The order of selection is based on choosing variables which add the most discriminating power, given the variables already selected. The first variable entered will therefore be the one which discriminates best between the groups, and the second will be the variable which adds to the discrimination achieved by the first. The second variable added may, therefore, not be the one with the second highest individual discriminatory power if, for example, it is highly correlated with the first. Selection of independent variables continues until no additional variables provide a significant improvement in discrimination.

The univariate F ratio of each variable indicates the extent of its power to discriminate between the *k* groups independently of any other variable; the *increment* in explanatory power produced by adding each variable is indicated by the Rao's V statistic, which is the criterion for the ordering of variables for inclusion in the discriminant functions. Each individual respondent is assigned to one of the *k* groups on the basis of his or her pattern of scores on the independent variables, and this assignment can be compared with actual group membership. In addition, the degree of association between the discriminant functions and group membership can be expressed as a canonical correlation.

To test the hypothesis that values as measured by the RVS can predict the allegiance of political activists, a discriminant analysis was conducted on the values of the four groups of political activists (those who designated themselves as activists on the questionnaire). The results of this analysis are shown in Table 10.5. *Equality* was the value which most clearly differentiated the four groups, but considerable extra discriminatory power was achieved by adding other values to the discriminant functions, particularly *national security*. Ultimately, a high canonical correlation (0.88) was achieved, indicating that the discriminant function based on values was very strongly related to group membership. This is borne out by an inspection of the classification table, which shows an overall correct classification of 77 percent, compared to a chance accuracy of 25 percent ($Z = 13.33$, $p < .0001$). The accuracy was, however, greater for extremist activists (91.7%) than for centrists (67.6%). There was no misclassification of Communists as National Front or vice versa.

DISCUSSION

The results of the values for *freedom* and *equality* are critical for the two-value model of politics. On the one hand, there is support for Rokeach's hypothesis that *equality* is the crucial value in distinguishing left- from right-wing political orientations, and that the divergence between the orientations would be more marked among activists than among all supporters. There was, however, no support whatever for his

TABLE 10.5.   Summary of Discriminant Analysis Using Values of Four Groups of Political Activists

Step No.	Value Entered	Univariate F Ratio	Change in Rao's V
1	Equality	59.18***	177.53***
2	National security	13.40***	39.09***
3	True friendship	4.76**	23.56***
4	A world of beauty	10.74***	40.51***
5	Family security	14.73***	29.87***
6	Freedom	3.88*	33.15***
7	Inner harmony	1.94	20.31***
8	Salvation	7.86***	19.05***
9	Pleasure	3.38*	16.94***
10	A world at peace	9.98***	11.40**
11	Social recognition	2.83*	10.94*
12	Happiness	1.62	9.96*
13	Self-respect	2.47*	8.50*
14	Mature love	0.13	7.99*
15	A comfortable life	3.55*	3.16
16	A sense of accomplishment	0.60	3.99
17	An exciting life	3.15*	3.44
18	Wisdom	0.31	4.58

RESULTS OF CLASSIFICATION

Actual Group	Predicted Group				
	Communist	National Front	Conservative	Socialist	Total
Communist	26	0	0	3	29
National Front	0	18	1	0	19
Conservative	1	6	32	5	44
Socialist	8	0	4	18	30
Total	35	24	37	26	122

* = $p < .05$
** = $p < .01$
*** = $p < .001$

other central hypothesis that the value *freedom* would distinguish political orientations on a moderate to extremist dimension. In fact, activist supporters of the National Front—an extreme right-wing party— apparently valued *freedom* more highly than did activists of the more moderate socialist orientation. This result conforms quite well with the results Rokeach himself found in the United States. There, supporters of George Wallace still ranked *freedom* quite highly, even though Wallace was considered a right-wing extremist. It appears that *freedom* is central to all political value systems, at least on a verbal level.

It is necessary to look at, and to rule out, possible methodological explanations of these findings before turning to a substantive discussion. Some problems encountered in collecting the data need to be considered. It is possible that the sample of respondents eventually obtained was unrepresentative of supporters of the political orientations. However, the crucial question is whether any possible unrepresentativeness could be related to the results obtained. For Rokeach's model to hold on this argument, it would be necessary to assume that a representative sample was achieved as far as the value *equality* goes, but not so far as *freedom* is concerned. This would be tenable if it were held that those communists and fascists who were against *freedom* were ashamed of saying so and thus refused to complete the questionnaire. This is unlikely, because a view which is considered to be shameful cannot be in accord with basic values, and also there is evidence from content analyses (Billig, 1978b) that the official propaganda of the National Front does stress the value *freedom*.

There are special difficulties in obtaining representative sampling from extreme left- or right-wing political groups. Research workers in this area are generally faced with unwilling or distrustful subjects, and are often forced to take their subjects where and when they can find them (Proshansky & Evans, 1963). Although on occasions criticisms are made of sampling procedures, studies of extreme right- and left-wing opinions do not typically use sophisticated sampling procedures for purely practical reasons.

An explanation based on the disproportionate number of activists among the supporters of the four political orientations is also untenable, because the results of the activists-only analysis even more strongly indicate the failure of *freedom* to discriminate between political orientations in the way predicted by Rokeach.

If these results are interpreted at their face value, the most obvious conclusions are that either the Communist Party and National Front Party supporters do not represent the communist and fascist quadrants of Rokeach's model or that the model itself is inadequate. If people indicating support for, or active participation in, a Communist Party are not to be considered as extreme left or indeed as communist, then we must ask to whom this label can be properly applied? A model which fits only a hypothetical group of left-wing extremists who do not actually exist is of very little use.

The situation concerning the National Front is more complicated because this party specifically denies that it is fascist. However, the term "fascist" should not be reserved only for those who style themselves as fascist; that would preclude Hitler, amongst others. Even a self-confessed fascist like Bardèche (1961) recognizes that postwar fascists will avoid the label of "fascism," although they might uphold the fascist ideal. The issue of defining fascism is itself contentious, but for our present purposes the basic definition of Jones (1974) can be accepted. Accordingly, the National Front should be classed as a fascist party because its ideology advocates a strong omnicompetent state and firm leadership, and rejects liberal optimism, Marxism–Leninism, and class war. One can also note that the party openly champions racialism and is fundamentally anti-Semitic, believing, like the Nazis, in the myth of a world Jewish conspiracy (see Billig, 1978a, 1978b; Edgar, 1977). Its present leaders, almost to a man, have in the past engaged in openly Nazi and fascist political activity (Walker, 1977).

Where, then, does this leave Rokeach's model? Given that adequate representation of the four quadrants has been achieved, the failure of the value *freedom* to discriminate as predicted has to be explained, or the model must be abandoned or modified.

A possible resolution lies in the meaning of the word "freedom" to the various political groups who use it. The value analysis on the purely verbal level seems to ignore the possibility that a word expressing a value—or, indeed, the value itself—might have several contradictory meanings. In particular, different political ideologies might interpret the same value in diametrically opposed ways. For instance, it is not difficult to find fascists valuing *freedom* (Billig, 1978a, 1978b; White, 1949). However, when fascists praise *freedom*, there is no reason to suppose that they mean the same thing as their opponents. In fact, as Orwell's *1984* demonstrated so convincingly, the language of freedom is not incompatible with the practice of repression.

The word "freedom" has its own connotation within the Marxist tradition, and this does not accord at all with the current Western use of the word. The related concept of "democracy" has a different meaning when applied by communists to Soviet states than when used by liberals to refer to Western countries. With the development of Eurocommunism, an attempt to reconcile these different meanings of freedom and democracy can be expected.

The implication is that under certain cultural and political conditions, there may be values which are uniformly championed by competing political ideologies, but this uniformity does not imply agreement or consensus. Perhaps, in these situations, it may be inappropriate to refer to "values": "symbols" might be a more apt term (Edelman, 1964). The same outward symbol may have deeply different interpretations, depending upon ideological context.

The power, and possibly the danger, of discriminant analysis is that it allows discrimination between groups to be made without specific prior hypotheses being necessary. Replication of such an analysis is essential before any conclusive results can be established.

The discriminant analysis of the four groups of political activists showed clearly that value symbols, as measured by the RVS, are apparently excellent predictors of political orientation. In particular, the more extreme groups were discriminated well. Several values, in addition to those incorporated in Rokeach's two-value model, emerged as powerful individual discriminators between political groups. With *equality*, 12 other values also varied significantly between groups.

A world at peace clearly differentiated the left from the right in this study, and was in fact the most important value to the communist and socialist activists. The relative importance assigned to *national security* by National Front supporters is the one value that most clearly distinguishes the fascist from the other orientations. If these findings can be replicated, it appears that, empirically and conceptually, a typology of political beliefs on these values, together with *equality*, may have more explanatory power than Rokeach's model.

11

The Two-Value Model of Political Ideology and British Politics

Milton Rokeach

Cochrane, Billig, and Hogg have provided us with an important state-ment about the value similarities and differences among partisans of four political parties existing in Britain today. While I have reservations about their sampling procedures, as do also the authors, I would be reluctant to dismiss their findings. Instead, on intuitive grounds, and also because I have no theoretical reason to think otherwise, I assume that their report on the values of British political partisans is basically accurate, and would not turn out to be substantially different even if replicated with a more sophisticated methodology. Their results are, moreover, in good agreement with Searing's findings (Chapter 9) of significant value differences between Labour and Conservative Mem-bers of the British House of Commons.

I differ with Cochrane, Billig, and Hogg, however, in their interpre-tation of the findings, and more particularly, about the implications of their findings for the validity of the two-value model of political ideol-ogy. Their question, "What are the main value differences distinguish-ing among partisans of existing political parties?", is not the equivalent of the question, "What are the main values underlying or explaining differences among major political ideologies?" Data about value differences between, say, Jews and Catholics are not necessarily pertinent to the question of value differences underlying Judaism and Catholicism. In the same way, data about differences between persons identifying themselves as Conservative, Labour, Communist, and National Front in Britain are not necessarily relevant for identifying the basic differences among the classical capitalist, socialist, communist, and fascist political ideologies. The main problem is one of establishing an unequivocal or isomorphic link between specified political or religious ideologies that transcend national boundaries and historical eras and specified political or religious groups that happen to exist in a particular country at a particular time. There are surely varying reasons for party identifications or voting patterns besides purely ideological reasons. It thus remains to be empirically determined rather than *assumed* whether those who align themselves with one or another political group are also followers of a particular political ideology.

The political parties classified in advance by Cochrane, Billig, and Hogg as representing one or another political ideology may not exhibit the value pattern hypothesized to characterize that ideology for one or more of several reasons: first, because the theory from which the prediction is derived is wrong; second, because one might be mistaken in one's initial classification of a political group as an advocate of a specified political ideology. It is especially difficult to distinguish unambiguously between communist and socialist groups, and between ultraconservative and fascist groups. Third, unpopular political groups, such as the Communist Party and the National Front in Britain, operating as minorities in a country that allows freedom of expression, may undergo significant deviations over time from classical ideological positions. They may have opportunistically endorsed the value of *freedom* as a temporary, self-defensive tactic, or they may have adopted a more genuinely independent line. Professor Donald MacRae, a sociologist at the London School of Economics, has observed, according to a recent report in *Science,* that "the Hungarian uprising of 1956 liberated Marxism from the Soviet mold . . . the new generation, liberated from the need to support Stalin and Bolshevik orthodoxy, became Marxist activists supporting a range of groups on the far Left" (Hawkes, 1977, p. 1230). Cochrane, Billig, and Hogg do not consider and thus possibly overlook the extent to which the present-day Communist Party of Britain is old left or new left. Major differences between old and new left would include differences in the advocacy of decentralization, participatory democracy, and "do your own thing" (Mauss, 1971; Rous & Lee, 1978), in short, differences in value for individual *freedom.*

Thus, results disconfirming the hypothesized value orientations obtained for existing political groups in Britain are necessarily ambiguous in their interpretation insofar as the validity of the two-value model is the issue. Because of such ambiguities, I was extremely reluctant in my own research to classify existing political groups in advance as representing one or another political ideology, and instead looked for a more unequivocal, less controversial way of testing the validity of the two-value model. Moreover, because of the difficulties of inference from political participation to ideological espousal, I was careful to identify the *equality-freedom* model as a model of political ideology and not as a model attempting to explain or account for political membership or participation. All I was willing to assume was that there is some minimum number of values that could parsimoniously describe fundamental differences in the major political ideologies. I hypothesized on theoretical grounds that the minimum number of such values was two, and identified them as the values of *equality* and *freedom*. The question then confronting me was how it might be feasible to test empirically the validity of this two-value model of political ideology, keeping in mind the methodological riskiness of prejudging the ideological position of adherents to existing political parties. I attempted to solve this problem by first identifying the best exemplifications of the major ideologies, namely, in documents written by Lenin, Hitler, Goldwater, and widely known socialists, and, then, by the method of content analysis, ascertaining how often the values of *equality* and *freedom* were advocated favorably in these writings, in comparison with their advocacy of all other values. I should emphasize: (a) that all the writings that were analyzed had been written prior to the assumption of political power; (b) that those carrying out the content analysis never heard of the two-value model and thus had no idea about the specific empirical hypothesis being tested; and (c) that the content analysts did not have to concern themselves with questions about the meaning of *equality* and *freedom*. All they did was to merely record the frequency of mention of these and related value terms as well as the frequency of mention of all other value terms.

It was the results of this content analysis that empirically confirmed the two-value model of political ideology. *Equality* and *freedom,* whatever these words might mean, were identified as the two values most often mentioned favorably in socialist writings, and as the two values least favorably mentioned in *Mein Kampf.* Lenin's most favored value, ascertained from a content analysis of his *Collected Works,* was *equality,* and *freedom* was identified as the value that he favored least. This picture was reversed in Barry Goldwater's *Conscience of a Conservative: freedom* was found to be his most favored and *equality* his least favored value.

Now, it is possible that my particular selections of ideological writings were ill chosen. But other selections written by other ideologists (Rokeach, 1973, p. 185; Rous & Lee, 1978) provide us with highly similar results, thus strengthening confidence in the validity of the two-value model of political ideology.

What, one might then ask, is the relevance for the two-value model of data obtained from various political partisans within a particular country at a particular time? In view of the fact that the precise ideological position of a given political group is not necessarily clear or self-evident, itself an issue over which there is often controversy, it is now possible to ascertain objectively, by measuring the values of various political partisans, which *equality–freedom* orientations they in fact subscribe to. Moreover, it is now possible to ascertain the extent to which observed ideological orientations actually conform to suspected ideological orientations. Are Wallace supporters in the United States of America really the fascists that many suppose them to be? How about the National Front in Britain, classified as fascist by Cochrane, Billig, and Hogg, notwithstanding the fact that it "specifically denies it is fascist"? Calling them fascist in advance hoists the chain of reasoning up by its own petard. Such a prejudgment may (or may not) be mistaken; it may (or may not) be politically biased. The empirical results are, however, clear. The *equality–freedom* orientations of Wallace and National Front supporters are indistinguishable from one another. Both groups inform us they care a great deal about *freedom* but not about *equality*. Such a value pattern is known to be correlated with extreme forms of racism and with a concern for economic and national security. There is therefore evidence here, at least, of a right-wing capitalist or ultraconservative value orientation, but no evidence of a fascist value orientation.

The data thus obtained are, of course, relevant to the validity of the two-value model, (1) providing we are willing to take into account the difficulties we often encounter when distinguishing between political groups alleged to be left-wing and alleged to be right-wing; and (2) providing that we are also willing to take into account the possibility of value shifts, ideologically or opportunistically motivated, among unpopular minority parties operating in Western democracies that allow multiple political parties. The positive regard for *freedom* actually manifested by Communist and National Front members can be plausibly accounted for, and is thus not nearly as embarrassing for the two-value model of political ideology as, say, a low regard for *freedom* by Labour and Conservative members might have been.

In any event, now that we have in hand the value data for political partisans in Britain, we are left with the problem of having to account not only for these data but also for a rather large body of other available data. How can the British data be reconciled and integrated with the data obtained from the content analyses of ideological writings (Rokeach, 1973; Rous & Lee, 1978), and with other data that have been reported for political partisans in the United States (Rokeach, 1973;

Bishop, Barclay, & Rokeach, 1972; Rawls, Harrison, Rawls, Hayes, & Johnson, 1973) and Britain (Searing, Chapter 9)?[1] Cochrane, Billig, and Hogg do not discuss or attempt to account for all such data; their conclusion about the "simplicity" of the two-value model, based only on the British data they themselves collected, is thus weakened. Nor do they offer an alternative model that might better account for all the known data.

Finally, what are we to make of the fact that partisans of the four British political parties differ significantly from one another not only with respect to their regard for *equality* but also with respect to their regard for a number of other values as shown in Table 10.5 of their chapter? Some but not all of these value rankings also differentiate significantly among political partisans in the United States, but not necessarily to the same extent or the same direction (Rokeach, 1973, p. 85; Rawls et al., 1973). Such differences between political partisans in Britain can, as was the case with the U.S. data, be readily interpreted as arising from such demographic differences as status, sex, or age among the political partisans, or as arising from local economic and social conditions prevailing in Britain in the late 1970s. These value differences are indubitably there, but do not necessarily arise from compelling ideological differences between political partisans—ideological differences that can reasonably be expected to replicate across national boundaries or historical time.

In sum, I think it reasonable to conclude the following from the data reported by Cochrane, Billig, and Hogg: (1) that for various local and demographic reasons there are many values that distinguish significantly among partisans of political parties in Britain; (2) that ideological divisions and conflicts in British politics, as also in U.S. politics, are mainly, but admittedly not solely, reducible to divisions and conflicts with respect to one value—*equality;* and (3) that the British data, when placed alongside all the other known data, do not embarrass and are, indeed, compatible with a two-value model of political ideology.

---

[1] I am excluding from consideration but wish to mention in passing Feather's data obtained in Australia (1977b) showing that many values are significantly related to Wilson's attitudinal measure of conservatism (1973). These data were not obtained for samples of known political partisans, and to date the extent to which this measure is able to distinguish between various left-wing or right-wing forms of "liberalism–conservatism" is unknown.

PART THREE

Value Change Through Self-Awareness

12

Human Values, Smoking Behavior, and Public Health Programs

William J. Conroy

The assertion that individuals are primarily responsible for their own health is a surprising one, one that appears initially to be either seriously in error or, at the very least, overstated. The statement is surprising because it challenges certain fundamental assumptions concerning the development of disease and the role of medical science in the restoration of health. These assumptions derive from the germ theory of disease, postulating that each disease is caused by a single identifiable germ and is, therefore, curable by a single appropriate medical therapy. This theory has proved to be a seminal one for medical science since the time of Pasteur. Unfortunately, however, the health problems most prevalent in American society today do not result from microorganisms. Rather, they result from behaviors, from life styles, and from the environment that we ourselves create.

John H. Knowles, M.D., President of the Rockefeller Foundation, has summarized our present health concerns in his statement:

> Over 99% of us are born healthy and made sick as a result of personal misbehavior and environmental conditions. The solution to the problem of

ill health in modern American society involves individual responsibility, in the first instance, and social responsibility through public legislative and private voluntary efforts, in the second instance. (1977, p. 58).

The health concerns referred to are numerous and include: stress, obesity, smoking, excessive use of alcohol and other drugs, environmental carcinogens, venereal disease, mental illness, and the carnage on our highways. For these problems, medical science is unable to offer the miracle remedies the public has come to expect. In fact, the only assured cure for some of these conditions is paradoxically—prevention. In other cases, only a fundamental change in emotional and behavioral habits will suffice. To quote Dr. Knowles again, "The next major advances in the health of the American people will come from the assumption of individual responsibility for one's health and a necessary change in habits for the majority of Americans" (1977, p. 60).

The problem of producing such large-scale alterations of the public's life styles and habit patterns constitutes a major challenge to all those who design or direct public health programs. It is a particularly difficult challenge, for a fundamental shift in the public's attitudes and values may be required prior to the acceptance of individual responsibility for personal health, as well as being a prerequisite to any significant level of behavioral change. In addition, past methods of affecting the public's behavior via various types of media appeals may not be sufficient to produce the required impetus to change. Rimer (1976) has noted the need for each public health program to be custom-tailored for the specific audience to which it is addressed. Also, programs designed to promote awareness or to educate differ from those that encourage one to visit a doctor or take a medical test, and both of these differ markedly from programs designed to produce a behavioral change, such as quitting smoking. Finally, Mendelsohn (1976) has observed that the image or model of humans underlying most media messages is based either upon a behavioristic stimulus-response psychology, in which exposure to communications is equated with effect, or upon the presupposition that humans are totally rational beings who will act appropriately in response to factual information. Both of these images are, of course, open to serious challenge.

Thus, the problems of designing effective public health programs are exceedingly involved, and the experience with past programs may not be a reliable guide for producing the large-scale changes envisioned by Knowles. What would seem to be required is a comprehensive design that would include a massive effort: (1) to educate the public as to its role and responsibility in health maintenance; (2) to identify through appropriate research the attitudes and values that sustain the various self-defeating behavioral patterns; and (3) to provide an effective method of altering not only the attitudes and values involved, but also the specific behaviors. A considerable body of knowledge and experience exists to assure the achievement of the first objective, but the attainment of the other two goals will require an innovative approach for which evidence exists attesting to its promise, appropriateness, and efficacy.

A HUMAN VALUES MODEL OF BEHAVIOR MODIFICATION

Rokeach (1968, 1973) has described a model in which individuals incorporate countless beliefs and thousands of attitudes, but only dozens of terminal and instrumental values. Further, these components vary in centrality, and at the core of this functionally interconnected belief system is the self or self-concept. In theory, a change in any part of the system should affect the other parts, and it should also affect behavior. Thus, any induced dissatisfaction implicating the self should lead to alterations of terminal and instrumental values, functionally related attitudes, and related behaviors.

The first extensive test of this model was reported by Rokeach (1971a) in an experiment in which he confronted university students with an inconsistency in their value rankings. Experimental subjects were shown the average terminal value rankings of Michigan State University students. Their attention was directed to the fact that the value *freedom* was ranked first but that the value *equality* was ranked eleventh. The experimenter interpreted these findings to mean that "Michigan State University students, in general, are much more interested in their own freedom than they are in the freedom of other people." Experimental subjects were then invited to compare their own rankings of the same 18 values. To increase the level of self-dissatisfaction further, subjects were asked to specify the extent of their sympathy with and participation in civil rights demonstrations. They were then shown a table that displayed a highly significant positive relationship between attitudes toward civil rights demonstrations and the rankings of the value *equality*. The experimenter interpreted these data as meaning that those who are against civil rights want freedom not only for themselves, but also for other people. Subjects were again asked to compare their own rankings for *equality* and *freedom* and their own position on civil rights, with the results depicted in the table.

This technique was designed to make subjects aware of certain inconsistencies in their value–attitude system and, thereby, to arouse conscious feelings of self-dissatisfaction. Control subjects were not so confronted. They merely filled out the value and attitude scales and were then dismissed. This confrontation technique produced significant changes in values and attitudes persisting for at least 17 months. Moreover, significant long-term behavioral differences were obtained in response to a

NAACP membership solicitation, in enrollment in ethnic core courses, and in changes in academic major.

Because of its brevity and because the technique appears to be effective as a single treatment, it appeared to be ideally suited for National Health programs that attempt to modify the public's behavior. Conroy, Katkin, and Barnette (1973) put the self-confrontation technique to a severe test. They inquired: Could this brief technique also produce changes in a behavior known for its resistance to change—cigarette smoking? And could this technique produce behavioral changes significantly better than those achieved in a typical smoking clinic design?

To elaborate on the rationale leading to these questions and the experimental design that followed, a few references to the smoking literature are in order. Schwartz (1969) reviewed 62 cessation studies conducted in the United States, Canada, Australia, England, Scandinavia, and other parts of Europe. "In summary," he concluded, "many investigators have tried 'methods' to help smokers give up cigarettes but few have shown high success rates" (p. 501). In another comprehensive review, Bernstein (1969) lamented the poor quality of smoking research in which there are frequent examples of "simultaneous manipulation of more than one independent variable in the same condition" (p. 431). McFall and Hammen (1971) compared a variety of major stop-smoking studies with their own design that utilized only nonspecific factors such as motivated volunteering, structure, and self-monitoring. They concluded that such factors "can yield outcome patterns comparable to those obtained with more elaborate, theoretically derived, and presumably more potent stop-smoking procedures" (p. 84).

The foregoing dictated an experimental design that would control for nonspecific factors and measure the effectiveness of the value confrontation technique over and above the results achieved in a typical smoking clinic. In the design adopted, both experimental and control groups completed a smoking clinic treatment, thereby equalizing the nonspecific factors and providing standard clinic data beyond which the effects of value confrontation could be assessed.

THE EXPERIMENT

Procedure

Announcements that a smoking-cessation clinic would be conducted at the State University of New York at Buffalo were entered in two local newspapers. Fourteen subjects, seven males and seven females, with a mean age of 37.8, provided estimates of their smoking rates for each hour of the day, with adjustments averaged in for higher rates of smoking on weekends and on social occasions. They also completed a slightly modified Form E of the Rokeach Instrumental Value Survey (wherein *self-discipline* was substituted for *self-controlled*). All experimental and control subjects were then exposed to a highly fear-inducing film concerning circulatory, heart, and respiratory illnesses that may result from smoking, a short lecture on the nature of habit, an explanation of Ellis' "ABC" method of examining internalized sentences (Ellis, 1962), and instructions on monitoring the times of day and cues associated with smoking.

Subjects were requested to cease smoking upon arising the following morning and to keep hourly records of their smoking rates, as well as of the cues and internalized sentences that accompanied any instances of smoking. At a second meeting two days later, procedures were clarified, and seven subjects were randomly assigned to control and also to experimental groups. The control group was instructed to mail in their records every three days, and to report back for two additional meetings 12 and 19 days later. Control subjects were then dismissed. At this point, all members of the experimental and control groups had participated equally in a smoking clinic that included many of the features of typical smoking clinic designs.

Members of the experimental group were advised that they would meet individually with the experimenter for approximately five minutes. They were instructed to report to the experimenter in any order they wished and to depart individually thereafter. They were informed that they would meet again 14 and 19 days hence. They were also requested to mail their smoking records to the experimenter every three days.

The first of the experimental subjects then appeared for a meeting with the experimenter. The following procedure was followed with each subject:

1. He or she was asked to view a chart showing the instrumental value rankings of "Smokers," on which the values *broadminded* and *self-discipline* were outlined in red ink. They were then shown a second chart showing the instrumental values of "Quitters," on which the same values were outlined in red ink. These two values were selected because earlier research had indicated that smokers and quitters differed significantly in their rankings of these two values. These charts (Table 12.1) showed that smokers had ranked *broadmindedness* third and *self-discipline* eighth on the average, whereas quitters had ranked *broadmindedness* eighth and *self-discipline* first.

2. The experimenter then interpreted these findings: "It would appear from our scientific research that people who have trouble quitting cigarette smoking are trying to be *broadminded* about a task that requires

rigid *self-discipline.*" The subjects were then handed the value rankings they had filled out at the first session of the clinic, and were asked to compare their own rankings with the rankings of smokers and quitters.

3. In order to increase self-dissatisfaction, the subjects were then asked to check one of the following three choices that best expressed their admiration of persons who have been able to cease smoking:

_____Yes, I admire those who have quit smoking and it has resulted in my attempting to quit.

_____Yes, I admire those who have quit smoking, but it has not resulted in my attempting to quit.

_____No, I don't especially admire those who have quit smoking, and their success has had no effect on my smoking behavior.

4. The subjects were then shown Table 12.1, which summarized the two separate charts they had been shown previously. Again, the subjects were asked to compare their own rankings with the summary data.

5. Subjects were then asked to indicate on an 11-point scale the extent of their self-satisfaction with their own values concerning their smoking behavior. They were also asked to consult their own instrumental value rankings, and invited to assign a new rank number to any individual value they might wish to change.

Twelve days later the control group returned for a short meeting, as did the experimental group 14 days later. These brief sessions were devoted to checking over the daily smoking reports sent by mail, and to the clarification or correction of any questionable data. Five days later the two groups met again. Final data were collected and checked, the instrumental values list was completed as a postclinic measure, the design of the experiment was explained, and further advice on contingency management techniques was offered. The telephone number of the experimenter was provided to the subjects, and they were invited to call if additional questions or problems developed.

Change in Value Rankings

Immediately following the experimental treatment, the experimental group recorded a mean increase of 6.14 in their ranking of *self-discipline.*

TABLE 12.1. Value Rankings of Smokers and Quitters

	SMOKERS	QUITTERS
Broadminded	3	8
Self-discipline	8	1
Difference	−5	+7

Seventeen days later, the mean increase over pretest was 4.57, which is significantly greater than the control group's postclinic mean increase of 1.71 ($t = 1.86$; df = 12; $p < .05$). Changes in rankings for other values, including *broadminded*, were not significant.

Increases in rankings of *self-discipline* were, moreover, systematically related to self-dissatisfaction. Immediately after the treatment, change in the subjects' rankings of *self-discipline* was perfectly correlated (rho = 1.00) with the amount of dissatisfaction expressed with preclinic value rankings. At postclinic, this relationship was .61 ($p < .05$).

Behavioral Effects

Preclinic base rates for the control and experimental groups were 51 and 41 cigarettes per day, respectively. A randomization test (Siegel, 1956) of these data showed that this difference is not significant.

The data for the 16 days of treatment, grouped into four blocks of four days each, are presented in Figure 12.1. As would be expected, cigarette consumption for both groups showed a marked decline for the first block. However, there was a steady increase in cigarette consumption on the subsequent blocks only for control group subjects. A mixed-design analysis of variance of these data, in which experimental and control groups were a between-subjects factor, and day-blocks was a within-subjects factor, confirmed the observation that the experimental and control groups diverged over day-blocks. While there was no significant effect for treatment, there was a significant effect for day-blocks ($F = 3.22$; df = 3/36; $p < .05$), and the interaction of groups by day-blocks was significant ($F = 2.97$; df = 3/36; $p < .05$). The significant day-blocks effect is attributable to the strong increasing effect for the control group; the absence of a main effect of treatments is attributable to the fact that although significant differences between experimental and control groups were obtained for the last two day-blocks, there were no significant differences between them during the first two day-blocks. At the conclusion of the clinic period the experimental group had reduced its smoking rate to 5 percent of its preclinic rate, whereas the control group had reduced to 28 percent of its preclinic rate.

Six months after the completion of the smoking clinic, all subjects were contacted and asked to estimate the amount of cigarettes they had consumed during each of the six months following the clinic. Analysis of these retrospective data indicated that the significant difference observed between groups at the end of the 16-day treatment period was maintained at a statistically significant level for two months following termination of the experiment ($F = 1.88$; df = 12; $p < .05$). After that, the experimental and control groups both returned to higher and equivalent rates of smoking.

Figure 12.1

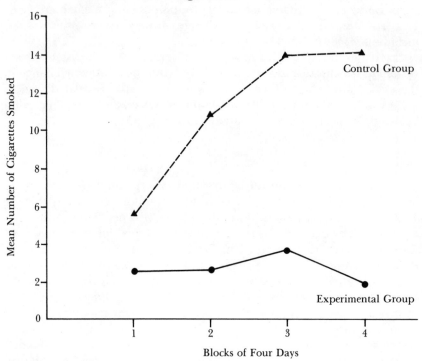

Discussion

The technique of value confrontation employed in this experiment was derived from a model of human behavior which suggests that behavior change may be effectively pursued by modifying core values. In this experiment, smoking behavior was selected for change because it is enormously resistant to change, both by short-term techniques and by more elaborate smoking clinic programs. Although the time period covered in this experiment was relatively short, the findings consistently supported the conceptualization being tested.

First, smokers and quitters were significantly distinguished on two core values—*broadmindedness* and *self-discipline*. Second, the treatment resulted in a significant increase in rankings of the value *self-discipline,* and this increase persisted during the course of the experiment. Finally, smoking behavior for subjects exposed to the treatment was maintained at a reduced level for a longer time period than for control subjects who participated in an identical antismoking clinic program.

While the follow-up data are dependent on the subjects' retrospective reconstruction of their smoking behavior over a relatively long time period, there is no reason to suspect that these self-reports are biased. These data suggest that the effects of the single experimental treatment persisted for about two months and then dissipated. The experimental effects can be assessed in the light of McFall and Hammen's research (1971). They compared eight prominent antismoking studies and converted the reported data to a common scale, percent of baseline, to facilitate comparisons. The resultant 27 V-shaped treatment curves tended to share an end-of-treatment rate of about 30 percent to 40 percent of baseline. In the present experiment, the control group achieved an end-of-treatment baseline rate of 28 percent, a result close to McFall and Hammen's 30 percent to 40 percent baseline rate, thereby serving as a typical smoking clinic group beyond which the effects of the value confrontation treatment can be assessed. The comparable baseline rate achieved by the value confrontation group was 5 percent, far exceeding the results attained by the typical smoking clinic control group, or by the eight antismoking clinic groups summarized by McFall and Hammen.

In summary, the value confrontation treatment produced significantly greater effects than a variety of other and more typical smoking clinic treatments. The results have implications not only for smoking cessation, but also for the cessation of other habitual behaviors or addictions, and, more generally, for psychotherapy. They seem to be particularly promising for public health programs that utilize brief media messages in the hope of producing large-scale behavioral changes.

A REPLICATION

Our confidence in the value confrontation approach to the reduction of smoking would be increased if our results were independently replicated. DeSeve (1975) conducted a similar experiment with 33 subjects. During a three-week antismoking clinic, he compared the effects of the value confrontation technique with the results obtained for three comparison groups.

The results he obtained for the value confrontation treatment were essentially as expected. Immediately following the confrontation, the ranking of the value *self-controlled* increased significantly and then declined to a posttest level that was still significantly higher than that recorded during the preclinic phase. Smoking behavior also declined markedly following the confrontation, to a level significantly lower than the preclinic rate. This decline in smoking was greater than that achieved by DeSeve's other comparison groups, but not significantly greater because all of DeSeve's groups had performed well as a result of participation in the clinic. Nonetheless, the overall pattern of DeSeve's results was remarkably consistent with that reported in our own experiment. Recall that the eight smoking studies summarized by McFall and Hammen (1971) shared an end-of-treatment smoking rate of 30 percent to 40 percent of baseline; the comparable rates for our own and for DeSeve's experiment were 5 percent and 5.9 percent, respectively.

The data from both experiments were combined by summing the probabilities, as proposed by Rosenthal (1978). Immediately following the value confrontation treatment, the ranking of the values *self-discipline* and *self-controlled* increased significantly for the combined groups ($p < .002$), and then declined somewhat to a posttest level still significantly higher than the preclinic rankings ($p < .005$). The combined smoking rates for the two experimental groups also declined from their preclinic levels to significantly lower levels following value confrontation ($p < .001$), and remained at these significantly lower levels for one additional month. Data for the DeSeve experiment was not recorded beyond that point but, as noted, the smoking rate for the value confrontation group in our own experiment continued to differ significantly from its control group for two months.

Thus, the overall results from both experiments exceed those recorded in other antismoking studies. Considering the briefness of the value confrontation technique, and the fact that smoking behavior is so highly resistant to modification that many researchers have labeled it an addiction, these results are particularly promising.

CONCLUDING COMMENTS

The research reported here is intended to illustrate the type of research that might contribute to future public health programs. This study as well as others (Straits, 1967; Waters, 1971; Conroy, 1976) focuses attention on various attitudes and values that are believed to be related to or to underlie smoking. Similar research is now needed to identify the attitudes and values that might be implicated in other health-destructive behaviors, such as automobile accidents, obesity, and drug abuse. It would then be possible to adapt and design self-confrontation techniques for the alleviation of specific health problems through the mass media, as the research by Sanders and Atwood (Chapter 14) suggests, and thereby produce desired reductions in various health-destructive behaviors.

In the final analysis, our present crisis in public health, as described by Knowles (1977), constitutes a challenge to our citizenry and our elected representatives. Two recent publications from the United States and Canadian governments *(Forward Plan for Health,* 1975; *New Perspective on the Health of Canadians,* 1974) reflect the fact that the officials of both governments are becoming increasingly concerned over the extent of this crisis. Both documents endorse large-scale public health programs, and they also support research efforts such as those discussed here to improve such programs. Knowles summarized our current health crisis as a conflict between an excessive level of personal freedom and an inadequate level of personal responsibility. Both *freedom* and *responsibility* are, of course, values. It would appear, therefore, that our current health crisis can be formulated to represent, at its very core, a crisis in values.

13

Long-Term Value Change Initiated by Computer Feedback

Milton Rokeach

Can a computer be programmed to induce long-term changes in human values? Can long-term value change be induced even when no target values are preselected for experimental treatment? These two questions arise as natural outgrowths of earlier work showing that certain kinds of feedback provided by a human agent can lead to long-term cognitive and behavioral change (Rokeach, 1973). This earlier research was concerned with certain conditions under which human values will undergo change, and with the question of the long-term cognitive and behavioral consequences following value change.

More specifically, white university students were provided with feedback about their own and about others' political values and attitudes. This feedback was deliberately designed to make many of them aware of certain contradictions chronically existing within their own value–attitude system. For instance, about 25 percent of the experimental subjects discovered that they supported civil rights for black Americans yet did not particularly care about the value *equality;* another 15 percent discovered that they placed a high priority on *equality* yet endorsed certain racist positions; and another 30 percent discovered that, even though they might regard themselves as citizens of a democratic society, they cared neither for civil rights for black Americans nor for the more general value of *equality*. Subjects who became aware through feedback of such contradictions within their belief systems subsequently exhibited significant increases in the importance they attached to the political values of *equality* and *freedom*, significantly changed related attitudes concerning civil rights for black Americans, and behaved significantly more often in an egalitarian manner. For instance, they responded significantly more frequently than did a control group to a direct solicitation to join the NAACP (National Association for the Advancement of Colored People). Such cognitive and behavioral effects were observed many weeks and months afterward—as long as 21 months after a single experimental treatment.

The available evidence indicates that the basic psychological mechanism that generates such a sequence of enduring change is the arousal of a specific state of self-dissatisfaction—that is, an affective state of self-dissatisfaction the nature or origin of which the subject can identify. Feedback of objective information about one's own and others' values, attitudes, and behavior made many of the experimental subjects consciously aware of the fact that they held certain values and attitudes or engaged in certain behaviors that, even though they happened to conform to those of their peer group, contradicted their self-esteem or their conceptions of themselves as moral or competent persons, arousing a specific state of self-dissatisfaction. To reduce such an emotional state, these experimental subjects reordered their value priorities and subsequently modified value-related attitudes and behavior to make them all more compatible with one another and, even more fundamentally, to make them all more compatible with their self-conceptions as tolerant citizens of a democratic society.

The above cited work has now been replicated and extended in several ways. Hopkins (1973) replicated this work with air force recruits (rather than college students) and has reported long-term change in attitude toward blacks following similar feedback procedures. Hamid and Flay (1974) have reported changes in political values two weeks after a similar experimental treatment in New Zealand. They found such changes in subjects who are internally as well as externally controlled and have reported changes in locus of control following value modification. Penner (1971) found that feedback resulted in long-term change in the value *equality* among white subjects, which in turn led to significant increases in frequency of eye contact between white and black subjects. Hollen (1972) has shown that the importance of *a world of beauty* can be significantly increased over a two-month period by employing similar feedback methods. Conroy, Katkin, and Barnette (1973) found that the importance of the instrumental value *self-controlled* can be experimentally increased in heavy cigarette smokers by feedback of information about the differences in the values of smokers and ex-smokers, and, moreover, that such an increase can lead to significant decreases in cigarette consumption over a two-month period. Greenstein (1976) has shown that a self-confrontation treatment concerning the values of good and mediocre high school teachers led to significant value and behavioral changes among teacher trainees 13 weeks later. Other research has demonstrated long-term cognitive and behavioral change under various conditions, such as following feedback about the values and attitudes of others even when subjects are not given feedback beforehand about their own values and attitudes (Rokeach & McLellan, 1972), under nonanonymous as well as anonymous conditions (Rokeach & Cochrane, 1972), when certain interpretations of the feedback data are offered to the experimental subjects (McLellan, 1974), and regardless of certain individual differences in personality (Cochrane & Kelly, 1971).

Each of these studies involved face-to-face interaction between human subjects and experimenters and, moreover, focused on specific target values that had been selected in advance for experimental treatment. One purpose of the research reported in this chapter was to determine whether the presence of a human experimenter is a necessary condition for inducing long-term cognitive change—that is, whether long-term value change can be initiated just as well by a computer without the presence of a human experimenter. A second purpose was to ascertain whether value change can be induced even when no specific target values are deliberately preselected for treatment.

It is reasonable to assume that people have a need to evaluate the information they acquire about themselves by comparing it with corresponding information about others (Festinger, 1954). The purpose of such evaluation and comparison is not necessarily to conform arbitrarily to whatever may be the normative values, opinions, and abilities of one's positive comparison groups but, rather, to serve as points of departure for self-evaluation—to affirm insofar as possible one's conception of oneself as a competent and moral human being, to maintain and, if possible, to enhance self-esteem. In the present research, college students were first invited to take a value-ranking test; then they were given the opportunity to ask a computer for information about how their own value rankings compared with those previously obtained for the educated and uneducated, the young and old, persons of the same and opposite sex, and persons who are prejudiced and unprejudiced. Then they compared their own value rankings with those shown for all of these comparison groups. It can be conjectured that, following such comparisons, persons who end up discerning no contradictions between their own values and their conceptions of themselves as moral and competent will have no compelling reason to become dissatisfied with themselves and, consequently, will have no compelling reason to change their values or value systems. In contrast, persons who discover contradictions or discrepancies between their values and self-conceptions should undergo value change designed to reduce or remove such discrepancies.

METHOD

Procedure for Inducing and Assessing Value Change via Computer

The subjects were students enrolled in introductory psychology classes at the University of Western Ontario in London, Ontario. They were all required to participate in a psychology experiment to fulfill a course requirement. All were tested individually. One hundred eight subjects were randomly assigned to an experimental group and 109 to a control group. There were approximately equal numbers of men and women in the experimental and control groups.

Pretest. The experimental subject first ranked the 18 terminal values (end-states of existence) shown in Table 13.1 "in order of their importance to YOU, as guiding principles in YOUR life" (Rokeach, 1967). The subject was then shown how to operate the terminal keyboard connected to a PDP-12 computer. The experimenter left the room, and all further interactions were between the computer and the experimental subject.

Experimental Treatment. The computer printed out the following instructions: "We will now ask you to type in, on the teletype, all your value rankings. We will then show you how your value rankings compare with the rankings obtained for various groups that you may be interested in."

The subject then recorded the rankings he or she had assigned to each of the 18 terminal values. "We have information on the value rankings of four groups. Each group has an identifying number (in brackets): educated–uneducated [1], males–females [2], pro–civil rights–anti–civil rights [3], and young (college students)–old (70s and over) [4]."

All subjects were exposed to these four sets of comparisons in whatever order they preferred. Table 13.1 shows the results displayed for one particular experimental subject, comparing his or her own values with those of the educated and uneducated. The same format was employed to provide feedback to all experimental subjects about the values of males and females, young and old, and people for and against civil rights.

The subject was then instructed to "circle the five largest differences in columns 1 and 5 [see Table 13.1]. These are the differences that you

TABLE 13.1. Typical Computer Display Shown to a Subject Requesting Comparison of Own Values with Values of the Educated and Uneducated

VALUE	MY DIFFERENCE WITH EDUCATED	VALUES OF EDUCATED	*ME*	VALUES OF UNEDUCATED	MY DIFFERENCE WITH UNEDUCATED
A comfortable life	5	15	10	3	7
An exciting life	6	14	8	18	10
A sense of accomplishment	5	4	9	13	4
A world at peace	3	1	4	1	3
A world of beauty	5	12	7	16	9
Equality	5	7	2	12	10
Family security	6	5	11	2	9
Freedom	2	3	1	4	3
Happiness	7	10	3	5	2
Inner harmony	4	9	5	9	4
Mature love	1	11	12	17	5
National security	1	13	14	10	4
Pleasure	5	18	13	14	1
Salvation	1	17	18	8	10
Self-respect	10	6	16	7	9
Social recognition	1	16	17	15	2
True friendship	7	8	15	6	9
Wisdom	4	2	6	11	5

will probably be the most interested in studying. Take 2 or 3 minutes to study the numbers you have circled." The sole purpose of this instruction was to focus the experimental subjects' attention especially on those values that they had ranked in a manner different from those given by the various comparison groups.

The value rankings displayed for the various comparison groups had been obtained previously from a national area probability sample over 1,400 adult Americans tested by the National Opinion Research Center in 1968. The data in Table 13.1 for the educated and uneducated were obtained from subgroups of adult Americans who reported that they had postgraduate and 0–4 years of education, respectively. These data, as well as the data on male and female values, young and old, and pro–civil rights and anti–civil rights groups are all reported elsewhere.[1]

Upon termination of the experimental session, the experimenter returned to dismiss the subjects. Half of the subjects were randomly selected to keep the computer printouts, and the other half were not allowed to keep the computer printouts.

The control subjects merely filled out the Value Survey (Rokeach, 1967) and were then dismissed. Half of them, again randomly selected, were allowed to keep a copy of their Value Survey, and the other half were dismissed without retaining a copy.

Posttest. Experimental and control subjects were all contacted by phone and requested to appear at a designated time and place for a posttest session two months after the original experimental session. Without exception, they appeared and were retested with the Value Survey. They also filled out a brief questionnaire designed to find out whether those who retained copies of the computer printout or the Value Survey had consulted them, and whether they had discussed the research with anyone.

RESULTS

Posttests obtained two months after the experimental treatment showed no differences in the amount of value change between the experimental subjects allowed and not allowed to keep the printouts; nor were there any significant differences between control subjects allowed and not allowed to keep their Value Surveys. Moreover, the order in which experimental subjects selected the various comparison group value data had no discernible effect. Accordingly, in all subsequent

---

[1]The data on education, sex, age, and civil rights attitude will be found on pp. 57, 64, 76, and 101, respectively, in Rokeach (1973).

analyses, order of comparison was ignored, and the data collected for both kinds of experimental subjects and, similarly, for both kinds of control subjects, were combined.

Overall Effects of Experimental Treatment

Did the experimental treatment—feedback by a computer, with no target values preselected for treatment—significantly affect the subjects? Table 13.2 shows the mean degree of similarity, as measured by rho, between the subjects' value rankings and the value rankings displayed by the computer printouts for the educated and uneducated, pro- and anti-civil rights groups, young and old, and same sex and opposite sex. These indices of similarity are shown separately for experimental and control groups, and separately for pretest and posttest value rankings. If the experimental treatment did indeed affect the subjects, we should find ignificant changes in value system similarity from pretest to post-test within the experimental group, but not within the control group, and significantly more changes in value system similarity within the ex-perimental group than within the control group.

Table 13.2 shows that the value rankings of the experimental subjects become significantly more similar from pretest to posttest to the value rankings displayed on the computer printout for the pro-civil rights comparison group and for the same-sex comparison group. In both cases, the t tests for correlated measures are significant beyond the .05 level. In contrast, no significant changes in similarity from pretest to posttest were obtained for the control group.

More crucial, however, is whether the changes in similarity from pretest to posttest are greater for the experimental than for the control group. The relevant data are shown on the two bottom rows of Table 13.2. Compared with the control group, the experimental group's value rankings became significantly more similar to the value rankings dis-played for the educated, the pro-civil rights, and the same-sex compari-son groups ($p < .05$). The experimental group's value rankings also became more similar to the value rankings displayed for the aged, but this difference did not reach statistical significance ($p < .07$).

These findings do not tell us whether certain experimental subjects were affected more than others; neither do they inform us whether certain specific values were affected. But they do tell us that the com-puter feedback had significantly affected the values of the experimental subjects considered as a whole over a two-month period.

Long-term Value System Change

The correlation between pretest and posttest value rankings provides us with a simple index of value system change, an index that we have

TABLE 13.2. Overall Value Similarity to Eight Comparison Groups for Subjects Measured by Rho

EXPERIMENTAL GROUP	COMPARISON GROUP							
	Educated	Uneducated	Pro–Civil Rights	Anti–Civil Rights	Old	Young	Same Sex	Opposite Sex
Experimental (N = 108)								
Mean pretest rho	.38	.15	.35	.12	.06	.49	.21	.20
Mean posttest rho	.41	.18	.39	.14	.09	.51	.25	.22
Difference	.03	.03	.04	.02	.03	.02	.04	.02
t	1.78	1.78	2.41*	1.15	1.72	1.35	2.31*	1.22
Control (N = 109)								
Mean pretest rho	.39	.15	.36	.12	.06	.51	.22	.20
Mean posttest rho	.37	.16	.34	.11	.05	.54	.21	.20
Difference	-.02	.01	-.02	-.01	-.01	.03	-.01	.00
t	1.10	.60	1.11	.57	.61	1.63	.62	.00
Experimental versus control								
Difference between differences	.05	.02	.06	.03	.04	-.01	.05	.02
t of difference	2.01*	1.06	2.10*	1.44	1.81	.07	2.17*	1.26

*$p < .05$.

used before and found to be valid (Rokeach, 1973, pp. 257–258): the lower this correlation, the more the value system change. We should find significantly more value system change among certain experimental subjects than among others—among those experimental subjects who discovered that their value systems were on the whole more similar to those shown for the less congruent comparison groups, when compared either with comparable control subjects or when compared with other experimental subjects who discovered that their value systems were on the whole more similar to those shown for the congruent comparison groups. Rho correlations were computed between each subject's own pretest terminal value rankings and those displayed on the computer printouts for the educated and uneducated, own sex and opposite sex, young and old, and for persons favoring and opposing civil rights— eight correlations in all for each subject. Because all of the subjects were college students, we assumed that four of these eight groups served as the congruent comparison groups (educated, own sex, young, and pro-civil rights), whereas the remaining four served as the less congruent comparison groups (uneducated, opposite sex, old, and anti–civil rights). Each subject, control as well as experimental, was then classified into one of the following three categories: (1) having a value system that was on the whole more similar to that of the less congruent comparison groups, if the rho correlation between the subject's own pretest value rankings and the average value rankings of the four less congruent comparison groups was larger than the rho correlation between own value rankings of the four congruent comparison groups; (2) having a value system that was on the whole somewhat more similar to that of the four congruent comparison groups, if the rho correlation between own pretest value ranking and the average value rankings of the four congruent comparison groups was .01 to .29 larger than the comparable correlation between own value ranking and the average of the four less congruent comparison groups; or (3) having a value system that was even more similar to that of the four congruent comparison groups, if the correlation between own pretest value rankings of the four congruent comparison groups exceeded by .30 the correlation between own value rankings and the average value rankings of the four less congruent comparison groups.

We reasoned that those experimental subjects who discovered, following computer feedback, that they had ranked their values rather differently on the whole from the way their congruent comparison groups had ranked them were more likely to be stimulated to think about their values, to become dissatisfied with themselves as they thought about them, to have a need to reexamine their values, and thus to undergo value system change. Conversely, those experimental subjects who discovered that they had ranked their values on the whole rather similarly to the way their congruent comparison groups had ranked them would have had no particular reason to question or reexamine their values or to become dissatisfied with themselves, and, consequently, they should have little or no reason to undergo value system change.

Table 13.3 shows that those experimental subjects whose value systems more closely resembled the four less congruent, rather than more congruent, comparison groups underwent the greater amount of value system change. The mean rho correlation between pretest and posttest value rankings is .618 for 10 experimental subjects whose value systems were on the whole more similar to those of the less congruent comparison groups; the mean correlation is .731 for 55 experimental subjects whose value systems were on the whole slightly more similar to those of the four congruent comparison groups; and the mean correlation is .782 for 43 experimental subjects whose value systems were on the whole even more similar to those of the four congruent comparison groups. Analysis of variance reveals that these value system differences are statistically significant beyond the .02 level, and a one-tailed t test comparison between the experimental mean rhos of .782 and .618 is significant beyond the .005 level. The comparable differences among the three control subgroup levels are not significant.

Table 13.3 further shows that those experimental subjects whose value systems were on the whole more similar to those of the four less congruent comparison groups underwent more value system change

TABLE 13.3. Mean Value System Change for Experimental and Control Subgroups Varying in Similarity to 4 Congruent and 4 Less Congruent Comparison Groups

CORRELATION OF SUBJECTS' PRETEST VALUE RANKINGS	EXPERIMENTAL		CONTROL	
	N	Mean rho	N	Mean rho
More with 4 congruent than with 4 less congruent comparison groups	43	.782	42	.754
Slightly more with 4 congruent than with 4 less congruent comparison groups	55	.731	59	.751
More with 4 less congruent than with 4 congruent comparison groups	10	.618	8	.705

than the comparable subgroup of control subjects. The mean pretest-posttest rho correlation between value rankings is .618 for the former and .705 for the latter. This finding does not, however, reach statistical significance, probably because of the small number of cases in these two subgroups.

Changes in Specific Values

Additional analyses enabled us to identify which values in particular had been affected by the treatment. The experimental subjects had been shown computer printouts comparing four pairs of contrasting groups on 18 values—72 comparisons in all. Of these 72 value comparisons, we selected for further analysis 10 values that were displayed by the computer as having been ranked in "markedly divergent" ways by contrasting comparison groups. Markedly divergent was defined as a displayed difference in rank of 9 or more. These are as follows: (1) four values—*a comfortable life, a sense of accomplishment, salvation,* and *wisdom*—were displayed by the computer as distinguishing markedly between the educated and uneducated; (2) two values—*equality* and *salvation*—distinguished markedly between persons for and against civil rights; (3) one value—*a comfortable life*—distinguished markedly between men and women; and (4) three values—*a world at peace, mature love,* and *salvation*—distinguished markedly between the young and old.

The most sensitive test of change in these specific values following the experimental treatment is a posttest comparison of differences in value rankings between experimental and control groups by an analysis of covariance that statistically equates experimental and control groups for initial pretest value rankings (Cronbach & Furby, 1970).

Table 13.4 indicates that three values in particular (of the 10 selected for analysis, as described above)—*a sense of accomplishment, equality,* and *a world at peace*—show significant posttest differences between experimental and control subjects whose initial value rankings differed markedly from those displayed by the computer for their own (congruent) comparison groups. Additional analyses reveal, however, that only the first two values, *a sense of accomplishment* and *equality,* had actually increased significantly in importance from pretest to posttest for these experimental subjects. *A world at peace* shows a significant posttest difference between experimental and control subjects (Table 13.4) not because the experimental subjects had increased their rankings from pretest to posttest, but because the control subjects had significantly decreased their rankings from pretest to posttest to a significantly greater extent than did the experimental group—a significantly smaller regression-toward-the-mean effect by experimental than by control subjects ($p < .03$). This

TABLE 13.4. Effect of Computer Feedback on the Values of Experimental and Control Groups

	A Sense of Accomplishment		Equality		A World at Peace	
	Educated	*Uneducated*	*Pro-Civil Rights*	*Anti-Civil Rights*	*Young*	*Old*
Mean rank shown on printout	4	13	4	14	10	1
Definition of "similar"	1–8	9–18	1–9	10–18	6–18	1–5
Number of experimental subjects "similar to"	61	47	49	59	70	38
Number of control subjects "similar to"	67	42	49	60	83	26
Adjusted posttest mean of above experimental subjects	7.21	10.00	6.69	11.19	11.23	3.80
Adjusted posttest mean of above control subjects	6.41	11.69	6.68	12.38	11.71	5.37
Level of significance	n.s.	.02	n.s.	.02	n.s.	.02

latter finding suggests that the computer feedback had the effect of inhibiting the initially high rankings for *a world at peace* of these experimental subjects from regression toward the mean.

DISCUSSION

Recall that half of the experimental subjects were allowed to retain the computer printouts following the experimental treatment, whereas the remaining half were not allowed to do so. Similarly, half of the control subjects retained copies of the Value Survey, and the remaining half did not. The fact that these variations did not lead to any differential effects might seem surprising, especially considering that the majority of those allowed to retain the test materials reported that they had consulted them (96% of the experimental and 71% of the control subjects) and, moreover, that they had discussed them with friends (90% and 73%, respectively). These findings suggest that it was the emotional impact of the computer feedback, and not what happened in the intervening two months, that affected their values.

The findings show, first, that the experimental subjects had been significantly affected by the computer feedback (Table 13.2). The experimental subjects' value systems had changed to become significantly more similar on the posttest to the value systems displayed by the computer for the pro–civil rights and the same-sex comparison groups. No such significant changes were found in the control group. Moreover, the experimental group had changed more than the control group from pretest to posttest, their value rankings becoming significantly more similar as a whole to those displayed for the educated, the pro–civil rights, and the same-sex comparison groups. Note further that the experimental group also became more similar on the whole to the values displayed for the old (rather than the young), but not significantly so.

Second, the findings show that some experimental subjects had been more affected than others by the computer feedback (Table 13.3). These experimental subjects who discovered that their value rankings were on the whole most discrepant from those of their own four comparison groups underwent more value system change than did those whose values were less discrepant.

Third, even though no values had been preselected in this experiment as specific targets for value change, we found that three values in particular showed significant posttest differences between experimental and control subjects whose value rankings were discrepant from their own reference group (Table 13.4). Further analyses revealed that the effect of the experimental treatment was to increase the importance of *a sense of accomplishment* and *equality* significantly from pretest to posttest among these subjects and, moreover, to inhibit regression toward the mean of *a world at peace* from pretest to posttest. These three effects were found primarily among those experimental subjects who discovered that they had ranked such values quite differently from the way others like them had ranked them.

All three of these significant effects, observed two months after the experimental treatment, can be interpreted as changes occurring in a direction of greater compatibility with self-conceptions or with the maintenance or enhancement of self-esteem. According to a theory of cognitive and behavioral change previously advanced (Rokeach, 1973, Chapter 8), values, attitudes, and behaviors will undergo long-term change if they are experienced as inconsistent with self-conceptions concerning competence or morality. For instance, even if a value and an attitude are wholly consistent with one another, they are both predicted, contrary to conventional consistency theories, to undergo change if both violate self-conceptions, and the changes should be in a direction of maintaining or enhancing self-conceptions or self-esteem. Experimental evidence supports such a prediction. College students who discovered through human-mediated feedback that they care little for the value *equality* and, moreover, that they have anti–civil rights attitudes (which logicians and consistency theorists alike would surely consider consistent), nonetheless underwent significant long-term increases in both *equality* and pro–civil rights attitude. Such experimental findings can readily be interpreted as changes that are in a direction of greater consistency with self-conceptions or self-esteem.[2]

Regardless of differences in interpretation of the specific value changes, it is clear that computer feedback led to significant effects over a two-month period, that these effects were stronger among certain experimental subjects, and that these effects were evident for certain values in certain experimental subjects—those who discovered dis-

---

[2]The present findings concerning computer-mediated value changes do not fit a conformity interpretation any better than do previously reported findings concerning human-mediated value changes. Previous experiments have shown, for example, that experimental subjects significantly increased their rankings of *equality* and *freedom* following feedback of the value rankings of their peer group, but such increases were in a direction opposite to that manifested by their peer comparison group, namely, in a direction toward a greater egalitarianism and libertarianism than that manifested by their peer group. Such findings can, however, most readily be explained as occurring in a direction of greater compatibility with self-esteem or, to put the matter in more social-psychological terms, of greater compatibility with self-conceptions as citizens of a democratic society.

For a more systematic discussion of the nonviability of a conformity interpretation, as well as the nonviability of some half-dozen other alternative interpretations of various experimental findings concerning long-term value change, see Rokeach (1973, pp. 313–319).

crepancies between certain of their own value rankings and those of the congruent comparison groups.[3]

The present study does not, however, enable us to conclude whether computer feedback will affect attitudes and behavior as well as values. Although theoretical considerations and empirical research cited at the beginning of this selection strongly suggest that value change, however it might be initiated, will lead also to attitude and behavioral change, we have no direct evidence thus far bearing on this point, and only further research with computer-initiated feedback will be able to answer this question more definitively.

When the present findings are considered alongside those obtained in earlier research, they suggest that (1) long-term value change can be induced by computers as well as by human experimenters, (2) value change can be induced by computers even when no target values are preselected, as was the case in earlier research, and (3) computers can be programmed to change different values in different people, depending on whichever values are discovered by particular subjects to contradict self-conceptions. Thus, the present findings are seen to be education oriented rather than persuasion oriented. In contrast to the deception that is so typical of many attitude change studies, the emphasis here is on the feedback of truthful information about various comparison groups and on self-examination of value inconsistencies. More specifically, the findings are seen as paving the way for computer-initiated value education, value therapy, and vocational counseling in high schools and colleges, expositions, and museums (Lee, 1968). A computer would be programmed first to "invite" persons to find out about their values, then to "help" them ascertain the extent to which their values are similar to and different from those of other groups they may be interested in, and,

---

[3]A question may be raised as to whether these significant computer-induced changes represent changes in meaning or definition rather than changes in the values themselves. This question can be raised in any experimental study in which verbal responses, and changes in verbal responses, are at the focus of attention—for example, changes in attitude, needs, personality traits, and interests. The logic of measurement theory requires us to assume that changes in verbal responses that purport to measure a specified variable, assuming it is reliable, represent changes in the measured variable. For extensive data on the reliability of the value measure employed here, see Rokeach (1973, Chapter 2). Perhaps more important, the posed issue boils down to a question of validity. In the present instance, it is possible to point to research by Rokeach (1971a, 1973), Penner (1971), Rokeach and McLellan (1972), Conroy, Katkin, and Barnette (1973), and Greenstein (1976) that shows that long-term changes in verbal responses elicited by the value measure are significantly associated with logically related behavioral changes, thus suggesting that the value changes obtained with verbal value tests represent genuine changes rather than mere changes in interpretation.

For a more systematic discussion of the meaning that respondents attribute to the values represented in the Value Survey, see Rokeach (1973, pp. 49–51), and for a more systematic discussion of the different kinds of evidence required to establish whether changes in value rankings represent genuine changes, see Rokeach (1973, Chapter 13).

finally, to "draw" their attention to the most salient similarities and differences between their own values and those of various significant reference groups in which they may be interested.

Katz (1969) and Katz, Chapman, and Godwin (1972) have recently reported similar work done at the Educational Testing Service, in which they employ computers to help students make vocational guidance decisions:

> The student interacts with a computer in such a way as to examine his own values, obtain and use relevant information, interpret predictive data, and formulate plans. . . . At the end of each value game, the student sees a display showing . . . the preferred value. . . . He is also given a display pointing out inconsistencies.

Their main purpose in feeding back such inconsistencies was to help clarify and hopefully to remove inconsistencies in the student's guidance decisions. It would thus appear that Katz's computer-based System of Interactive Guidance and Information (SIGI) is designed to change not only guidance decisions but also values. An evaluation of the long-term effects of SIGI, which has thus far apparently not been attempted, should inform us about the extent to which this computer-based program does have long-term effects on human values as well as on vocational guidance decisions, as would be expected from the present findings.

If it is indeed the case that the basic mechanism that generates a process of long-term cognitive and behavioral change is the arousal of an identifiable state of self-dissatisfaction, then feedback via any medium that successfully arouses such a state should lead to lasting change. Thus, not only face-to-face interactions between subjects and humans, and between subjects and computers, but also between subjects and such mass media as television, might also be employed to bring about value change. However accomplished, the capacity to bring about lasting value change raises grave ethical issues. These issues are too complex to discuss in this chapter, and the interested reader is therefore referred to the more comprehensive earlier work which discusses more extensively the ethical issues involved (Rokeach, 1973).

14

Value Change Initiated by the Mass Media

Keith R. Sanders and L. Erwin Atwood

During the past several years, scholars interested in speech communication have rather dramatically changed their thinking about the nature of the phenomena which they study. Prior to about 1965, most empirical speech-communication scholars were laboratory experimentalists. The independent variables in their research tended to be message and source variables, and their dependent variables tended to be attitude change and information gain. For the most part, their research reflected a linear view of human communication with influence flowing from sources, usually "establishment" sources, through messages, toward receivers (Cronkhite, 1974).

However, during the recent past, there has been an increasingly strong reaction to this narrow perspective. Recently theorists and researchers have called for more research in naturalistic settings (Clevenger, 1969), and for a more inclusive view of human communication as process (Smith, 1972) which could eventually account for a larger

The authors wish to thank Professors Milton Rokeach and Theodore Greenstein for their thoughtful critiques of this selection, Professor Jerry Allen for help in data collection, and the College of Communication and Fine Arts, at Southern Illinois University at Carbondale, for financial support. It was first presented as a paper at the International Communication Association Convention, Berlin, Germany, June, 1977.

number of variables, their interactions, their uses (Blumler & Katz, 1974), their functions (Swanson, 1976), and their effects on overt behavior (Miller, 1967).

One of the most salient presuppositions of this new movement is the view that significant attitudes, values, and behavior are not likely to be substantially and permanently changed by the kinds of "one-shot" communication situations which, for some time, constituted the corpus of research on oral communication. It is reasoned that since significant attitudes, values, and behavior are the products of a series of interacting events which form the total personal history of the individual, it is unlikely that permanent changes can be wrought by momentarily manipulating a single stimulus among the many in each person's total stimulus field. For example, it is argued that while a single speech by a political candidate may change an audience's attitudes toward him, this change may not persist and, even if it does, may have no impact on the audience's voting behavior, unless it is reinforced by other stimuli (Swanson, 1976).

Just as speech-communication scholars and others (McGuire, 1969) had begun to settle comfortably into their new theoretical position, Rokeach began publishing the results of a series of experiments which diametrically contradicted the basic presupposition of the approach. Rokeach produced long-standing changes in attitudes, values, and behavior during a single 40-minute experimental session, concluding that "it now seems to be within man's power to alter experimentally another person's basic values and to control the direction of the change" (Rokeach, 1971b, p. 68).

The prime assertion of the theory out of which the original Rokeach experiments were drawn is that when individuals become aware, through self-confrontation, of contradictions between their conceptions of self and their values, attitudes, or behavior, they will reorganize their values and attitudes, and, thus, their behavior in order to make them more consistent with their conceptions of self. The theory (Rokeach, 1973, Chapter 8) is based on the assumption that individuals hold a hierarchically ordered, interconnected belief system in which the most central elements are the conceptions or cognitions that individuals hold about themselves. The "Master Function" of the entire belief system is to maintain and, when possible, to enhance one's total conception of oneself.

The next most central group of elements in the belief system are hierarchically arranged values which are of two types. Some few are "terminal" values which are composed of beliefs concerning desirable end-states of existence such as a world at peace and human equality. A somewhat larger number of "instrumental" values are concerned with modes of conduct such as courage and honesty. One presumably engages in certain modes of conduct in order to achieve certain desirable end-states of being. Terminal values are nearer the center of the belief system than are instrumental values.

Attitudes hold a still less central position in the belief system and are different from values. An attitude is "an organization of several beliefs around a specific object or situation" (Rokeach, 1973, p. 18). A value, on the other hand, whether instrumental or terminal, "refers to a single belief . . . that has a transcendental quality to it, guiding actions, attitudes, judgments, and comparisons across specific objects and situations beyond immediate goals to more ultimate goals" (Rokeach, 1973, p. 18).

In order to test some of the fundamental implications of this theory, Rokeach and his colleagues hypothesized that when persons compare their self-conceptions with objective feedback about their terminal values, and notice sufficient inconsistency to produce a state of dissatisfaction, they will (1) alter their less central terminal values so as to make them more consistent with their self-conceptions, and (2) these alterations will induce enduring changes in functionally related attitudes and behavior. (For a provocative challenge to this sequence of events, see Grube, Rankin, Greenstein, & Kearney, 1977.)

They conducted three experiments in which they asked several groups of students at Michigan State University to rank, in order of priority, a set of terminal values including *freedom, equality, pleasure,* and so on. Tabulations revealed that *freedom* had been ranked first and *equality* much lower, sixth in one experiment and eleventh in the other two. The experimenters presented this latter finding to a second group of students, and, in order to arouse self-dissatisfaction, conjectured that "MSU students in general are much more interested in their own freedom than they are in freedom for other people" (Rokeach, 1973, p. 237). Experimental subjects were then invited to compare their value rankings with the value rankings of the other Michigan State students.

Experimental subjects were then asked to indicate on a three-point scale how sympathetic they were with the aims of civil rights demonstrators. They were informed that the previously tested group of students had answered the same questions, and that those who were sympathetic to civil rights also tended to rank *freedom* and *equality* much more highly than did those who were not sympathetic to civil rights. A table showing these findings was presented, and the experimenter concluded that those who were against civil rights were more indifferent to other people's freedom than those who were for civil rights. Subjects were invited to compare their degree of sympathy with civil rights to their values, and were invited to compare again their value rankings with those of their peers.

All predictions were confirmed. One application of the experimental treatment produced statistically significant changes in value rankings and in attitudes held toward civil rights. Moreover, these changes held when posttesting was extended to include intervals of three weeks, three to five months, and 15 to 17 months. Behavioral change also occurred. The experimental group showed a significantly greater willingness to join the NAACP when asked to do so three to five months after the administration of the treatment. Rokeach interpreted these findings to mean that it is now within the power of man to alter enduringly values, attitudes, and behavior during a 40-minute period of time. One of the motivations behind the study reported here was to replicate the basic features of Rokeach's experiments in an effort to confirm or disconfirm this startling conclusion.

Several researchers have replicated Rokeach's original work, producing value or attitude change in all instances, and subsequent behavioral change in some instances (Penner, 1971; Hollen, 1972; Hopkins, 1973, Conroy, Katkin, & Barnette, 1973; Hamid & Flay, 1974; Sherrid & Beech, 1976; Greenstein, 1976). One purpose of the study reported here was to replicate the essential features of the original Rokeach experiments. However, the primary objective of this research was to determine whether self-confrontation, as a method for changing values and behavior, could be generalized beyond the interpersonal channel. All of the experiments referred to above were conducted using face-to-face communication as the primary channel, with print media playing a secondary role. The value rankings and attitudinal measurements of previously tested groups, of the subjects themselves, and the interpretations of these data were presented orally, with the experimenter physically present, and with the same information available to subjects in print. It is obviously of much practical and theoretical significance to know whether the dramatic results achieved in previous studies can also be achieved via the mass media.

Partly because they have not been theoretically interesting, channel variables have been one of the most neglected areas in communication research (McGuire, 1973). However, some thought and research have been devoted to the matter (Weiss, 1969). For example, Rogers' (1973) work on the diffusion of innovation has indicated that mass channels are superior to interpersonal channels in their ability to change audience cognitions, but interpersonal channels predominate when attitude change is the goal of the communicator. These data have led Rogers (1973, p. 291) to assert that "messages transmitted over the mass media are *alone* unlikely to effect *substantial* changes in strongly held attitudes or overt behavior," with the exception of instances wherein the audience already feels a strong need for change. This absence of effect, Rogers posits, may be due to the more efficient functioning for the individual of selective exposure, perception, and retention in mass communication settings than in face-to-face encounters.

On the whole, however, experimental studies which have sought to identify direct effects attributable to media variables have produced results which are difficult to interpret. Croft, Stimpson, Ross, Bray, and Breglio (1968) exposed students to either a live or video-taped persuasive speech, and found that the live presentation was more effective in producing attitude change. On the other hand, five other studies (Frandsen, 1963; Keating, 1972; Kennedy, 1972; Sawyer, 1955; Tannenbaum & Kerrick, 1954) found no important differences among television, radio, and written messages in terms of their ability to produce attitude change, and Sprague (1970) found that audio, written, and face-to-face channels were equally effective in conferring resistance to moderately and strongly held beliefs. Adding to the confusion is the finding by Wall and Boyd (1971) that a written presentation was superior to either a live or video-taped presentation in changing attitudes.

More coherent findings emerge from studies which do not anticipate effects due singularly to channel variables but anticipate interactions among source, channel, message, and receiver variables. Becker (1969) reported interactions between channels and sources. Some politicians produced more favorable attitudes toward themselves on television, while others were more favorably received on radio, or in print. Likewise, Cohen (1976) found no direct effects but reported interactions between channel variables and sources. Worchel, Andreoli, and Eason (1975) reported no main effects but concluded from their data that audience attitudes toward the topic discussed in the message, and audience attitudes toward the source, interacted powerfully with channel variables.

Thus, studies from the field and the laboratory suggest, without consistent or compelling theoretical rationales, that channel variables may play a role in attitude formation and change. These studies are, however, difficult to relate to Rokeach's theory and to the research which it has inspired. Rokeach and his colleagues view attitudes as peripheral elements in the belief system, and are not surprised when they are changed. They would contend that such changes are fleeting, when unaccompanied by changes in functionally related terminal and/or instrumental values. None of the studies just described, with the possible exception of some of those upon which Rogers (1973) drew, would permit a determination of the duration of the change, nor of the relationship between attitude change and behavioral change. These studies do indicate, however, that the matter is worth pursuing.

Three studies reported by Rokeach and his colleagues are highly relevant to the question of whether differences in message and medium are significant in the inducement of value change. Rokeach and Cochrane (1972) conducted an experiment to determine whether attempts to change values would be less successful under conditions of confrontation with a significant other than under conditions of private self-confrontation. All previous studies had been conducted under entirely anonymous conditions in which the experimenter did not interact directly with each subject, nor was he aware of each subject's values, attitudes, or behavior. The results of this experiment, however, indicated that private self-confrontation and self-confrontation with a significant other produced the same long-term value changes which had been observed in earlier studies.

Must the message communicated contain information about the subjects' values, so that they can compare their stated values with their self-conceptions, or can the message simply contain information on how others have ranked values? The answer to this question obviously holds important practical and theoretical implications. In educational settings, and in scholarly publications such as this one, persons are exposed, implicitly and explicitly, to the values of other people without obtaining information about their own values. Moreover, in most mass communication contexts, it is impractical to require members of the audience to obtain objective information about their values, attitudes, or behavior. But is such information necessary? Can the values, attitudes, and behavior of millions of television viewers be made to undergo enduring changes by presenting the value profiles of "significant other" groups?

The results of an experiment by Rokeach and McLellan (1972) indicate that objective feedback about one's values is *not* a necessary condition for value change. Significant changes in values and behavior were induced when subjects were given objective feedback only about the value rankings of others. This finding suggests that this modified form of self-confrontation could be applied in mass media contexts.

If variation within the interpersonal channel can take place with no discernible reduction in the impact of self-confrontation, and if confrontation need not be explicitly with self, are human beings necessary as experimenters? Can value change be induced via interactive computer? And, if so, can it be done when specific values are not preselected for change? These two questions motivated a study, reported in Chapter 13, in which subjects completed the Value Survey and then obtained information from a computer terminal which allowed them to compare their own value rankings with those obtained from various reference groups. This procedure induced value change which endured over a two-month period, even though no particular values were targeted. The computer, with its displays of graphic information, is clearly a different feedback channel from that used in previous studies. The inducement of self-dissatisfaction may not be channel bound. It may be as easily accomplished on television and in newspapers as it has been via interpersonal communication. Further clarification of this issue is the primary objective of the research reported here.

HYPOTHESES

This study was designed to test five hypotheses. They are stated here in the specific terms of this experiment. However, one should keep in mind that any terminal value, instrumental value, or attitude which is found by an individual to be inconsistent with his or her self-conceptions, and which, therefore, produces dissatisfaction, could be substituted for the values *freedom* and *equality* investigated here.

1. Subjects who become dissatisfied with their original ranking of *freedom* will (a) increase their ranking of *freedom* from pretest to first posttest more than will subjects who remain satisfied with their original ranking of *freedom,* and (b) this change will persist.

2. Subjects who become dissatisfied with their original ranking of *equality* will (a) increase their ranking of *equality* from pretest to first posttest more than will subjects who remain satisfied with their original ranking of *equality,* and (b) this change will persist.

3. Subjects who become dissatisfied with their original ranking of *freedom* will, when invited, join the NAACP in proportionately larger numbers than will subjects who remain satisfied with their original ranking of *freedom*.

4. Subjects who become dissatisfied with their original ranking of *equality* will, when invited, join the NAACP in larger numbers than will subjects who remain satisfied with their original ranking of *equality*.

Rokeach's value theory does not predict that all persons who are induced to engage in self-confrontation will change their values. The theory asserts only that those persons who experience self-dissatisfaction will be motivated to change. Hypotheses one through four are designed to test this assertion more parsimoniously than have several earlier studies.

In addition, the hypotheses for *freedom* and *equality* have been separated in the attempt to gain parsimony, especially in terms of the behavioral variable. Previous research is not clear as to whether change in both *freedom* and *equality* must take place if functionally related behavior is to occur, or whether change in one or the other would be sufficient. Theoretically, a change in either one would eventuate in behavior change. This investigation, therefore, looks at each separately.

5. There will be no differences among the three channels—interpersonal, television, and print—in terms of (a) the amount of value

change induced, or (b) the number of subjects who, when invited, join the NAACP.

METHODS AND PROCEDURES

Subjects. One hundred and eighty-one volunteer subjects were drawn from 17 undergraduate classes during the summer session, 1972, at Southern Illinois University at Carbondale. Eleven of the courses were sections of the basic Speech course. The remaining six sections were more advanced courses taught in the same department. One hundred and eleven subjects were assigned randomly to three treatment groups involving four different channels for the presentation of the stimulus message, and to a control group. The remaining 80 students were not available to attend all four sessions; thus, they could not be assigned at random. This group was assigned randomly to those sessions which they could attend. In a few instances, random assignment was not possible because there was but one session which the subject could attend.

The Measuring Instrument. The Rokeach Value Survey, Part I (Rokeach, 1973, p. 422), and related measures of attitudes and satisfaction were used in this study. This instrument has produced encouraging results from studies of its face validity (Shotland & Berger, 1970) and from reliability studies. One study indicated that while values listed high in alphabetical order tend to receive higher rankings, this appears to be a valid indicator of preference rather than an order effect (Cochrane & Rokeach, 1970). A more direct test (Greenstein & Bennett, 1974) for order effects also produced negative results. Rokeach (1973) reported test–retest reliability coefficients of .78 and .80 with an interval of three to seven weeks between tests. Penner, Homant, and Rokeach (1968) reported a reliability coefficient of .74 with an interval of three weeks, using the same form of the Value Survey which was used in this experiment.

Procedures. In general, this experiment was conducted in the same manner as Rokeach (1973, pp. 236–244) conducted his original three experiments at Michigan State University. During the first week of the summer session, June 20–23, the experimenter and a graduate student assistant solicited volunteer subjects, assigning them to the treatment and control groups. On June 26 and 27, the pretest and treatment were administered to the experimental subjects and the pretest was given to the control group. Treatments were administered to each group as a unit in similar classrooms in the same building.

In the experimental sessions, pretesting was followed by the presentation of Table 1 (Rokeach, 1973, p. 236) showing the average rankings given to each of the 18 values by previous "Southern Illinois University students." In the table, *freedom* was ranked "1" and *equality* was ranked "11." After subjects had silently reviewed the table, the experimenter described its contents and observed that "apparently, Southern Illinois University students value *freedom* far more highly than they value *equality*. This suggests that SIU students in general are much more interested in their own freedom than they are in the freedom of other people." Subjects were then given a brief period during which to compare their value rankings with those of the students shown in Table 1.

A three-point scale (Rokeach, 1973, p. 237) was administered to measure subjects' attitude toward civil rights demonstrations. When this task was completed, the experimenter presented Table 2 (Rokeach, 1973, p. 238), which showed that the previously tested SIU students who were strongly for civil rights valued *equality* higher but that those who were against civil rights ranked *equality* lower; however, both pro- and anti-civil rights students tended to rank *freedom* highly. The experimenter concluded that "this raises the question as to whether those who are against civil rights are really saying that they care a great deal about their own freedom but are indifferent to other people's freedom." Subjects were then asked to compare their own rankings with those of the previously tested SIU students.

Subjects then completed four 11-point scales (Rokeach, 1973, p. 427) measuring their response to the experimental session and their degree of satisfaction with their rankings of the 18 values. They were then asked to indicate whether they were satisfied or dissatisfied with their ratings of each of the 18 terminal values (Rokeach, 1973, p. 428). After being reassured of the confidentiality of their responses and thanked for their time, subjects were dismissed.

In all three experimental sessions all subjects received a test booklet with instructions for completing the Value Scale and the other scales, and tables 1 and 2. In the interpersonal session, the experimenter described the tables, interpreted the tables, and invited subjects to compare their values with those of previous SIU students. In the television treatment session, the experimenter presented the same messages in the same order, via black-and-white video tape. The tape was made using a single, stationary camera. The image presented was of the experimenter standing with notes in hand delivering a lecture in the same manner which he used in the live session.

A group of seven instructors and graduate students in Speech viewed the live presentation and the video tape, rating each on seven dimensions of delivery and style. Their ratings, when analyzed by the "t" test, indicated no overall differences in style and delivery between the two presentations.

In the print treatment session, the test booklet contained instructions for completing the Value Survey and the other scales, and tables 1 and 2, just as it had in the other two sessions; however, in this instance, it also contained, verbatim, the descriptions of the tables, interpretations of the tables, and the invitations to subjects to make value comparisons. In the control session, subjects were given the pretest and dismissed.

A first posttest, using the terminal value scale only, was administered to all groups two weeks after the pretesting and treatment sessions. A second posttest was administered four weeks after the treatment session, and a third posttest was administered six weeks after the treatment session.

By the end of the third posttesting period, attrition had reduced the number of subjects to a total of 135, 76 percent of the 181 who had initially volunteered for the study. It was on this group of subjects that all statistical tests were calculated.

One week after the third posttesting period, all 135 subjects were sent a form letter on NAACP stationery from the National Education Director of the NAACP Special Contribution Fund. The letter invited subjects to join the organization for a fee of two dollars. Enclosed in the mailing envelope, postmarked in Chicago, Illinois, was a self-addressed return envelope.

RESULTS

One-way analysis of variance of the pretest mean rankings for *equality* and *freedom* show no significant difference among the four groups—control, interpersonal, television, and written. The mean rank for *equality* was 9.54 across the four groups (F = 0.82, $p > .05$). The mean rank for *freedom* was 6.76 (F = 0.38, $p > .05$). Analysis of the control group across the four testing periods showed no significant difference in the rankings of either *equality* or *freedom*. The mean rank for *equality* was 9.00 (F = .09, $p > .05$), and the mean for *freedom* was 6.98 (F = 0.23, $p > .05$). These outcomes suggest that the assignment of subjects to treatment conditions was successful in establishing groups with substantially equivalent pretest value rankings for the two test values, and that no external influences appear to have been operating that would produce changes in ranking of the test values. Hence, any change in the rankings of the test values by the treatment groups is likely to be due to the independent variables. Hypotheses were tested in an analysis of variance design with two between-groups dimensions (Channel [B] and satisfied–dissatisfied [C]) and one within-groups dimension (pretest-posttest [A]).

Hypothesis 1. Hypothesis 1 asserted that subjects who became dissatisfied with their original ranking of *freedom* would (a) increase their ranking of *freedom* from pretest to first posttest more than would subjects who remain satisfied with their original ranking of *freedom,* and (b) that this change would persist. Both parts of this hypothesis were confirmed.

Twenty-two of the 89 experimental subjects became dissatisfied with their initial ranking of *freedom,* while 67 remained satisfied. As predicted, the AC interaction (pretest–posttest by satisfied–dissatisfied) was significant ($F = 5.09$, $p < .01$). The "A" main effect of the repeated measures within groups was also significant ($F = 15.06$, $p < .01$). Figure 14.1 presents, graphically, the trends which were under way during the experiment.

As shown in Figure 14.1, the pretest mean for the dissatisfied group was 9.09. This score moved upward by 5.23 rankings to 3.86 at posttest 1. The pretest mean for the satisfied group was 6.00. This score moved upward by one ranking to 5.00 at posttest 1. The Scheffe test (Kirk, 1968, pp. 266–269) indicates that the difference of 5.23 between the pretest mean and the first posttest mean for dissatisfied subjects was significantly larger ($F = 53.43$, $p < .05$) than the difference of 1.00 between the pretest mean and the first posttest mean for the satisfied subjects. These findings, and a significant AC interaction, confirm part

Figure 14.1   Means for Satisfied and Dissatisfied Subjects for Pretest and Three Posttests: Freedom

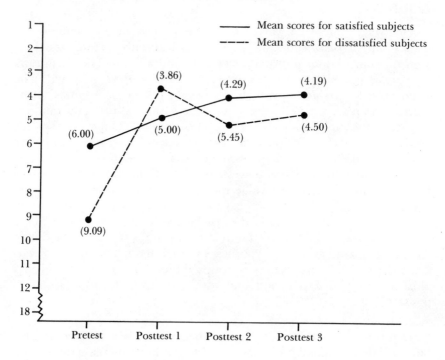

"a" of Hypothesis 1. Dissatisfied subjects increased their ranking of *freedom* from pretest to first posttest more than did satisfied subjects.

In addition, for dissatisfied subjects, the differences between the pretest mean (9.09) and the third posttest mean (4.50) was significant. However, the difference (3.64) between the pretest mean (9.09) and the second posttest mean (5.45) was slightly less than the Scheffe smallest significant difference of 3.68. This latter finding should be discounted, considering the number of significance tests performed. It is clearly contrary to the trends illustrated in all of the other data presented here. Thus, taking into account the significant "A" main effect, the lack of significant differences among the three posttest means for either satisfied or dissatisfied subjects, and a lack of significant difference between the pretest mean for satisfied subjects and any of the posttest means, one should accept part "b" of Hypothesis 1. The changes produced by self-confrontation persisted.

Hypothesis 2. Hypothesis 2 predicted that subjects who became dissatisfied with their ranking of *equality* would (a) increase their ranking from pretest to first posttest more than would subjects who remained satisfied with their original ranking, and (b) this change would persist. Parts "a" and "b" of Hypothesis 2 were confirmed.

Twenty-six of 89 subjects expressed dissatisfaction with their initial ranking of *equality*, after self-confrontation, and 63 remained satisfied. As predicted, the AC interaction (pretest–posttest by satisfied–dissatisfied) was significant ($F = 9.89$, $p < .01$). The "A" main effect, pretest–posttest, was also significant ($F = 24.35$, $p < .01$). The outcomes depicted in Figure 14.2 for *equality* mirror those depicted in Figure 14.1 for *freedom*.

Application of the Scheffe test indicated that the difference (5.15 rankings) between the pretest mean (11.69) and the first posttest mean (6.54) for dissatisfied subjects was significantly larger ($F = 46.78$, $p < .05$) than the difference (1.84) between pretest mean (9.19) and the first posttest mean (7.35) for satisfied subjects. This finding, and the significant AC interaction mentioned earlier, confirm part "a" of Hypothesis 2. Dissatisfied subjects increased their ranking of *equality* more than did satisfied subjects.

In addition, for dissatisfied subjects, the difference between the pretest mean (11.69) and each of the three posttest means was significant. In the case of satisfied subjects, none of the differences between the pretest mean and the posttest means were significant. There were no significant differences among any of the posttest means for either the satisfied or dissatisfied groups. These findings confirm part "b" of Hypothesis 2. The changes produced in the ratings of *equality* persisted through the second and third posttests.

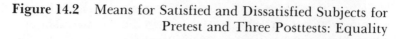

Figure 14.2   Means for Satisfied and Dissatisfied Subjects for
Pretest and Three Posttests: Equality

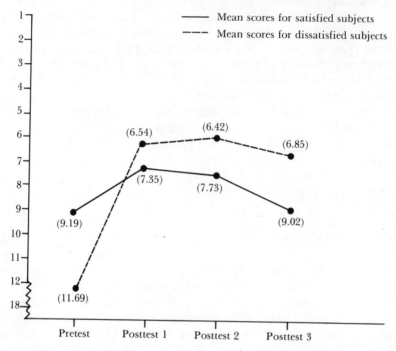

Hypotheses 3 and 4. Hypotheses 3 and 4 asserted that for *freedom* and *equality,* subjects who became dissatisfied with their original rankings would, when invited, join the NAACP in larger numbers than would those who remained satisfied with their original rankings. Only one of the 135 experimental and control subjects who were invited to join the NAACP did so, and he was in the control group! Hypotheses 3 and 4 are, therefore, rejected.

Hypothesis 5. Hypothesis 5 predicted that there would be no differences among the interpersonal, television, and print groups in terms of (a) the amount of value change induced, or (b) the number of subjects who, when invited, joined the NAACP. This prediction was confirmed. Analysis of variance results indicated that the channel main effect (B) for *freedom* was not significant ($F = 0.14$, $p > .05$) nor did the channel (B) main effect for *equality* yield a significant outcome ($F = 0.36$, $p > .05$). There were, of course, no differences, for either value, in the number of persons who joined the NAACP.

DISCUSSION

The value changes produced in this study confirm the findings of Rokeach and several other researchers. Self-confrontation produced self-dissatisfaction in some subjects. Self-dissatisfaction, in turn, led to value shifts which persisted for six weeks. The time period involved in this study was considerably shorter than the 15- to 17-month periods used in earlier experiments, but the outcomes, in terms of value change, were remarkably similar.

The theoretical explanation of the changes reported here, and in previous studies, cannot be as clear as are the consistencies displayed by their results. Self-confrontation is said to produce self-dissatisfaction when one's value rankings are inconsistent with one's conceptions of self. Unfortunately, neither this study, nor any of those referred to earlier, speak directly to this proposition. There are no data here on the conceptions which subjects held of themselves. Given the cultural context of this study, we assume that many of our subjects saw themselves as fair-minded, just persons and that their disparate ratings of *freedom* and *equality* might conflict with these perceptions. However, such assumptions are a poor substitute for data. Until the notion of self-concept is better operationalized, in this theoretical context, explanations as to why some persons experience self-dissatisfaction and others do not, and explanations as to why self-dissatisfaction leads to long-term value change will be less than satisfactory. This deficiency should not, however, detract from the several studies which indicate that, for some subjects, self-dissatisfaction does, indeed, produce profound value change.

The value changes reported here were produced regardless of the channel through which self-confrontational information was presented. These results, plus the work of Rokeach and McLellan (1972) indicating that objective feedback about one's values may not be a necessary precondition to value change, and the Rokeach study (Chapter 13) indicating that the interactive computer, with no targeted values programmed, can produce such changes, suggest that the self-confrontational technique holds dramatic implications for communication theory and practice. Can public speeches, of short duration, produce enduring changes in the values of the audience through self-confrontation? Are interpersonal communication classes regularly producing value change due to their self-conscious effort to get students to examine their values, attitudes, and behaviors, particularly in regard to self and significant others?

Can fundamental changes be made in national values through the mass media? Why could there not be a national values test just as easily as there was a national drivers' test? Could not a mass audience be asked to rank values, if necessary, and be presented with rankings of several groups of significant others, with predictable and sustained results? If one takes the evidence at face value, these are provocative, ominous questions.

One aspect of the earlier studies was disconfirmed in this study. Anticipated behavioral changes were not observed. Only one subject joined the NAACP. Earlier researchers sent a personal letter on NAACP stationery, addressing the subject by first name, and asking for a one-dollar membership fee. This study sent a form letter on NAACP stationery, addressing the subject generally, and asked for a two-dollar membership fee. These differences, however, probably did not account for the absence of a meaningful response. It is more likely that, by the summer of 1972, joining the NAACP was not perceived as being functionally related to increases in appreciation for *freedom* and *equality*. Civil rights may simply not have been as relevant to college students in 1972 as they were in the late 1960s when Rokeach and his colleagues were conducting their experiments. However, this should not be a matter for speculation in future studies. Researchers must determine *in advance* what behaviors are perceived to be functionally related to the values and attitudes they intend to study. The theory does not predict that behaviors perceived to be functionally relevant by the experimenter will undergo change. It predicts, rather, that behaviors which are functionally relevant to subjects will undergo change. Such determinations can and should be made in advance if further light is to be shed on the apparently complicated relationship between value change and subsequent overt behavior.

Finally, some will contend that this study, for the purposes of control, so reduced differences among channels that they were not allowed to exert measurable influence. For example, the interpersonal presentation did not involve feedback between subjects and the experimenter, as would be the case in a naturalistic setting. The televised treatment did not utilize elaborate production techniques. These decisions may not have, to say the least, maximized experimental variance. In any case, value change was induced by all channels, indicating that value theory, and the research it has stimulated, deserves attention from students of human communication.

15

Can Values Be Manipulated Arbitrarily?

Milton Rokeach and Joel W. Grube

Can human values be arbitrarily manipulated? This is a question of considerable theoretical and ethical importance that has arisen in connection with recent research investigating the nature of human value systems and the conditions under which they will undergo change. A number of experimental studies now suggest that long-term changes in human values can be brought about as a result of a *self-confrontation* treatment in which individuals are given certain feedback and interpretations concerning their own and significant others' values. It has been proposed (Rokeach, 1973) that this feedback makes some individuals aware of chronically existing contradictions between their values and their self-conceptions. It is further proposed that the awareness of such inconsistencies arouses a state of self-dissatisfaction and, moreover, as one means of reducing this negative affective state some individuals will change their values to become more consistent with self-conceptions.

All told, 23 experiments have thus far reported long-term value

Study 1 was carried out by Milton Rokeach, and Study 2 by Joel W. Grube. A report of Study 2 was presented by Grube at the meetings of the Western Psychological Association, Los Angeles, Calif., in April, 1976, under the title: "The Unidirectional Nature of Value Change: An Experimental Test." We wish to thank Theodore N. Greenstein, William L. Rankin, Kathleen A. Kearney, and Barry J. Coyne for their help in conducting one or both of these studies.

241

changes as a result of such feedback about contradictions existing within the subjects' own belief systems (Rokeach, 1979). Most of these studies have focused on long-term value changes brought about as a result of feedback concerning two political values, *equality* and *freedom* (Rokeach, 1968, 1971a, 1973; Rokeach & Cochrane, 1972; Rokeach & McLellan, 1972; Penner, 1971; McLellan, 1974). But changes have also been reported in other values. In an experiment concerned with ecological issues, Hollen induced significant long-term changes in the target value *a world of beauty* (1972). In an experiment designed to persuade smokers to quit smoking, Conroy, Katkin, and Barnette (1973) induced significant long-term changes in the target value *self-controlled* (Chapter 12). In another experiment designed to improve the quality of student teachers, Greenstein (1976) induced significant long-term changes in the values *mature love, loving,* and *self-respect*. Finally, Rokeach (Chapter 13) has reported significant long-term changes in the values *a sense of accomplishment, a world at peace,* and *equality* when feedback was initiated by a computer rather than by a human experimenter.

The implications of such findings have raised important ethical questions as to possible abuses of the self-confrontation treatment. In particular, concern has been expressed that the technique might be used to manipulate values arbitrarily. However, certain theoretical considerations would suggest that direct attempts to modify any particular value within any person is an inherently unidirectional rather than bidirectional process. Previous research has already shown that long-term value change can be initiated by inducing a state of self-dissatisfaction concerning contradictions implicating self-conceptions (Rokeach, 1973); the value change is presumably motivated by a desire to maintain and, if possible, enhance one's conception of oneself as moral and competent. Thus, to reduce or remove felt dissatisfactions, a person should be willing to undergo an increase or decrease with regard to any given value mainly in one direction—in whichever direction a person perceives to be defined as competent or moral by the particular social institutions and reference groups with which he or she most identifies. Self-conceptions are social in origin, reflecting what Mead called a socially constructed self (1934) or what Cooley called a "looking glass" self (1956). They will suffer, be maintained, or be enhanced within some normative framework set by society, society's institutions, and, most of all, by various primary groups and reference groups that define morality and competence for the individuals by specifying how they ought to behave and the end-goals for which they ought to strive. Thus, the extent to which individuals will remain satisfied or become dissatisfied with themselves will depend on the extent to which they perceive themselves as conforming to the unidirectional demands of the social groups with which they most identify.

On theoretical grounds, therefore, it seems unlikely that value change (and associated cognitive and behavioral changes) could be brought about in either direction by arbitrary experimental manipulations. However, this is a question that needs to be answered empirically. This selection reports the results of two studies which attempt to test the unidirectional hypothesis. In the first study, individuals with known values were presented with a hypothetical situation in which they were asked to imagine that they were endowed with unlimited power to change other people's values, and then they were asked to indicate which of other people's values they would want to increase or decrease in importance. Second, they were asked to imagine that others were endowed with unlimited power to change values, and then to indicate whether they would oppose attempts by others to increase or decrease various values. It was believed that the responses to such hypothetical questions would reflect the direction of value change that would be tolerated by respondents—that is, reflect the extent to which such changes would be consistent with respondents' self-conceptions. The second study attempted to test the assumption that these verbal reports reflect the direction of value change that could actually be initiated in any given individual by experimental means through self-confrontation. In this study, the effectiveness of a self-confrontation treatment designed to increase the importance of the value *equality* was compared for two groups: (1) respondents who reported that they would increase the importance of *equality* for others if they had the power to do so and, moreover, would resist attempts by others to decrease its importance; and (2) respondents who reported that they would decrease the importance of *equality* for others if they had the power to do so and, moreover, would resist attempts by others to increase its importance. In the first group, increases in the importance of *equality* should be consistent with self-conceptions. It was therefore expected that the self-confrontation would result in significant increases in *equality*. In the second group, increases in the importance of *equality* should be inconsistent with self-conceptions. It was therefore expected that the self-confrontation would have no effect, that is, should not result in increases in *equality*.

A failure to support the unidirectionality hypothesis would have at least two implications. On a theoretical level, it would seriously challenge a theory which postulates that value change after self-confrontation can best be understood as the resolution of inconsistencies between value priorities and self-conceptions. A test of the unidirectionality hypothesis can be seen as a central test of this theory. If the unidirectionality hypothesis is found not to hold, it would imply that value change involves processes other than those aimed at resolving such inconsistencies. On an ethical level, a failure to support the unidirectional hypothesis might indicate that self-confrontation may potentially be abused to manipulate an individual's values arbitrarily. Such a finding would have serious social, political, and ethical implications.

STUDY 1

Method

Two hundred sixty students in introductory sociology classes at Washington State University first ranked the 18 terminal and 18 instrumental values in the Rokeach Value Survey (1967) "in order of their importance to YOU, as guiding principles in YOUR life." Both sets were presented to the students in alphabetical order. These values, along with their defining phrases, are shown in Table 15.1. Students then filled out the same two value scales "as you think they would be ranked by American Society." Rankings were completed anonymously and then collected, thus preventing the students from referring back either to their own value rankings or to the value rankings that they had attributed to "American Society."

The students were then instructed:

> Imagine that you have discovered the secret of how to change other people's values. You have the power to increase or to decrease the importance of any and all values that other people have.... Assume that you are profoundly dissatisfied with the values of American Society and that you have the power to change these values, either by increasing or decreasing their importance.
>
> You may feel that certain values in American Society are *over-emphasized* and should be made less important, and that other values in American Society are *under-emphasized* and should be made more important.
>
> For each of the values shown below, please indicate, with a check in the appropriate column, whether you would consider it desirable to increase or decrease its importance in American Society. Work carefully in checking each and every value.

The student then chose for each of the 36 values on the Rokeach Value Survey one of the following three options: "I would INCREASE the importance of this value for American Society"; "I cannot decide"; "I would DECREASE the importance of this value for American Society."

The last part of the questionnaire was designed to elicit the student's opinions about how he or she might react if others attempted to increase or decrease various values:

> Please assume now that some individuals or organizations are deliberately attempting to change people's values. Please indicate below whether you would (a) oppose efforts to *increase* the importance of a particular value, (b) oppose efforts to *decrease* the importance of a given value, or whether (c) you are undecided.

The student then responded to each of the 36 values shown in Table 15.1 by choosing one of these three options.

Results and Discussion

Table 15.1 shows the proportions of subjects ranking each value high (1-6), middle (7-12), and low (13-18) who reported they "would increase" the importance of each of the 36 values if they had the power to do so, and it also shows the proportions of subjects reporting they "would oppose decrease," if initiated by others. Also shown for each value is the correlation between subjects' self-reports about the direction of change they would themselves initiate (increase, cannot decide, decrease) and the direction of change they would resist if initiated by others (oppose increase, cannot decide, oppose decrease). The correlations shown are coefficients of contingencies, corrected for number of categories (Siegel, 1956). Inspection of Table 15.1 reveals the following:

1. The subjects' own ranking of a particular value is a significant predictor of the likelihood that he or she would increase, and oppose attempts by others to decrease, its importance. Typically, larger proportions of subjects ranking a value high report they would increase, and also that they would oppose decrease of its importance. These relationships are statistically significant in virtually all comparisons. By chi square (df = 4), 52 of the 72 high-middle-low comparisons shown in Table 15.1 are significant beyond the .001, 13 beyond the .01, and 6 beyond the .05 level.

2. These significant relationships notwithstanding, we nonetheless note that there are many values that sizable majorities of all subgroups report they would increase and oppose decrease, regardless of where they themselves had ranked these values. Thus, 96, 93, and 62 percent of the subjects ranking *a world at peace* high, middle, and low, respectively, report they would increase it if they could, and 96, 93, and 75 percent, respectively, report they would resist attempts by others to decrease the importance of *a world at peace*.

Similar findings are obtained for *a world of beauty, equality, freedom, happiness, true friendship, wisdom,* being *broadminded, cheerful, forgiving, helpful, honest, loving,* and *responsible.* Regardless of where the subjects had ranked these values, a majority reported that they would increase their importance, and also that they would oppose attempts by others to decrease their importance.

It should be noted that *equality* and *freedom,* the most frequent targets for change in previous research, are included in the above list. Because these two are distinctively political values (Rokeach, 1973), it would not be surprising if the greatest ethical concern were expressed about the possibility of a manipulator decreasing the importance of these particu-

TABLE 15.1. Percent of Subjects Ranking Each Value High, Medium, and Low Who Would Increase and Who Would Oppose Attempts by Others to Decrease Each of 36 Values

	% Who Would Increase			% Who Would Oppose Decrease			
	High	Middle	Low	High	Middle	Low	C
Terminal values							
A comfortable life (a prosperous life)	38	18	18	54	42	27	.71
An exciting life (a stimulating, active life)	72	53	28	80	61	34	.80
A sense of accomplishment (lasting contribution)	86	59	37	73	72	40	.65
A world at peace (free of war and conflict)	96	93	62	96	93	75	.66
A world of beauty (beauty of nature and the arts)	90	89	70	93	90	65	.81
Equality (brotherhood, equal opportunity for all)	100	90	72	98	93	74	.72
Family security (taking care of loved ones)	84	67	45	91	81	57	.73
Freedom (independence, free choice)	79	75	56	91	85	82	.55
Happiness (contentedness)	85	70	67	93	76	68	.54
Inner harmony (freedom from inner conflict)	91	74	49	91	80	53	.63
Mature love (sexual and spiritual intimacy)	79	57	37	83	67	53	.72
National security (protection from attack)	17	53	17	67	64	26	.74
Pleasure (an enjoyable, leisurely life)	47	49	23	60	67	41	.63
Salvation (saved, eternal life)	94	67	16	94	64	20	.83

Self-respect (self-esteem)	88	62	50	89	70	58	.65
Social recognition (respect, admiration)	25	17	7	42	32	19	.71
True friendship (close companionship)	96	83	83	97	88	87	.69
Wisdom (a mature understanding of life)	91	85	57	86	81	58	.67

Instrumental values

Ambitious (hard-working, aspiring)	67	58	37	73	63	39	.73
Broadminded (open-minded)	97	93	76	94	89	73	.72
Capable (competent, effective)	74	58	42	93	64	56	.69
Cheerful (lightheard, joyful)	86	77	66	95	80	64	.60
Clean (neat, tidy)	76	62	34	87	73	42	.78
Courageous (standing up for your beliefs)	74	77	50	81	81	53	.70
Forgiving (willing to pardon others)	96	90	72	92	92	71	.77
Helpful (working for the welfare of others)	96	94	76	91	94	78	.72
Honest (sincere, truthful)	96	90	83	97	94	79	.38
Imaginative (daring, creative)	85	70	36	81	76	54	.73
Independent (self-reliant, self-sufficient)	79	59	34	81	71	46	.69
Intellectual (intelligent, reflective)	76	48	27	80	67	40	.72
Logical (consistent, rational)	85	68	37	82	71	48	.73
Loving (affectionate, tender)	93	90	53	94	91	58	.77
Obedient (dutiful, respectful)	80	74	30	70	76	35	.77
Polite (courteous, well-mannered)	98	70	43	95	79	45	.82
Responsible (dependable, reliable)	90	85	68	91	82	68	.75
Self-controlled (restrained, self-disciplined)	84	75	40	90	80	47	.75

247

lar values. Thus, it is somewhat reassuring to note that the majority of the subjects reported they would want to see these two values increased and not decreased. Presumably, experimental attempts to decrease their importance would be directed mainly toward persons ranking them middle or high rather than low. Such experimental attempts are not likely to prove successful in view of the large majorities reporting that they prefer to see these values increased, and in view of the fact that these majorities become even larger as we proceed from low to middle to high rankings of *equality* and *freedom.*

Similarly, the data suggest that sizable majorities of the subjects would be receptive to an increase, and unreceptive to a decrease, in the importance of the other values mentioned above—*a world at peace, a world of beauty,* and so on. In view of these findings, it is again difficult to envision what sort of experimental procedure or feedback might persuade subjects to decrease whatever importance they might attach to all such values.

3. Two values—*a comfortable life* and *social recognition*—provide us with similar results except that they are in the opposite direction. Regardless of whether subjects ranked these two values high, middle, or low, only a minority report that they would want to increase their importance. Most subjects report they would rather decrease their importance or that they are "not certain," and, moreover, that they would resist efforts to increase their importance.

4. Most of the remaining values shown in Table 15.1 fall somewhere in between the two types of values just discussed. Consider the findings for *salvation.* Over 90 percent of the subjects ranking *salvation* high report that they would increase and, also, that they would oppose a decrease in the importance of *salvation.* These proportions decline to two-thirds for those ranking *salvation* in the middle, and to about 20 percent for those ranking *salvation* in the bottom third of the value scale. In other words, a majority of subjects ranking this value high would like to see others rank it high too, and a majority of those ranking it low would like to see the converse.

Several other values show a similar pattern. Note especially the findings for *an exciting life, a sense of accomplishment,* being *ambitious, clean, independent, logical, obedient, polite,* and *self-controlled.* Subjects ranking them high generally report they would like to see others rank them high too, and also that they would oppose attempts by others to reduce their importance; subjects ranking them low generally report the converse.

In summary, three kinds of values are shown in Table 15.1: (1) There are certain values that large majorities of subjects report they would increase and oppose decrease, regardless of their own value rankings. Thus, it seems unlikely that attempts to manipulate these values downward would prove to be generally successful. (2) There are other values that most subjects would decrease and oppose increase, regardless of their own value rankings. Thus, it seems unlikely that attempts to manipulate such values upward would prove successful. (3) There is a third class of values that most subjects would increase and oppose decrease if they are ranked high, and, conversely, would decrease and oppose increase if they are ranked low. Thus, it seems unlikely that a person ranking such values high could be persuaded to reduce their importance and, conversely, it is unlikely that a person ranking them low could be persuaded to increase their importance.

The data considered thus far show only that the proportion of subjects who report they would increase a value's importance parallel closely the proportions reporting they would oppose attempts by others to decrease its importance. They do not, however, inform us about the extent to which it is the same subjects who consistently do both. This information is given in the last column of Table 15.1— the correlation (corrected coefficient of contingency) between direction of change that the subjects report they would initiate if they could, and the direction of change they would resist if initiated by others. These correlations are usually high, averaging around .70, and they provide us with compelling evidence for the unidirectionality hypothesis.

To help us interpret these correlations, consider the following three examples: (1) *Equality* shows a correlation of .72 between the direction of change that the subjects would initiate and the direction of change they would resist if initiated by others. The great majority of all subjects (85%) reported that they would increase *equality*'s importance, and only a handful (6%) reported they would decrease its importance. But a majority of both groups (95 and 53%, respectively) reported they would oppose changes in the opposite direction. (2) *Salvation* shows a correlation of .83 between direction of change initiated by self and others. Fifty percent of all subjects reported that they would increase *salvation*'s importance, and 25 percent reported they would decrease its importance. But, here again, a majority of both groups (87 and 70%, respectively) reported they would oppose changes in an opposite direction. (3) Finally, *a comfortable life* shows a correlation of .71 between direction of change initiated by self and others. About one-fourth of all subjects reported that they would increase and about one-half reported that they would decrease the importance of *a comfortable life* if they could. And, once again, a majority of both groups (82 and 70%, respectively) reported they would oppose attempts to change this particular value in the opposite direction.

In other words, regardless of the degree or direction of consensus expressed about a particular value, regardless of whether a subject ranked a particular value high or middle or low, and regardless of whether a subject ranked it as others do, the findings suggest that a great majority of the subjects have definite opinions about wanting either to increase or to decrease a particular value, and would resist efforts by others to alter that value in the opposite direction.

These correlational data lead us to conclude that it is unlikely that any of the 36 values shown in Table 15.1 could be arbitrarily manipulated to conform to some experimenter's whims. Rather, they suggest that each person, perhaps because of his or her having been influenced or socialized by certain social institutions and reference groups, has become highly partial about the direction of value change he or she would be willing to tolerate. Presumably, this tolerance will be in one direction or the other—in whatever direction a person anticipates a certain mileage or gain for his or her self-conception. Thus, the data reported here provide at least some reassurance to those who might be concerned about the possibility that the previously reported value change procedures via feedback of one's own and others' values might be put to sinister uses. Such reassurance is, however, somewhat tentative, since the data are correlational rather than experimental in nature. Study 2 was designed to provide experimental evidence about the unidirectional nature of value change. In this experiment, we first identified individuals who reported that they would welcome or that they would resist a change in the value *equality,* and we subsequently exposed these individuals to a self-confrontation treatment designed to increase the value for *equality.* If the unidirectional hypothesis is valid, we should expect a significant increase in *equality* in the former group, but not in the latter group.

STUDY 2

Method

Eight hundred and fifty students in introductory sociology and psychology classes at Washington State University first filled out the Rokeach Value Survey (Rokeach, 1967), ranking the two lists of 18 values in order of importance as guiding principles in their own lives. Then, as in Study 1, the participants were asked to imagine that they had discovered the secret of changing other people's values. Their task was to indicate whether they would increase or decrease the importance of each of the 36 values from the Rokeach Value Survey if they had the power to do so. The participants were next asked to imagine that certain other individuals or organizations were attempting to change people's values, and to indicate for each value if they would (1) resist efforts to increase the importance of that value or (2) resist efforts to decrease the importance of that value.

Approximately one week later, 64 of these students were contacted by phone and invited to participate in another study that was to be conducted within two or three days. These were solicited from among the original 850 participants because they had all ranked the value *equality* low, that is, 13 or lower on the 18-value ranking scale.

One experimental group consisted of 30 individuals who had (1) indicated that they would decrease the importance of the value *equality* for American society if given the chance to do so, and (2) indicated that they would oppose attempts by others to increase the importance of this value. It was assumed that this group's low rankings of the value *equality* were consistent with their self-conceptions, and it was therefore hypothesized that this group—the value-consistent group—would not be affected by a self-confrontation treatment designed to influence them to increase the importance of *equality*.

A second experimental group—the value-inconsistent group— consisted of 34 individuals who had (1) indicated a week before that they would increase the importance of the value *equality* for American society if given the chance, and (2) indicated that they would oppose the efforts of others to decrease the importance of *equality*. It was assumed that these individuals had self-conceptions that were inconsistent with their low rankings of the value *equality*, and it was therefore predicted that these individuals would increase their rankings of *equality* as a result of self-confrontation, in order to make this value more consistent with their self-conceptions.

A third group—the control group—consisted of 32 individuals randomly selected from another pool of 100 introductory sociology and psychology students. All these 32 subjects had also ranked *equality* 13 or lower. This group did not complete the questionnaire asking them whether they would welcome or resist increasing or decreasing the importance of the values, nor did they undergo the self-confrontation treatment. This control group was included in order to provide a baseline against which to compare the results obtained for the two experimental groups.

During the treatment session, the participants in the experimental groups were first asked to rank the 18 terminal values from the Rokeach Value Survey. They were then shown a chart (Table 15.2), which depicted the average value rankings that had been previously obtained from Washington State University students. Their attention was drawn to the finding that previously tested college students had, on the average, ranked *freedom* fourth, and *equality* eleventh. To arouse feelings of dissatisfaction, the experimenter interpreted these findings to mean that "Washington State University students, in general, are much more concerned with their own freedom than they are with the freedom of other people." The experimental participants were then asked to spend a few moments comparing their own rankings of the same 18 values with the tabular results presented.

Then, to increase the level of self-dissatisfaction even further, the participants were asked to state the extent of their sympathy with the aims of civil rights movements by checking one of three options: (1) I am sympathetic, and I have personally participated in a civil rights demonstration, (2) I am sympathetic, but I have not participated in a civil rights demonstration, or (3) I am not sympathetic with the aims of the civil rights movement. Immediately afterward, they were shown a second chart (Table 15.3), which displayed a highly significant positive relationship between attitude toward civil rights demonstrations and ranking of *equality.*

The experimenter interpreted these results as follows: "This raises the question as to whether those who are against civil rights are really saying that they care a great deal about their own freedom, but are indifferent to other people's freedom. Those who are for civil rights are perhaps saying that they not only want freedom for themselves, but for other people too."

Once again, the participants were invited to compare their own rankings of *freedom* and *equality,* and their own position on the civil rights issue with the tabular results they were shown.

TABLE 15.2. Average Value System of 216 Washington
State University Students Shown to Experimental
Participants to Arouse Self-Dissatisfaction

14	A COMFORTABLE LIFE
12	AN EXCITING LIFE
10	A SENSE OF ACCOMPLISHMENT
9	A WORLD AT PEACE
15	A WORLD OF BEAUTY
11	EQUALITY
8	FAMILY SECURITY
4	FREEDOM
1	HAPPINESS
2	INNER HARMONY
5	MATURE LOVE
18	NATIONAL SECURITY
13	PLEASURE
16	SALVATION
6	SOCIAL RECOGNITION
17	SELF-RESPECT
3	TRUE FRIENDSHIP
7	WISDOM

TABLE 15.3. Information Presented to Experimental Participants to Arouse Self-Dissatisfaction

	AVERAGE RANKINGS OF *Freedom* AND *Equality* BY STUDENTS FOR AND AGAINST CIVIL RIGHTS		
	Sympathetic and Have Participated	Sympathetic but Have Not Participated	Not Sympathetic
Freedom	1	6	5
Equality	5	9	15

The treatment session for the control group followed the same basic procedure as for the experimental groups. The control participants ranked their own values and were shown the average value rankings of the Washington State students, as presented in Table 15.2. However, their attention was not focused on the values *freedom* and *equality*. In addition, they indicated their degree of sympathy with the civil rights movement, but were given neither the information presented in Table 15.3 nor the experimenter's interpretation of the value rankings.

The value posttest was mailed to the participants five weeks after the treatment sessions. The posttest consisted of the Rokeach Value Survey (Rokeach, 1967), and several additional measures of attitude and personality which were employed for other purposes, and will therefore not be further discussed here. The posttest was mailed by Washington State University's Social Research Center; it was identified as the Fall 1974 Student Information Survey. A cover letter explained that the survey was being conducted in order to assess student opinion on a number of school-related, local, and national issues. To protect further against artifact, the survey was completely anonymous, matched with pretest data on the basis of several demographic questions (e.g., sex, birthdate, and city and state of birth). A postage-paid return envelope was enclosed with the surveys.

Results and Discussion

The most appropriate analyses for these data is an *a priori* t test comparing the mean *equality* rankings at the posttest adjusted for the *equality* rankings obtained at the treatment session. To obtain these adjusted means and a pooled estimate of the variance to be used in calculating the t tests, an analysis of covariance was applied to the data before proceeding with the planned comparisons. This analysis revealed an overall effect for groups, $F(2,86) = 2.87$, $p < .06$. The adjusted means obtained from this analysis of covariance are presented in Table 15.4. As predicted, the planned comparisons revealed that the adjusted mean

TABLE 15.4.   Mean *Equality* Rankings at the Posttest Adjusted by Analysis of Covariance for *Equality* Rankings at the Treatment Session*

Group	Posttest
No treatment control	13.34
	(31)
Value-consistent	13.55
	(26)
Value-inconsistent	11.47
	(30)

*Numbers in parentheses indicate the number of participants in each group who completed and returned the posttest.

equality ranking for the value-inconsistent group was significantly higher than for either the control group, $t(86) = 2.15$, $p < .05$, or the value-consistent group, $t(86) = 2.29$, $p < .05$. The adjusted mean *equality* ranking for the value-consistent group did not differ significantly from that of the control group, $t(86) = 0.23$.

The important finding of Study 2 is that the self-confrontation treatment led to significant increases in the rankings of the value *equality* only for those experimental participants who had previously stated that they would initiate an increase in *equality* in others if given the opportunity to do so, who, moreover, would not resist attempts by others to increase the importance of *equality*. In the context of our theory of cognitive change (Rokeach, 1973), these individuals were those for whom low rankings of *equality* were inconsistent with self-conceptions. For these individuals, increases in *equality* rankings should serve to maintain and enhance self-conceptions or self-esteem.

In contrast, no such increases in the rankings of *equality* were found for those experimental participants who had previously stated that they would decrease the importance of *equality* for others if they had the power to do so, who, moreover, would resist attempts by others to increase the importance of this value. For these individuals, such increases would not serve to enhance or maintain self-conceptions. The finding that this group did not increase its value for *equality* is consistent with the predictions and supports the unidirectional hypothesis.

GENERAL DISCUSSION

One of us has proposed earlier (Rokeach, 1973) that individuals will organize their beliefs and behaviors in ways that will serve to maintain and enhance their self-conceptions as moral and competent human beings. To the extent that an individual's beliefs or performances in a specific situation are realized to be inconsistent with such self-conceptions, a negative affective state of self-dissatisfaction will be aroused. To alleviate or reduce this negative affective state, individuals will change their beliefs or behaviors so that they will become more consistent with self-conceptions.

An easily applied cognitive and behavior change technique called "self-confrontation" has been developed from this theory. This treatment is designed to provide individuals with information that will lead to awareness of chronically existing inconsistencies within the belief–behavior system. To the extent that these inconsistencies implicate self-conceptions, a state of dissatisfaction is expected to be aroused and cognitive–behavioral changes will follow. Numerous studies have demonstrated that value, attitude, and behavior changes can be initiated by this process, and that such changes can persist as long as 21 months after a single treatment (Rokeach, 1973). Research also indicates that the primary psychological mechanism that leads to these changes is the arousal of a state of self-dissatisfaction. Such studies have uniformly shown that value changes following self-confrontation are directly related to reported levels of self-dissatisfaction for experimental participants who received a self-confrontation treatment. In one study (Grube, 1978), value changes were found to be systematically related to level of self-dissatisfaction, even among persons who were not exposed to an experimental treatment. In addition, while most of the research in this area has addressed value change and value-mediated behavior change, recent evidence (Grube, Greenstein, Rankin, & Kearney, 1977) suggests that self-dissatisfaction also leads to non-value-mediated behavior change following self-confrontation.

While the preponderance of evidence strongly supports this theory and indicates a practical method for initiating cognitive and behavioral change, some aspects of the theory have remained untested. Specifically, it would follow from the theory that cognitive and behavior change following self-confrontation should be unidirectional—that is, possible only in the direction that reduces self-dissatisfaction and increases consistency with self-conceptions. However, some concern has been expressed that this might not be the case, and that self-confrontation may potentially be abused to manipulate values, attitudes, and behaviors arbitrarily (Schwartz, 1974). The studies presented in this selection represent an attempt to test the hypothesis that value change following self-confrontation is of a unidirectional nature, and that this direction is determined by any given individual's own self-conceptions, not by experimenter whim.

The findings of these two studies strongly support the unidirectional hypothesis. It is apparent that individuals are selective about the direction of value change that they say they are willing to tolerate and, further, that the actual changes initiated by self-confrontation seem to conform to these verbal reports. These findings are most easily interpreted as being consistent with the proposition that the major determinant of value change is self-dissatisfaction, resulting from awareness of inconsistencies between values and socially defined self-conceptions. Thus, it seems unlikely that self-confrontation can be abused to initiate arbitrary changes in values, attitudes, and behavior.

PART FOUR

Value Education Through Self-Awareness

16

Value Education in Educational Settings

Milton Rokeach

A great deal has been written in recent years about value education—a burgeoning field that has attracted and generated wide interest and controversy. Various theories and strategies have been proposed about the best way to advance value education—values clarification, moral development, moral education, focusing on the valuing process, and teaching value skills.[1]

What is value education, and what ought it to be? To what extent should value education be value-free, and to what extent should it frankly try to inculcate students with certain values? Is it possible to make students aware of their values without at the same time modifying them? Who else besides teachers in educational settings can properly and improperly be concerned with value education? My purpose in this chapter is to propose a view of the functions of value education in various institutional settings in general and within educational settings in particular. This view derives from considerations about the role that

[1]A good summary of various approaches to values education can be found in works edited by Meyer, Burnham, and Cholvat (1975), and by Meyer (1976). In 1975 the *Phi Delta Kappan* published a special issue on various approaches to and critiques of moral education.

social institutions play in inculcating and implementing various subsets of human values, as discussed in Chapter 3, and the social antecedents and consequents of individual values, as discussed in Rokeach (1973). It will differ in a number of respects from certain prevailing views about value education. More specifically, I will propose that value education within educational settings cannot and should not remain value-free, and that educators are not performing their educational functions unless they attempt to change certain values in certain directions, and unless they convey factual information to students about their own and about others' values. To prepare the groundwork for my advocacy of such views, I will first discuss in a general way the major functions that I believe are served by all social institutions, and then consider in particular the main functions of educational institutions.

INSTITUTIONAL VALUES

A main point of departure is the premise that the major determinants of human values are culture, society, and society's institutions. All societies can be conceptualized as having a more or less common set of social institutions—for instance, religious, economic, and educational institutions. And each institution can further be defined or conceptualized as specializing in the transmission of certain subsets of values from generation to generation, and as engaging in various activities designed to implement these values. Thus conceived, an educational institution is one that specializes in the transmission and implementation of a certain cluster of values that are called educational values, a religious institution is one that specializes in the transmission and implementation of another cluster of values that are called religious values. And so on for other social institutions. The total spectrum of human values has, in essence, been divided up among the various social institutions in order to facilitate their transmission and implementation. Presumably, such a differentiation of function or division of labor is functional, both for the society that makes various demands upon individuals, and for individuals that depend upon society to help meet their various needs.

If it is indeed the case that all social institutions have a value-transmission function, then it can be expected that they will each exhibit some sort of value inculcation program—a program designed to inculcate their specialized values among those falling under their jurisdiction. From the standpoint of a particular social institution, inculcation will typically be seen as education, but from the standpoint of critics it may be seen as indoctrination or propaganda. Thus, military institutions will set up "educational programs" designed to inculcate military values among their recruits, religious institutions will set up schools designed to inculcate religious values, and educational institutions will set up schools designed to inculcate students with educational values. In some cases, value inculcation will proceed formally—as, for example, through the Sunday school, the military academy, or the grade school—while in other cases it will proceed informally—as, for example, through the values transmitted by the family and the economic or political institutions of society.

The particular day-to-day activities that are engaged in to implement the value-transmission function will differ, of course, from one social institution to another. Whereas the military institution will train soldiers to obey orders, to conform to various military norms, and to fight, religious institutions will engage in various sacred and ritualistic activities, and economic institutions will engage in various commercial or financial activities. In each case, we may anticipate that institutionally related activities will be coordinated with and instrumentally related to the realization of whatever are the values in which the institution specializes.

Like other components of social systems, social institutions are interrelated and interdependent. In order for societies to survive, there must be a certain amount of cooperation between them. However, as Gouldner (1970) and other conflict theorists have noted, interinstitutional relations are also characterized by conflict. They will compete with one another for priority in drawing upon a society's resources, and they will also compete with one another for influence or control over individual value systems. The hierarchical structure of an individual's or group's value system is, in some part, an end result of interinstitutional competition. Thus, to the extent that one social institution succeeds in influencing an individual, we may anticipate that the values of this institution will exhibit a high priority within this individual's value system, and the specialized values of other social institutions will necessarily exhibit a lower priority. If the religious institution of our society were the most powerful of all social institutions, we should exhibit individual value systems wherein religious values have the greatest priority; if, instead, the military institution is the most powerful, we should all exhibit individual value systems wherein military values are the most important.

It is not necessary to assume, however, that all the values in which any one social institution specializes are altogether different from those of all other institutions. There will be cooperation as well as competition among social institutions, as Parsons' structural–functional theory of society suggests (1951). Institutions may overlap, share, or have mutually supportive values. Two or more social institutions may reinforce one another in transmitting and implementing certain human values, as is the case with the family and the educational and religious institutions within the United States.

EMPIRICAL IDENTIFICATION OF INSTITUTIONAL VALUES

If it is indeed the case that each social institution transmits certain values to succeeding generations, then it would be helpful if we were able to identify them more specifically. It would be especially helpful in the present context if we were able to identify those that we call "educational values." As suggested in Chapter 3, it is possible to do so in five ways: (1) by measuring the values of the "gatekeepers" of the various social institutions, such as ministers and priests, military officers, corporation executives, school superintendents, and teachers; (2) by measuring the values of those who can be assumed to have been especially influenced by one or another social institution, such as regular church-goers, seminary students, and military cadets; (3) by measuring the perceived values of the social institution by gatekeepers; (4) by measuring the perceived values of the general clientele of the institution; or (5) through a content analysis of the values contained in institutional documents, such as religious writings or educational journals.

By employing a combination of these methods, we are in the process of compiling comprehensive lists of various institutional values. In some cases we have ascertained the distinctive values of certain social institutions by content analysis. In most cases we have relied on a standardized value test (Rokeach, 1967) that employs preselected lists of values, as previously described in this volume. This instrument, typically employed to measure individual values, is now also being employed to identify institutional values—by ascertaining the value rankings of gatekeepers, by ascertaining the value rankings of those known to have been especially influenced by social institutions, and by measuring value image, that is, the perceived values of an institution.

While the empirical research we are engaged in is by no means complete, it is possible from our present findings and also from Feather's (1975b) findings to identify certain values as being distinctively the values of one or another social institution. For instance, the terminal value *salvation* and the instrumental value *forgiving* are found to be the two main religious values, distinguishing most clearly the religious from the nonreligious. Other values like being *loving* and *helpful* are apparently not religious values, since rankings of these values do not distinguish the religious from the nonreligious. Similarly, *freedom* and *equality* are found to be distinctively political values, distinguishing most clearly people of different ideological persuasion (Rokeach, 1973; Rous & Lee, 1978; see also the chapters by Searing and by Cochrane, Billig, and Hogg in this volume). We also find that *a world of beauty* is a distinctively aesthetic value, *a comfortable life* a distinctively economic value, *family security* a distinctively family value, and *national security* a distinctively mililtary value.

Since my main focus here is on value education in educational rather than other institutional settings, it is appropriate to mention in greater detail the values that have thus far been identified as being distinctively educational ones. We find general agreement about what are the most important educational values, as determined by measurements of the perceived values of educational institutions, and as determined by rankings assigned to certain values by professors of education and by school administrators. The top four terminal values for education are *a sense of accomplishment, self-respect, wisdom* and *freedom,* and the top four instrumental values are being *responsible, capable, broadminded,* and *intellectual.* Thus, if students were to rank these values at the top of their hierarchy, it would suggest that educational values are the most important for them; conversely, if students were to rank these values at the bottom, it would suggest that educational values are far less important for them. In the latter case, there would be cause for concern and value education would be legitimately directed to changing such values.

The values mentioned above are, however, not the only ones that could properly be called educational values. We have some evidence that the terminal values *equality, inner harmony,* and *family security,* and the instrumental values, being *honest, courageous, imaginative, independent, logical,* and *helpful* are also educational values. Some of these values are also shared with other social institutions. For instance, *family security* is also a main value of the family institution, and *equality* is also a main value of the political and the judicial–legal institutions.

Thus, even though we cannot as yet be sure that we have succeeded in identifying all the values that each of the social institutions specializes in, it is nonetheless clear that there is some subset of the total spectrum of human values that can reasonably be called educational values, and that this subset is conceptually and empirically distinguishable from other subsets of human values. It is this subset that I conceive educational institutions to specialize in, to transmit, and to implement in their day-to-day institutional activities.

However tentative our present ability to identify the full range of educational values, an inspection of the ones we have been able to identify thus far suggests that the inculcation of students with educational values requires more than a mere preoccupation with their moral development. Some educational values have to do with questions or morality, while others have to do with questions of competence. If it is indeed valid to argue that a major function of the educational institution is to inculcate students with educational values, then it is also valid to argue that the educational institution is mandated to inculcate students with certain values that have nothing whatever to do with ethics or questions of right and wrong. There is nothing immoral or unethical, for instance, about behaving illogically or unimaginatively, yet the educational institution has a legitimate stake in discouraging such behavior because they are manifestations of incompetence. The inculcation of educational values requires the inculcation of competence values no less than of morality values, or, put the other way around, it requires the discouragement of incompetent behavior no less than of immoral behavior. Thus, in my view, the reduction or equating of the whole domain of value education with moral development is unwarranted. The concept of value education is a generic one that includes training in moral development, on the one hand, and training in competence development, on the other. Both kinds of development can be implemented by inculcating students with certain values that we call educational values.

TWO TYPES OF VALUE EDUCATION

Consistent with the preceding analysis, educational institutions can be said to have two closely interrelated missions: to inculcate a specific subset of values identified as educational values, and to implement the realization of these values by teaching students all sorts of substantive information and skills.

This substantive information consists of the Three Rs and all their elaborations from grade school through graduate school. They have practical purposes—to train students for a vocation or profession, to train teachers to transmit knowledge and skills to succeeding generations, and to train succeeding generations so that they will become sufficiently knowledgeable and skillful to add their own contributions to previously acquired knowledge and skills. Substantive teaching also has a more intrinsic purpose—to teach knowledge and skills "for their own sake." Really, such teachings are for purposes of self-realization or self-actualization—to enable students to better understand themselves and the world they live in, and to better appreciate their cultural heritage. All such substantive teachings will be facilitated if students are successfully inculcated with educational values, and they will be hindered if the educational institution fails to inculcate students with these values.

One of the many subjects that can be, but is typically not, taught in the school is a substantively oriented course on human values designed to increase awareness and understanding of one's own and others' values. Obviously, it would be desirable for students to be made aware of their own values; of the extent to which their own values are similar to and different from various cultural, ethnic, racial, socioeconomic, sexual, occupational, religious, political, regional, and age groups; of the extent to which their own values and the values of others are related to and determine specific social outlooks and behavior; and of the conditions under which the students' own values and others' values are undergoing change. A great deal of information is available in the social science literature that can be legitimately brought into such a course, information based on many viewpoints and methods.

We may identify this sort of value education by calling it *substantive value education.* Its purpose is informational, its method is objective, and its content can be taught just like any other subject matter. It can be contrasted with the first kind of value education that pervades all educational subject matter—the *inculcation of educational values.*

COMPARISON WITH VALUES CLARIFICATION

The two kinds of value education that I have described and that I am advocating can be further elaborated by contrasting them especially with another form of value education that they resemble superficially—the movement popularly known as "values clarification." Proponents of the values clarification movement advocate a form of value education that cannot readily be identified either as substantive value education or as the inculcation of educational values. Harman and Simon write: "Teachers have three main alternatives in dealing with value development. One alternative is to do nothing about such development. Another is to transmit a pre-existing set of values to students. A third is to help students find their own values" (1973, p. 5). These authors reject the first two alternatives and, of course, prefer the third, using all sorts of "strategies" to help students in their quest for values clarification. But the values that these authors would like to help students to "find" are private, unmeasurable, and provide no basis for comparison between one individual or group and another. Little or no consideration is given to the cultural, societal, or institutional origins that shape the values of large numbers of people in similar ways, or to the fact that a basic property of human values is that they are shared, or to the fact that there is an intimate connection between institutional and individual values. Different types of institutional values—aesthetic, political, religious, nationalistic, economic, and so on—are rarely identified as such or discussed in values clarification exercises. Not even educational values are acknowledged to exist. Nor is there an explicit acknowledgment of the special responsibility that the educational institution has to transmit or inculcate educational values. The approach is one that Stewart (1975) has called "absolute relativism."

From a values clarification perspective, the school is seen to have a "value-clarifying" function, but not value-transmitting or value-implementing functions. In fact, the latter functions are more or less explicitly denied, because the only social institutions that are recognized to have such functions are the family and organized religion:

> In our society, families and organized religions will not allow the school to usurp their role and teach a particular set of values. Therefore, modern values education as it has evolved in the school has, for the most part, emphasized the teaching of a *process* of valuing, rather than any one value or value system.
>
> Values clarification, stemming from the pioneer work of Louis Raths, is one approach to teaching a process of valuing—in schools, in homes, or in any setting where values issues may be present. (Simon & Kirschenbaum, 1973, p. 2)

Not all educators would agree that the family and religion are the main or sole transmitters and implementers of values. Wagschal, for instance, writes that "a society transfers values to its members through its political, social, and educational structures" (1974). But for those educators who do accept this view, and for those who feel that the school should not usurp the family's and the church's traditional functions, it is perhaps inevitable that they would adopt a doctrine of value neutrality, and a concomitant opposition to moralizing, value inculcation, and value modification. About all that is left is to focus on the "process of valuing" and the teaching of "value process skills."

Values clarification's insistence about value neutrality notwithstanding, an examination of its basic tenets suggests that it has certain value commitments that remain silent, and that it attempts to inculcate students with these values through the back door. The seven "valuing process" skills that it attempts to teach—(1) seeking alternatives when faced with a choice, (2) looking ahead to probable consequences before choosing, (3) making choices on one's own, without depending on others, (4) being aware of one's own preferences and valuations, (5) being willing to affirm one's choices and preferences publicly, (6) acting in ways that are consistent with choices and preferences, and (7) acting in these ways repeatedly—can readily be translated as attempts to inculcate students with the following value preferences: (1) broadmindedness or openmindedness rather than narrowmindedness or closedmindedness, (2) a future rather than a past or present time perspective, (3) independence and freedom rather than dependence or obedience, (4) self-awareness rather than self-deception, (5) courage in standing up for one's beliefs rather than cowardice, (6) logical consistency rather than indifference to logical consistency, and (7) reliability and dependability rather than unreliability and undependability. All these refer to values that are not all that different from those that many would identify as educational values. But a question remains: Is it not value-obfuscating rather than value-clarifying to teach such values through the back door, and at the same time give the impression of value neutrality through the front door?

Closely related to values clarifications's position on value neutrality is its position on value change: The purpose of values clarification is alleged to be the clarification, but not the modification, of values. Such a view is, I believe, an untenable one. How would one proceed to demonstrate the effectiveness of a classroom procedure that seeks to clarify but not to change values? If it is demonstrated not to affect values, can one claim it is effective? If it does have effects, it must surely affect values to one extent or another, in which case, can one claim it is value-free?

Thus far, my comments have been directed to the ways in which the values clarification movement has dealt with the issue of inculcating students with educational values. Let me now try to analyze the way it has approached the problem of substantive value education. Students are taught that they have a value, providing the following seven criteria are met: (1) prizing and cherishing, (2) publicly affirming, (3) choosing after thinking about alternatives, (4) choosing after considering their consequences, (5) choosing freely, (6) acting, and (7) acting with a pattern, repetition, and consistency. Thus, there is an all-or-none quality about values; either you have a value or you do not. Such an all-or-none conception makes it difficult to think in terms of such notions as value importance, value hierarchy, value priority, or value conflict. More important, it makes value measurement virtually meaningless and, consequently, comparison with others impossible. Whereas students are left to decide for themselves whether or not they have a value, they will be unable to decide how many values they have, whether their values are hierarchically organized, in what ways their values are similar to and different from those of others, or in what ways the values of any one culture, society, institution, or reference group are similar to and different from those of any other.

If we are to accept the definition of value proposed by advocates of values clarification, we would be forced to the untenable view that many classes of people have no values at all, because they probably cannot meet all seven criteria; for instance, the mentally retarded, the mentally ill, people in preliterate societies, the authoritarian personality, the Machiavellian personality, a member of the Mafia, and the professional politician. Indeed, it is difficult to see exactly who *would* qualify as meeting all seven criteria. In the end, we would be forced to the extreme view that even teachers and value clarifiers would not qualify as having any values.[2] An alternative view, one consistent with theoretical assumptions held by most social scientists, is that all people, without exception, can be said to have values, just like they can be said to have beliefs and attitudes, and that their existence can be inferred from behavior and expressed

---

[2]In a similar vein, Stewart (1975) has characterized the values clarification movement as inheriting from Raths "a theory that is philosophically indefensible and psychologically inadequate" (p. 686).

opinions, regardless of whether they are held consciously or unconsciously, regardless of whether they are determined or freely chosen, or publicly or privately held; in short, regardless of whether they meet any or all of the seven criteria so dear to values clarification proponents.

It is unlikely that the objectives of values clarification will be achieved by a movement in education that defines values so subjectively and arbitrarily, by a movement that, moreover, conceives of values in so elitist a manner as to preclude us from seeing the vast majority of humankind as possessing values. Values clarification's popularity in educational circles seems to derive from the fact that its exercises and strategies are easy for teachers pressed to plan out class assignments in advance, and fun for students who need not prepare for such class assignments in advance. It is doubtful that teachers who impose such exercises and strategies on their students in a "value-free" classroom need to be particularly knowledgeable about their own or about their students' values, and it is equally doubtful that students, as a result of engaging in values clarification exercises or strategies, will end up any the wiser about their own or others' values.

I believe that the school should abandon the position of value neutrality advocated by values clarification proponents because such a position can be defended neither theoretically nor philosophically, nor substantiated empirically. The educational institution's mandate to inculcate students with educational values is every bit as strong as the family's and the religion's mandate to inculcate members with their specialized values. Consistent with such a view, Wagschal (1975) has noted: "Some modern writers and theorists have begun to see the school as more of a 'value-producing' agency than an information-dispensing institution." I should emphasize that what I am advocating is that the school should abandon its position of value neutrality only with respect to educational values, but not with respect to other institutional values. The school has not only always been in the business of inculcating, shaping, and modifying certain values, but it should be in this business. Society *depends* upon the educational institution to inculcate educational values successfully. Consider the consequences for the economic life of the society if students were uniformly to rank those identified as educational values at the bottom of their value hierarchy.

Moreover, it seems unlikely that the school can remain value-free even when it is engaged in substantive value education. If we teach students about the substantive differences between the values of achievers and nonachievers, bigots and nonbigots, addicts and nonaddicts, the starving and the well fed, do we not also manage to convey to them that certain values are preferable to others? And should we not, if only we could, attempt to change the values of underachievers to become more like those of achievers, the values of bigots to become more like those of nonbigots, and so on?

Finally, I believe that a value education program will turn out to be illusory or self-deceptive if the sole focus is on the students' own values. Such a focus, which is the main focus of the values clarification movement, is likely to be too egocentric to be educationally effective. Self-awareness and self-understanding are but the opposite sides of the coin of social awareness and understanding. A more genuine self-awareness will, I believe, be achieved as a result of stimulating a comparison process, in which what we find out about ourselves is compared with what we find out about significant others. Experimental evidence discussed elsewhere in this volume and in earlier works (Rokeach, 1973) suggests that, in the process of making such comparisons between self and others, we will often become dissatisfied with what we have found out about ourselves, because it violates our conceptions of ourselves as competent and moral human beings. Such states of self-dissatisfaction are empirically found to lead to long-term value change and, as a consequence, to long-term changes in related values, attitudes, and behavior. Thus, it seems to me that value education should attempt to provide substantive information about the students' own values and about the values of others in their society in order to encourage students to compare what they find out about others with what they find out about themselves. Such a value education would encourage what John Dewey has called the experience of a "felt difficulty," a basic condition of learning and change, and also a basic condition for the realization of what are perhaps the ultimate educational values—individual growth and self-realization.

17

An Approach to the Teaching of Philosophy

Ronald H. Epp

One of the characteristics many academics share, and too few of us ever mention in print, is the inadequacy of our preparation for the teaching of philosophy. Our graduate student days provide the opportunity for colleges and universities to draw upon this cheap labor force for the teaching of elementary courses. By their own example, our mentors illustrate methods that we find successful in our learning experience, yet there is little—if any—direction or supervision of our initial attempts to teach. Unfortunately, those first few courses that we teach do more in the way of educating the novice teacher than the new student. In a nutshell, we learn what is effective by the slow, laborious, and solitary process of trial and failure.

The unique series on the Teaching of Philosophy which was recently inaugurated in *Metaphilosophy* partially remedies this deficiency in graduate education. What I would like to share with you is a method-ological approach which I have found enormously successful in my re-peated attempts to be an effective teacher of philosophy. In structure this approach may be workable in a variety of courses, yet I have found it most effective in a problematic approach to Introduction to Philosophy and Problems in Ethics.

My introductory course was structured in terms of key philosophical problems, divided into the traditional areas of epistemology, meta-physics, philosophy of religion, political philosophy, and ethics. With varying approaches I had achieved success in all areas, save ethics. In traditional fashion I covered various types of ethical theories and their foremost representatives. However, not only examinations but the temper of the class made it abundantly clear that my students were not reflecting on their *own* value commitments. Ethics remained for them an inquiry into conflicting and irresolvable ethical commitments of *other* men.

In April of 1970, the popular periodical *Psychology Today* published Milton Rokeach's "Faith, Hope and Bigotry" (1970). As a social psychologist, Rokeach was deeply interested in the origin and nature of value preferences, especially as they are revealed by representative opinion sampling. In this article he was concerned with the relationship of religious belief and bigotry, and his methodology seemed applicable to my struggles in teaching ethics.

Paraphrasing Rokeach, I developed a questionnaire which was given to each student prior to any discussion of ethical commitments. The instructions on this questionnaire were as follows:

> This questionnaire is directed toward revealing what *you* believe to be of worth, of value to you as an individual. The questionnaire is composed of parts A and B. Part A lists 18 End Values, terminal values or goals that most of us strive for. Part B consists of 18 Mean Values, the tools or instrumental values that we employ to attain End Values. Working with these value terms and what they mean to you, arrange the values of each list hierarchically according to their importance to you as guiding principles in your life. Keep each list separate and work only with the value options that I have given you.

The end values were randomly listed on page one, which was blocked into sections to facilitate the cutting of the sheet into 18 separate pieces of paper, each labeled with a value. Page two repeated this schemata with the mean values. The student was instructed to spread these values on a table and proceed to arrange them in order of their importance, and I cautioned them that there would be frequent shuffling of paper slips until they arrived at a satisfactory ranking. The student was verbally instructed to bear in mind the consequence of ranking. Namely, would he be willing to sacrifice end value number three in order to preserve end value number two, and risk number two in order to preserve end value number one? The students were asked to complete this questionnaire at their leisure before the next class meeting, listing on a separate sheet the results of their value card shuffling. Lastly, the student was assured that there would be no public disclosure of their personal value hierarchy. The list would not be seen by either the instructor or their fellow students, for I hoped that this insistence on the privacy of the questionnaire would insure a more authentic response.

The next class meeting was marvelous! The students were "sitting on the end of their seats" in anticipation, and before I could initiate my presentation they queried me as to the origin, function, and ends of the questionnaire. I informed them that their personal value scale would now be contrasted with a representative sample of the American public (the results of the Rokeach Value Survey). However, rather than listing on a handout or the blackboard the Rokeach results, I employed the following pedagogical tool.

I began by asking the class to offer verbal suggestions of what they believed the public might hold to be the highest ranked end value. Past experience indicated that several values would be suggested before the correct answer (i.e., number one on the Rokeach survey) would be identified. As each suggestion was offered it was listed beside the appropriate number on the blackboard until the end value scale was completed. This process of soliciting their suggestions had a threefold effect: (1) it brought even the least vocal students into the search; (2) it encouraged the students to question and weigh the various values in light of their appraisal of social norms; and (3) the impact of the survey was more dramatic, due to the frequency of their errors. However, the meaningfulness of this approach to the survey is best attested by the gasps, moans, and opinions that soon reverberated in the classroom. Most members of the class were surprised and annoyed at their failure to correctly identify public value preferences. Yet this surprise and annoyance was heightened when I pressed them to identify the public preferences in the mean value survey.

The results of the Rokeach Value Survey show that honesty was valued more highly than any of the 18 mean values. However, more than a dozen other values were suggested before I listed honesty beside number one. The class reaction was spontaneous outrage. As I proceeded to complete the mean value list the class queried me with the following questions: How can the public rank honesty first when they repeatedly sacrifice it for the sake of ambition (number two on the mean value scale)? Do people correctly understand what honesty involves? How can the public respond so hypocritically?

Before I continue with an account of the next stage in administering this questionnaire, I would like to share several observations that should be anticipated by the teacher who employs this survey. First, the media repeatedly reports that today's college student is apathetic and indifferent. Consequently, to discover the shock that is written on their faces proves instructive to both teacher and students. Furthermore, anticipate striking differences between student value preferences and the Rokeach profile. Yet it is not the differences that are unanticipated; rather, it is the class reaction to these differences. With all the proud affirmations of today's counterculture—the strong individualism in dress styles, sexual habits, occupational preferences, and the like—it is curious to discover that students actually dislike their alienation from commonly accepted values. Lastly, anticipate probing questions concerning the motives which prompted the responses of those who participated in the Rokeach survey. Students become intensely curious as to the reasons for value commitments, besieging me with questions such as: What are the sources of one's ethical commitments, how strongly is the public committed to these preferences, and what grounds do they have for their convictions? It does not take much ability to turn these same questions back on the very beliefs of students themselves.

Another line of inquiry that I pursue concerns the nature of the questionnaire. I suggest that they examine the following hypothesis—that the character of the questionnaire is responsible for the oddness of both the Rokeach profile and their own personal value scale. The student critique of the questionnaire not only encourages them to be more critical of statistical analyses, but also leads them to observations which open more comprehensive axiological problems. Student criticism comes in the form of questions: How was the test administered? Orally or in written form? Was the party questioned confident that his responses were not open to public airing? Was a time limit imposed on completion of the questionnaire? Yet if the method of testing was under review, so were the motives of those examined: Were those tested stating what they did value or what they would ideally prefer to value? Did they regard the questionnaire as a cute game or an opportunity for serious introspection? However, the most pointed criticism aligned them with Socrates' renowned concern. That is, how can one know what is to be valued if one has not examined the adequacy of ethical grammar? In brief, the Rokeach survey is premised on a standardized grammar. Yet common usage is notoriously confusing and one man's freedom is another man's slavery. The able dialectician has enabled his students to discover the need for clarity in ethical terminology, and without some accompanying glossary for selecting one's value preferences, the questionnaire is rendered useless by the ambiguity of moral grammar.

At this point the class usually ends with the resounding shrill of the bell. Students are often annoyed that we cannot continue and here and now resolve these perplexing problems. In subsequent class periods the interest generated in this initial meeting usually sustains us as we cover some of the traditional ethical theorists. Kant, Bentham, and Sartre are no longer viewed as historical curiosities pontificating on problems of small consequence. To the contrary, not only are the students sympathetic with the struggles of these theorists, but they are intensely demanding in their desire to discover solutions that are personally meaningful.

Readers of *Metaphilosophy* should be conscious of the repeated pedagogical message that has been stated, argued, and echoed throughout these essays on the Philosopher as Teacher. Namely, what is preferable to traditional lecturing is the application of the Socratic technique of midwifery which enables the "teacher" to elicit ideas born in the mind of the student and delivered through the ministration of the "teacher." It has been my contention that the Rokeach profile coupled with a dialectical approach enables both student and teacher to experience many of the features that are the substance of a liberal education:

1. *Discussion.* The contrast of personal values (often newly discovered) with the Rokeach profile encourages a heightened degree of interaction and personal involvement among all participants.

2. *Exploration.* The instructor who implements this questionnaire does not begin with the proverbial blank slate, but with the convictions and assumptions of those surveyed. The students are not exploring uncharted territory, but rather are critically assessing commitments that were previously unknown or unexamined. This survey not only opened the student to consciousness of his basic commitments, but may have encouraged a partial *liberation* from the unsatisfactory edifice that supported his value preferences.

3. *Sharing.* Unlike Descartes, who searched in solitary fashion for some indubitable truth, the use of this approach precipitates the involvement of many minds in a common quest. Whereas at the outset of the survey I noted that each student's value scale would remain in his possession, the reaction of the students was such that they volunteered their personal ranking preferences and encouraged others to do the same.

4. *Theorizing.* Not only were students critical of both public and personal value preferences, but they were able to sense the need to stand apart from the values of their culture and consider whether any abstract ethical principles would hold universally.

5. *Relevance.* What may have appeared at the outset to be a trite exercise, became in time an issue of crucial importance. In fact, many students requested additional copies of the questionnaire. Later I discovered that these budding dialecticians broadened their knowledge by encouraging their acquaintances, friends, and relatives to take part in the survey.

I am still refining the above technique and recognize that it should be altered and amended as befits the temper of the class and its teacher. I have offered this account not only to encourage its use elsewhere, but to stimulate the publication of other methodologies that might be helpful to teachers in their quest for relevant and stimulating aids in the teaching of philosophy.

18

Improving the Quality of
Teaching Psychology

James R. Lundy and Milton Rokeach

Various reviewers of the literature (Eckert & Neale, 1965; Gagne & Rohwer, 1969; McKeachie, 1962; Johnson & Daniel, 1974) agree that there appears to be no conclusive or best answer to the question of how best to teach at the college level. Buxton (1956) notes that "we presently know of no one method of instruction which is best for all subject matters or for all instructors" (p. 363). Dubin and Taveggia (1968), after examining the data from 91 studies, concluded that there are apparently no real differences in effectiveness between different teaching methods. The implications of such studies are well expressed by Lee: "Improving teaching is a continuing concern . . . on every college campus. It is imperative that ways to improve college teaching be devised, explored, and appraised . . . a painstaking search obviously is demanded" (1967, p. 1).

Keller (1963) was perhaps among the first to suggest that a course taught in a "personal" manner might be more productive. But, thus far, apparently little progress has been made that makes use of this suggestion. Blackburn (1969) informs us that "the most striking aspect of these interviews is the extent to which they reveal how profoundly students are concerned about themselves, with their own personal and social development" (p. 6). However, Blackburn adds, "Their courses for the most part teach them incidentally and apparently not by design." In a similar vein, MacLeish notes: "Undergraduates... complain... over and over, that their education does not respond to their needs.... It is relevance to their lives, to themselves as men and women living" (1969, p. 18).

While many studies have demonstrated the important effect of nonintellectual factors upon academic performance (Briney & Taylor, 1959; Fricke, 1956; Garret, 1949; Garverick, 1964; Neidt & Hedlund, 1967; Stein, 1963; Wofford & Willoughby, 1968), the employment of personal relevance as an independent variable is a relatively neglected aspect of research on factors influencing academic performance. The purpose of the research to be described here is to investigate the effects upon academic performance of providing undergraduate social psychology students with course content designed to enhance personal relevance.

Rokeach (1973) has observed that one of the main ways psychology courses in particular (and social science courses in general) differ from courses in the natural sciences is in their inherent potential to be personally relevant. Psychology courses have, however, typically not been taught in a manner designed to exploit or capitalize on such a potential. The student is informed, through textbooks and lectures, about concepts and functional relationships among variables as demonstrated in empirical research carried out with *others*.

> But, curiously, great pains are usually taken to keep students in the dark about their own position on the social and personal variables they are required to learn, and this may be tantamount to throwing away our best teaching tool—personal relevance—a teaching advantage the natural sciences do not possess. The way psychology is typically taught thus discourages students from making personal applications of empirical knowledge. Thus, they stand little chance of discovering, for instance, whether they are high, middle, or low on prejudice compared with others; or that they are authoritarian, dogmatic, rigid, Machiavellian, or aggressive; or achievement or affiliation-oriented; externally or internally controlled; intolerant of ambiguity; or repressed, impulsive, extroverted, neurotic, or psychopathic.
>
> Beyond the issue of self-knowledge about single variables, there is the issue of self-knowledge about relationships between two or more variables. Relationships between psychological variables are always far from perfect, which means that there are always individuals who fall into the "wrong" cells. Because we do not give students in psychology courses (or in other social science courses) the opportunity of finding out about such relationships as they might exist within themselves, we pass up many valuable teaching and change-inducing opportunities. All such personal knowledge is typically ruled out as not relevant to the conceptual understanding of relationships and generalizations derived from research with human subjects. (Rokeach, 1973, p. 333)

What characteristics must a course possess if it is to be personally relevant? Maxwell (1969) asked his students this question and reported that relevance of a course can be evaluated only in terms of the unique individual's viewpoint, goals, aspirations, and expectations; in other words, a course that is relevant is one that tells students something specific about themselves. Woodring (1969) informs us that most undergraduates study psychology not to become sophisticated in techniques of laboratory experimentation, but because they hope to better understand their own behavior or that of others close to them.

EXPERIMENT 1

Thirty undergraduates, enrolled for the first time in a social psychology course at Grand Valley State College, participated in the study. They were randomly chosen in the Fall of 1969 from 76 students enrolled in the course. Half of these (seven females and eight males) were randomly assigned to the experimental condition, and the other half (nine males and six females) to the control condition. The two groups did not differ in age or grade point average.

The textbooks that were used in this course were *Principles and Methods of Social Psychology,* First Edition, by E. P. Hollander, and *Current Perspectives in Social Psychology,* Second Edition, by E. P. Hollander and R. G. Hunt. The following books were placed on closed reserve in the library: *The Open and Closed Mind* and *Beliefs, Attitudes, and Values* by M. Rokeach; *The Authoritarian Personality* by T. W. Adorno, E. Frenkel-Brunswik, D. J. Levinson, and R. N. Sanford; *Basic Studies in Social Psychology* by H. Proshansky and B. Seidenberg; *Current Studies in Social Psychology* by I. D. Steiner and M. Fishbein; and *Theories of Personality,* First Edition, by C. Hall and G. Lindzey.

In anticipation of the fact that certain personality and social-psychological variables would be covered in the course, the following instruments were administered during the first four class meetings to the subjects in the experimental (but not control) group, scored, and then returned and discussed for purposes of giving the students information about their own standing on the variables indicated: *The F Scale,* the *Dogmatism Scale,* the *Edwards Personal Preference Schedule,* Rokeach's *Value Survey,* and the *Sixteen Personality Factor Test.*

In an attempt to reduce the likelihood of the experimental subjects responding to what Orne (1962) called "the demand characteristics" of an experiment, the subjects assigned to the experimental group were asked to remain after the remaining students were dismissed on the first day of the semester. This was done by a faculty member other than the instructor of the course, a faculty member who was unaware of the purpose of the study. He informed the students that he was conducting a research project, and that they had been picked at random from the class for participation in his study. He then distributed the previously mentioned instruments, with the request that the students take them home and return them no later than the second class meeting.

This same faculty member returned the scored instruments to the subjects during the third and fourth class meeting. When the scored instruments were returned, he gave an explanation—using a prepared script—of the meaning of the variables that had been measured, how the tests were scored, and norms for each of the tests. Then he informed the students that they might keep the tests if they so desired. At the end of the term he returned once again and, after dismissing the rest of the class, informed the experimental subjects that they had participated in an ongoing research project designed to determine the characteristics of students enrolled in certain courses at Grand Valley State College. Thus, the experimental subjects had no reason to think that the experimental treatment was specifically related to the social psychology course in which they were enrolled.

Experimental subjects, control subjects, and the remaining members of the class were given a 100-item multiple choice examination, and responded also to a brief questionnaire during the regularly scheduled final examination period. The latter included a question designed to measure the perceived degree of personal relevance of the course on a five-point rating scale. The examination itself had been previously pretested. Its corrected odd–even reliability ranged between .61 and .82, as determined for four sections taking the course the year before. Twenty-five of the 100 items substantively concerned the particular variables used in the experimental treatment (to be called "contaminated" items), that is, they made explicit reference either to the instruments used in the experimental treatment or to the conceptual variables measured by those instruments.[1]

Results

The main findings are summarized in Table 18.1. The mean ratings for personal relevance for experimental and control groups were 1.26 and 2.26, respectively; this difference is significant beyond the .01 level ($t = 3.86$). Thus, the experimental group perceived the course to be significantly more personally relevant than did the control group.

More important, however, are the findings concerning differences in performance between experimental and control groups on the final examination. The respective means for the 100-item examination are 69.26 and 59.00, respectively. This difference is again significant beyond the .01 level ($t = 3.02$). These results indicate that the experimental

---

[1]Each item was mentioned twice during the lectures, thus insuring that all subjects, experimental and control, were equally exposed.

TABLE 18.1.   Means for Experimental and Control Groups for Personal Relevance for 100-Item Final Examination, for 75 "Uncontaminated" and 25 "Contaminated" Items

	EXPERIMENTAL GROUP	CONTROL GROUP	p
Personal relevance	1.26	2.26	.01
100-item final examination	69.26	59.00	.01
75 "uncontaminated" items	55.67	47.00	.01
25 "contaminated" items	13.59	12.00	—

group had significantly outperformed the control group by better than 10 items on a 100-item examination.

These findings cannot be attributed to extra coaching or to an advantage that experimental subjects might have had because of greater exposure to at least certain variables or concepts mentioned in the final examination. Seventy-five of the 100 items concerned course content wholly unrelated to the variables or concepts involved in the experimental treatment ("uncontaminated" items), while the remaining 25 items specifically concerned them ("contaminated" items). Table 18.1 shows that the experimental and control groups differed significantly beyond the .01 level ($t = 3.71$) on the 75 "uncontaminated" items, ruling out extra coaching as a possible alternative explanation.

But how to account for the finding (Table 18.1) that the three groups did not differ significantly from one another on the 25 "contaminated" items, those specifically concerning the variables covered in the experimental treatment? It is reasonable to suppose that the experimental group would have performed better on this portion of the final examination, since it had been exposed more than the control group to their content. On the surface, this appears to be a rather odd finding. There are, however, two reasons why this material was highly salient for all students, whether they were experimental or control subjects: (1) all students had been sensitized to material covered in both text and lecture that dealt with the psychological instruments, either because they had been administered at the beginning of the semester (as was the case for the experimental group), or because they had heard they were being used (as was the case for the control group); (2) each of the "contaminated" items had been discussed in the lectures by an instructor whose campus reputation included the fact that "he emphasizes his lectures on his examinations." Both these factors, we believe, resulted in both groups achieving approximately the same score on these items. That this "selective exposure" and "campus reputation" did not generalize to the other items on the final examination can be interpreted to mean that it was the exposure of students to their own standing on the psychological tests that led to the improved academic performance.

The instructor was, however, aware of the identities of the students in the experimental and control groups. Thus, we are not able to rule out the possibility that the differences in perception of personal relevance and academic performance arise from differences in the treatment—personal relevance—or are, instead, a result of special attention given to the experimental subjects—a "Hawthorne effect" (Roethlisberger, Dickson, & Wright, 1939). Alternatively, it has been demonstrated that the expectancies of the experimenter may significantly influence the outcome of experiments (Rosenthal, 1966) and, more particularly, it has been shown (Meichenbaum, Bowers, & Ross, 1969) that the expectancies of the experimenter can manifest themselves even on objective test results. Thus, it would be methodologically desirable to rule out the possibility of Hawthorne and experimenter effects.

EXPERIMENT 2

Thirty-six undergraduates, enrolled in social psychology at Grand Valley State College during the 1970–1971 academic year, served as subjects. They were randomly selected from the 57 students initially enrolled in the course. Twelve were randomly assigned to the experimental group (six males and six females); as in Experiment 1, they filled out the same psychological tests, which were then scored, returned, and discussed with the subjects. Another 12 (five females and seven males) were randomly assigned to control group 1; they underwent the same procedure of filling out the several psychological tests, except that the tests were returned to them unscored, on the grounds that there had not been enough time to score all the tests. The same explanations of the meaning of the tests were given, however. This control group was employed to check on a possible Hawthorne effect. Finally, a third group of 12 subjects (six males and six females) were randomly assigned to control group 2; they did not receive any treatment.

All subjects were selected by a second faculty member, not the course instructor. Thus, the instructor was prevented from knowing which of his students were subjects, or which students were in what group.

Experiment 2 was essentially identical in procedure to Experiment 1. Several additional measures of academic performance were, however, obtained: (1) an essay examination was given to the three groups six months after the course had ended; (2) several unobtrusive measures of performance (Webb, Campbell, Schwartz, & Sechrest, 1966) were added: number of classes missed, number of questions asked in class discussions, number of closed reserve books used, and number of tutorials attended. These measures were recorded by the instructor for all students.

The second faculty member came to class the first day and, after the instructor had left the room, gave each student copies of the several psychological tests to take home, fill out, and return on the second day of class. Only the students in the experimental group were given copies of Rokeach's Value Survey, however. This was done in order to prevent the subjects in control group 1 from seeing their own rankings—their own hierarchical arrangements of values—when the tests were returned, scored, to the experimental group, and unscored to control group 1. Subjects in control group 1 were then given copies of the Rokeach Value Survey at this time.

The faculty member gave a brief explanation during the third and fourth class hours of the meaning of the variables that had been measured, again using a prepared script. This constituted the experimental treatment.

At the regularly scheduled final exam period, the 100-item multiple-choice exam was again administered and scored by the instructor. Personal relevance ratings were also obtained at this time.

The same faculty member contacted the subjects six months afterward by mail, asking them to take part in a research project being carried out by the Psychology Department. The letter stated that each student would be paid three dollars. All but two of the 36 subjects appeared. The two missing persons, both control subjects, were contacted by phone and were successfully persuaded to take the essay examination five days after it was given to the other subjects. They both assured the examiner that they had not been told anything about the examination or what they were to do, but there was no way to verify that this was actually the case.

Subjects were given a maximum of one-and-one-half hours to complete the essay examination. The second faculty member monitored the exam, removed names and other identifying marks, coded each examination, and gave the papers to the course instructor to be graded.

Results

Table 18.2 shows that the three groups differed in their perceptions of the personal relevance of the course, and these differences are again significant beyond the .01 level ($F = 16.1$). Subjects in the experimental group, those who had filled out the tests and then received feedback on their test scores, judged the course to be the most relevant. Subjects in control group 1—those who had filled out the same tests but did not receive feedback on their own test scores—judged the course as being the least personally relevant, even less so than subjects in the second control group that had received no treatment. These data suggest that the experience of taking the tests, but then not being able to see their own test scores, produced a generally negative reaction.

More important, of course, are the findings concerning performance on the final examination. Table 18.2 shows that the experimental group obtained scores on the 100-item test that were on the average 7.5 to 11.5 points higher than the two control groups, findings that are significant beyond the .01 level (F = 6.86). These findings are essentially the same as those obtained in Experiment 1, and, moreover, they show that the performance of control group 1, of those who filled out the test but did not see their test scores, fell in between the experimental group and control group 2, which had received no treatment.

It is unlikely that these differences can be attributed to special treatment since the instructor did not know which students were subjects in the experiment, or which subjects were in experimental or control groups. Nor can the effects be attributed to extra coaching since the experimental and control groups, as before in Experiment 1, did not differ on the 25 "contaminated" items, yet did differ significantly on the 75 "uncontaminated" items (F = 11.08).

These findings are supported by the results obtained by the essay examination given six months afterward. The mean grades obtained by the experimental group, control group 1, and control group 2 were 76.08, 67.50, and 53.99, respectively. These differences are again significant beyond the .01 level (F = 7.27).

Other Findings. The three groups did not differ significantly on three of the four unobtrusive measures: number of books checked out from the reserve library, number of classes missed, and number of tutorials. But they did differ dramatically on number of questions asked in class during the semester. Experimental subjects asked an average of 9.25 questions each during the semester; control group 1 subjects asked

TABLE 18.2. Means of Experimental and Control Groups for Personal Relevance, for 100-Item Final Examination, for 75 "Uncontaminated," and 25 "Contaminated" Items, and for Essay Examination Given 6 Months Later

	EXPERIMENTAL GROUP	CONTROL GROUP 1	CONTROL GROUP 2	p
Personal relevance	1.20	1.83	1.70	.01
100-item final exam	71.91	64.41	60.25	.01
75 "uncontaminated" items	55.83	49.16	45.00	.01
25 "contaminated" items	16.08	15.25	15.25	—
Essay exam: 6 months later	76.08	67.50	53.99	.01

an average of 1.91 questions; and control group 2 subjects asked an average of .33 questions. The differences are highly significant (F = 30.11).

DISCUSSION

The results from both experiments strongly suggest that the experimental treatment had (1) increased student perceptions of the course as personally relevant, (2) increased student level of participation in class discussions, and (3) increased academic performance, not only as measured by an objective final examination given at the end of the semester, but also as measured by an essay examination given six months later.

The experimental treatment exposed students to information about their own standings in comparison with others (Festinger, 1954) on important personality variables, their value systems, their achievement motive, and their levels of dogmatism and authoritarianism. Why should such a pedagogical technique lead to increases in perception of the course as personally relevant, to increases in class participation and academic performance? Clearly, all the variables covered in the experimental treatment are central components of self-conceptions and important for the maintenance or enhancement of self-esteem. Thus, it is easy to see that the experimental subjects generally increased their perceptions of the course as personally relevant because the course content was now made salient for their self-conceptions and self-esteem. The treatment increased their motivation to obtain a better understanding of themselves, first, by informing them in relatively objective terms about themselves and then providing them with many additional opportunities—through textbook assignments, lectures, and class discussions—to obtain additional information that was relevant for their self-conceptions and self-esteem. Such an increase in academic motivation is missing from most psychology courses, wherein students are typically not provided with opportunities to find out anything important about themselves, or to compare themselves on significant dimensions with others.

Over and above such a general increase in motivation for self-understanding, we believe there is an additional explanation of the findings—an explanation that concerns the arousal of a need for consistency with self-conceptions. Experimental evidence discussed in this volume and elsewhere (Rokeach, 1973) shows that providing people with information about themselves through self-confrontation creates opportunities for discovering possible contradictions between cognitions concerning one's values, or attitudes, or other personal attributes, on the one hand, and self-conceptions, on the other. For instance, some experimental subjects might discover that they were more dogmatic or authoritarian or less achievement oriented than they had thought. The discovery of such contradictions arouses feelings of dissatisfaction with oneself. It is conjectured that to reduce such feelings of self-dissatisfaction a person will be more likely to seek out and to be receptive to new information, either to rationalize his or her shortcomings or to provide a better basis for removing them. It is such new information that is provided by the course content and it is now personally relevant in a way that such course content, as typically taught, is not personally relevant.

The present study goes beyond other experimental studies primarily concerned with issues of value, attitude, and behavioral change following the arousal of feelings of self-dissatisfaction by feedback of information about oneself. Here the main concern is not with cognitive and behavioral change, but with the question as to whether feedback of information about oneself can lead to increases in academic motivation and performance. The findings from both experiments strongly suggest that such a method of teaching can be fruitfully employed to improve academic motivation and performance.

Let us now consider some more specific findings. The experimental group that received the personal relevance treatment perceived the course as being more relevant than either of the control groups. But the control group that filled out the instruments but did not receive feedback (control group 1) perceived the course as even less personally relevant than did the control group that had received no treatment at all (control group 2). This finding is perhaps best explained by assuming that the experience of taking the tests but then not being able to find out the scores produced enough frustration and anger to result in a negative evaluation of the course.

The experimental group in both experiments, it will be recalled, scored substantially higher on the objective multiple-choice examination than did the control groups; these differences disappeared when only the scores on the "contaminated" items were compared. This apparent paradox can be explained by the fact that these "contaminated" items contained material which was highly salient for all students: (1) all students were sensitized to this material either because they had taken the test or had heard that such testing was being carried out; (2) it was "common knowledge" that the course instructor placed heavy emphasis upon lecture material in his examinations, all 25 "contaminated" items having been mentioned twice in the lectures.

While there were no significant differences found among experimental and control groups on three of the unobtrusive measures (number of class cuts, number of books consulted in library, number of tutorials), the differences were in the predicted direction. On the fourth measure—number of questions asked in class—the experimental subjects asked significantly more questions. Thus it can be said that the experimental treatment motivated the students to ask more questions because the material was more personally relevant. This is a particularly interesting finding when viewed within the context of the rather widespread hesitancy shown by college students to speak out in relatively large classes.

The findings on the essay examination in Experiment 2 suggest that an increase in personal relevance will not only lead to an increase in academic performance immediately after the course had ended, but also six months later. This finding parallels other experimental findings showing long-term *changes* in cognitions and behavior following self-confrontation—effects that have thus far been reported to persist for as long as 21 months after an experimental treatment. The finding that the experimental treatment produced measurable long-term effects on academic achievement is an important one in view of the fact that it is a result so rarely found.

To summarize: Students in undergraduate courses in social psychology who were exposed to information about their standing on particular variables to be covered in the content of the course (1) reported the content of the course to be more personally relevant than students not so exposed; (2) asked more questions during class discussion; (3) achieved higher scores on their final examination; and (4) achieved higher scores on an examination six months afterward. The difference in academic performance between the experimental and control groups was roughly one letter grade, that is, from a "C" to a "B," or from a "B" to an "A." Speaking more generally, the results of the present experiments suggest that academic performance in undergraduate psychology courses can be significantly enhanced, both immediately and over time, by increasing the personal relevance of the course content.

Another conclusion that appears to be warranted is that social-psychological theory and research can be applied to the improvement of the teaching process. This is of particular importance in view of the criticism made of most of the research being done on instructional processes and techniques. Gagne and Rohwer (1969), for instance, comment that "remoteness of applicability to instruction . . . characterizes many studies of human learning, retention and transfer, appearing in the most prestigious of psychological journals" (p. 381). The present study suggests that social-psychological theory and procedures are available to investigate educational processes without creating a degree of contrivance or artificiality that would make the findings of questionable usefulness when applied to the real world.

Perhaps one of the more important implications of this study, for purposes of structuring a social psychology of education, concerns the problem of the long-term impact of the education experience. If increasing the personal relevance of a course in social psychology will indeed increase the length of retention time of course content, it is now necessary to determine in more detail the dynamics of this increase. What is the span of time over which such an influence can last, and under what conditions can the maximal time span be obtained? It is just this area—enhancing academic performance by means of increasing personal relevance—that appears to hold great promise for contributing to a productive social psychology of education.

References

ABELSON, R. P., ARONSON, E., MCGUIRE, W. J., NEWCOMB, T. M., ROSENBERG, M. J., & TANNENBAUM, P. H. (Eds.), *Theories of cognitive consistency: A sourcebook.* Chicago: Rand McNally, 1968.

ABERBACH, J. D., CHESNEY, J. D., & ROCKMAN, B. A. Exploring elite political attitudes: Some methodological lessons. Paper presented at the 1974 Annual Meetings of the Midwest Political Science Association.

ACKERMAN, C., & PARSONS, T. The concept of "social system" as a theoretical device. In G. J. Direnzo (Ed.), *Concepts, theory, and explanation in the behavioral sciences,* pp. 24–40. New York: Random House, 1966.

ADORNO, T. W., FRENKEL-BRUNSWIK, E., LEVINSON, D. J., & SANFORD, R. N. *The authoritarian personality.* New York: Harper, 1950.

AHAMMER, I. M., & BALTES, P. B. Objective vs. perceived age differences in personality: How do adolescents, adults and older people view themselves and each other? *Journal of Gerontology,* 1972, *27,* 46–51.

ALBERT, E. M. Value systems. In D. L. Sills (Ed.), *International encyclopedia of the social sciences,* vol. 16, pp. 287–291. New York: Macmillan and Free Press, 1968.

ALLPORT, G., VERNON, P., & LINDZEY, G. *Study of values,* 3rd ed. Boston: Houghton Mifflin, 1960.

ALMOND, G. A., & VERBA, S. *The civic culture.* Princeton, N.J.: Princeton University Press, 1963.

ARONSON, E. Dissonance theory: Progress and problems. In R. P. Abelson et al. (Eds.), *Theories of cognitive consistency: A sourcebook.* Chicago: Rand McNally, 1968.

ARONSON, E. The theory of cognitive dissonance: A current perspective. In L. Berkowitz (Ed.), *Advances in experimental social psychology.* New York: Academic Press, 1969.

BALES, R. F., & COUCH, A. S. The value-profile: A factor-analytic study of value statements. *Sociological Inquiry,* 1969, *39,* 3–17.

BALL-ROKEACH, S. J. Receptivity to sexual equality. *Pacific Sociological Review,* 1976, *19,* 519–540.

BALL-ROKEACH, S. J., & DEFLEUR, M. L. A dependency model of mass media effects. *Communication Research,* 1976, *13,* 3–21.

BALTES, P. B., & GOULET, L. R. Exploration of developmental variables by manipulation and simulation of age differences in behavior. *Human Development,* 1971, *14,* 149–170.

BALTES, P. B., & SCHAIE, K. W. (Eds.), *Life-span developmental psychology: Personality and socialization.* New York: Academic Press, 1973.

BALTES, P. B., & WILLIS, S. L. Toward psychological theories of aging and development. In J. E. Birren & K. W. Schaie (Eds.), *Handbook of the psychology of aging.* New York: Van Nostrand Reinhold, 1976.

BARBER, B., & INKELES, A. (Eds.), *Stability and social change.* Boston: Little, Brown, 1971.

BARDÈCHE, M. *Qu'est-ce que le Fascisme?* Paris: Les Sept Couleurs, 1961.

BARNES, L. B. *Organizational systems and engineering groups.* Boston: Graduate School of Business Administration, Harvard University, 1960.

BARNETT, J. H. The Easter festival: A study of cultural change. *American Sociological Review,* 1949, *14,* 62–70.

BAUER, R. A. (Ed.), *Social indicators.* Cambridge, Mass.: MIT Press, 1966.

BAUM, R. C. Values and democracy in Imperial Germany. *Sociological Inquiry,* 1968, *38,* 176–196.

BECKER, H. S., GEER, B., HUGHES, E. C., & STRAUSS, A. *Boys in white: Student culture in medical school.* Chicago: University of Chicago Press, 1961.

BECKER, S. L. The impact of mass media on society. In R. V. Wimen & W. C. Mererhenry (Eds.), *Educational media: Theory into practice.* Columbus, Ohio: Merrill, 1969.

BEECH, R. P. Value systems, attitudes, and interpersonal attraction. Ph.D. thesis, Michigan State University, East Lansing, Mich., 1966.

BEER, S. H. *British politics in the collectivist age.* New York: Knopf, 1965.

BERK, R. A gaming approach to collective behavior. *American Sociological Review,* 1974, *39,* 355–373.

BERNSTEIN, D. A. Modification of smoking behavior: An evaluative review. *Psychological Bulletin,* 1969, *71,* 418–440.

BERREMAN, G. D. Stratification, pluralism, and interaction: A comparative analysis of caste. In A. de Reuck & J. Knight (Eds.), *Caste and race: Comparative approaches.* London: Churchill, 1968.

BESWICK, D. G., & HILLS, M. D. A survey of ethnocentrism in Australia. *Australian Journal of Psychology,* 1969, *21,* 211–225.

BILLIG, M. The new social psychology and "fascism." *European Journal of Social Psychology,* 1977, *4,*393–432.

BILLIG, M. *The Fascist revival: A social psychological view of British Fascism.* London: Academic Press, 1978.

BILLIG, M., & COCHRANE, R. Values of British political extremists and potential extremists: A discriminant analysis. Unpublished manuscript, 1978.

BISHOP, G. F., BARCLAY, A. M., & ROKEACH, M. Presidential preferences and freedom–equality value patterns in the 1968 American campaign. *Journal of Social Psychology,* 1972, *88,* 207–212.

BLACKBURN, R. T. Live and learn? A look at students in their setting. In *Memo Number 32 of the Center for Research on Learning and Teaching at the University of Michigan,* Ann Arbor, Mich., 1969.

BLAU, P. M., & SCHOENHERR, R. A. *The structure of organizations.* New York: Basic Books, 1971.

BLONDEL, J. *Voters, parties, and leaders.* Baltimore: Penguin Books, 1965.

BLUMLER, J. G., & KATZ, E. (Eds.), *The uses of mass communication: Current perspectives on gratifications research.* Beverly Hills, Calif.: Sage Publications, 1974.

BOTTOMORE, T. B. *Elites and society.* New York: Basic Books, 1964.

BOWERS, W. J. Normative constraints on deviant behavior in the college context. *Sociometry,* 1968, *31,* 370–385.

BRAUNSTEIN, D. N., & HAINES, G. H. Preference scaling of careers and organizations. *Journal of Applied Psychology,* 1968, *52,* 380–385.

BREER, P. E., & LOCKE, E. A. *Task experience as a source of attitudes.* Homewood, Ill.: Dorsey Press, 1965.

BREIN, M., & DAVID, K. H. Intercultural communication and the adjustment of the sojourner. *Psychological Bulletin,* 1971, *76,* 215–230.

BRIM, O. G. Life-span development of the theory of oneself: Implications for child development. In H. W. Reese & L. P. Lipsitt (Eds.), *Advances in child development and behavior,* vol. 2. New York: Academic Press, 1976.

BRINEY, R. C., & TAYLOR, M. J. Scholastic behavior and orientation to college. *Journal of Educational Psychology,* 1959, *50,* 266–274.

BROGADIR, P. Discussion. In *Proceedings, Second Annual New Congress for Mental Health, New York State Journal of Medicine,* 1967, *67,* 1996.

BRONOWSKI, J. *Science and human values.* New York: Free Press, 1956.

BUCKLEY, W. (Ed.), *Modern systems research for the behavioral scientist: A sourcebook.* Chicago: Aldine, 1968.

BUXTON, C. C. *College teaching—a psychologist's view.* New York: Harcourt, Brace, 1956.

CAMPBELL, D. P. *Handbook for the Strong Vocational Interest Blank.* Stanford, Calif.: Stanford University Press, 1971.

CAMPBELL, D. T. The indirect assessment of social attitudes. *Psychological Bulletin,* 1950, *47,* 15–38.

CAMPBELL, D. T. Common fate, similarity, and other indices of the status of aggregates of persons as social entities. *Behavioral Science,* 1958, *3,* 14–25.

CAMPBELL, D. T., & FISKE, D. Convergent and discriminant validation by the multitrait–multimethod matrix. *Psychological Bulletin,* 1959, *56,* 81–105.

CAMPBELL, A., CONVERSE, P. E., & RODGERS, W. L. *The quality of American life.* New York: Russell Sage Foundation, 1976.

CARROLL, S. H. Elitism and reform: Some anti-slavery opinion-makers in the era of Civil War and Reconstruction. Ph.D. thesis, Cornell University, Ithaca, N.Y., 1969.

CAUDILL, W., & SCARR, H. A. Japanese value orientations and culture change. *Ethnology,* 1962, *1,* 53–91.

CHRISTOPH, J. B. Consensus and cleavage in British political ideology. *American Political Science Review,* 1965, *59,* 629–642.

CHURCHMAN, C. W. *Prediction and optimal decision: Philosophical issues of a science of values.* Englewood Cliffs, N.J.: Prentice-Hall, 1961.

CLARK, J. P., & WENNINGER, E. P. Goal orientations and illegal behavior among juveniles. *Social Forces,* 1963, *42,* 49–59.

CLEVENGER, T. Research methodologies in speech–communication. In R. J. Kibler & L. L. Barker (Eds.), *Conceptual frontiers in speech communication.* New York: Speech Association of America, 1969.

COBB, R. V., & ELDER, C. D. Symbolic identifications and political behavior. *American Politics Quarterly,* 1976, *4,* 305–332.

COCHRANE, R., BILLIG, M., & HOGG, M. Politics and values in Britain: A test of Rokeach's two-value model. *British Journal of Social and Clinical Psychology,* 1979.

COCHRANE, R., & KELLY, K. Personality and the differential effectiveness of an experimental value change procedure. Unpublished paper, 1971.

COCHRANE, R., & ROKEACH, M. Rokeach's Value Survey: A methodological note. *Journal of Experimental Research in Personality,* 1970, *4,* 159–161.

COHEN, A. A. Radio vs. TV: The effect of the medium. *Journal of Communication,* 1976, *26,* 29–35.

COLEMAN, J. S. Relational analysis: The study of social organizations with survey methods. In A. Etzioni (Ed.), *Complex organizations.* New York: Holt, Rinehart, and Winston, 1961, pp. 441–452.

COLLINS, R. *Conflict sociology.* New York: Academic Press, 1975.

CONNOR, P. E., & BECKER, B. W. Values and comparative organizational research. *Proceedings of the Academy of Management,* 1974, *18,* 88–94.

CONNOR, P. E., EGAN, D. M., & KARMEL, B. Organizational relationships: Context, action, and effectiveness. *Proceedings of the Mountain-Plains Management Association,* 1973.

CONROY, W. J. A multi-variate analysis of the psychological and associated characteristics of former cigarette smokers. *Dissertation Abstracts,* 1976, *36,* 5251B.

CONROY, W. J., KATKIN, E. S., & BARNETTE, W. L. Modification of smoking behavior by the use of a self confrontation technique. *Proceedings, Southeastern Division, American Psychological Association,* 1973, p. 56.

COOLEY, C. H. *Two major works: Social organization and human nature and the social order.* Glencoe, Ill.: Free Press, 1956.

COUGHLAN, R. J. An assessment of teacher work values. *Educational Administration Quarterly,* 1969, *5,* 53–73.

COUGHLAN, R. J. Job satisfaction in relatively closed and open schools. *Educational Administration Quarterly,* 1971, *7,* 40–59.

COURNAND, A. F., & ZUCKERMAN, H. The code of science: Analysis and some reflections on its future. *Studium Generale,* 1970, *23,* 941–962.

CRAWFORD, B. F. *Changing conceptions of religion as revealed in 100 years of Methodist hymnology,* 2 vols. Carnegie, Pa.: Carnegie Church Press, 1938.

CROFT, R. G., STIMPSON, S. V., ROSS, W. L., BRAY, R. M., & BREGLIO, V. J. Comparison of attitude change elicited by live and videotaped classroom presentations. *AV Communications Review,* 1968, *17,* 315–321.

CRONBACH, L. J., & FURBY, L. How should we measure "change"—or should we? *Psychological Bulletin,* 1970, *74,* 68–80.

CRONKHITE, G. L. Rhetoric, communication, and psychoepistemology. In W. R. Fisher (Ed.), *Rhetoric: A tradition in transition.* East Lansing: Michigan State University Press, 1974.

CROSLAND, C. A. *The future of socialism.* New York: Schocken Books, 1963.

DAHRENDORF, R. *Class and class conflict in industrial society.* Stanford, Calif.: Stanford University Press, 1959.

DAVID, K. H. *Intercultural adjustment and applications of reinforcement theory to problems of "culture shock."* Hilo: Center for Crosscultural Training and Research, University of Hawaii, 1972.

DAVIS, D. B. *The problem of slavery in western culture.* Ithaca, N.Y.: Cornell University Press, 1966.

DAVIS, D. B. Some recent directions in American cultural history. *American Historical Review,* 1968, *73,* 696–707.

DeCHARMS, R., & MOELLER, G. H. Values expressed in American children's readers: 1800-1950. *Journal of Abnormal and Social Psychology,* 1962, *64,* 136–142.

DENITCH, B. Elite interviewing and social structure: An example from Yugoslavia. *Public Opinion Quarterly,* 1972, *36,* 149.

DERMINE (HENSHEL), A. M. The relationship between values and behavior: An experiment. Ph.D. thesis, Cornell University, Ithaca, N.Y., 1969.

DeSALVIA, D. N., & GEMILL, G. R. An exploratory study of the personal value systems of college students and managers. *Academy of Management Journal,* 1971, *14,* 227–238.

DeSEVE, K. L. An examination of the relationship between values and smoking behavior. Unpublished Ph.D. dissertation, Washington State University, Pullman, Wash., 1975.

DEUTSCH, K. W. *The nerves of government.* New York: Free Press, 1963.

DEXTER, L. A. *Elite and specialized interviewing.* Evanston, Ill.: Northwestern University Press, 1970.

DILL, W. R., HILTON, T. L., & REITMAN, W. R. *The new managers.* Englewood Cliffs, N.J.: Prentice-Hall, 1962.

DORNBUSCH, S. M., & HICKMAN, L. C. Other-directedness in consumer-goods advertising: A test of Riesman's historical theory. *Social Forces,* 1959, *38,* 99–102.

DOWNES, A. *An economic theory of democracy.* New York: Harper, 1957.

DRAKE, J. W. The backgrounds and value systems of transportation modeling project participants and their effects on project success. *Transportation Research Forum Proceedings,* 1973, 659–672.

DUBIN, R., & TAVEGGIA, T. *The teaching–learning paradox.* Eugene, Ore.: Center for the Advanced Study of Educational Administration, University of Oregon, 1968.

DUKES, W. F. Psychological studies of values. *Psychological Bulletin,* 1955, *52,* 24–50.

DUVERGER, M. *Party politics and pressure groups.* London: Nelson University Paperbacks, 1972.

DuWORS, R. E. Persistence and change in local values of two New England communities. *Rural Sociology,* 1952, *17,* 207–217.

ECKERT, R. E., & NEALE, D. C. Teachers and teaching. *Review of Educational Research,* 1965, *35,* 304–317.

ECKHARDT, W. *Compassion.* Oakville, Ontario: Canadian Peace Research Institute, 1972.

EDELMAN, M. *The symbolic uses of politics.* Urbana: University of Illinois Press, 1964.

EDGAR, D. Racism, fascism, and the National Front. *Race & Class,* 1977, *19,* 111–131.

EISENSTADT, S. N. *The absorption of immigrants.* London: Routledge & Kegan Paul, 1954.

EISENSTADT, S. N. Social institutions. In D. L. Sills (Ed.), *International encyclopedia of the social sciences,* vol. 14, 409–429. New York: Macmillan and Free Press, 1968.

ELLIS, A. *Reason and emotion in psychotherapy.* New York: Stuart, 1962.

EMMERICH, W. Socialization and sex-role development. In P. B. Baltes & K. W. Schaie (Eds.), *Life-span developmental psychology: Personality and socialization.* New York: Academic Press, 1973.

ENGLAND, G. W. Organizational goals and expected behavior of American managers. *Academy of Management Journal,* 1967, *10,* 107–117.

ENGLAND, G. W. Personal value systems of managers and administrators. *Proceedings of the Academy of Management,* 1973, 81–88.

ERIKSON, E. H. *Childhood and society.* New York: Norton, 1950.

ERSKINE, H., & SIEGEL, R. L. Civil liberties and the American public. *Journal of Social Issues,* 1975, *31,* 13–30.

EVANS, R. I. Personal values as factors in anti-Semitism. *Journal of Abnormal and Social Psychology,* 1952, *47,* 749–756.

FALLDING, H. The empirical study of values. *American Sociological Review,* 1965, *30,* 223-233.

FEATHER, N. T. A structural balance approach to the analysis of communication effects. In L. Berkowitz (Ed.), *Advances in experimental social psychology,* vol. 3. New York: Academic Press, 1967.

FEATHER, N. T. Organization and discrepancy in cognitive structures. *Psychological Review,* 1971a, *78,* 355-379.

FEATHER, N. T. Test-retest reliability of individual values and value systems. *Australian Psychologist,* 1971b, *6,* 181-188.

FEATHER, N. T. Factor structure of the conservatism scale: Results from an Australian survey. *Australian Psychologist,* 1975a, *10,* 179-184.

FEATHER, N. T. *Values in education and society.* New York: Free Press, 1975b.

FEATHER, N. T. Generational and sex differences in conservatism. *Australian Psychologist,* 1977a, *12,* 76-82.

FEATHER, N. T. Value importance, conservatism, and age. *European Journal of Social Psychology,* 1977b, *7,* 241-245.

FEATHER, N. T., & RUDZITIS, A. Subjective assimilation among Latvian adolescents: Effects of ethnic schools and perceptions of value systems. *International Migration,* 1974, *12,* 17-87.

FEATHER, N. T., & WASYLUK, G. Subjective assimilation among Ukrainian migrants: Value similarity and parent-child differences. *Australian and New Zealand Journal of Sociology,* 1973, *9,* 16-31.

FESTINGER, L. A theory of social comparison processes. *Human Relations,* 1954, *7,* 117-140.

FINER, S. E., BERRINGTON, H. B., & BARTHOLOMEW, D. J. *Backbench opinion in the House of Commons.* London: Pergamon Press, 1961.

FIREY, W. Conditions for the realization of values remote in time. In E. A. Tiryakian (Ed.), *Sociological theory, values, and sociocultural change: Essays in honor of Pitirim A. Sorokin,* pp. 147-159. New York: Free Press, 1963.

FLAVELL, J. H. Cognitive changes in adulthood. In L. R. Goulet & P. B. Baltes (Eds.), *Life-span developmental psychology: Research and theory.* New York: Academic Press, 1970.

Forward plan for health, FY 1977-81, U.S. Department of Health, Education, and Welfare, Public Health Service, Washington, D.C., June, 1975.

FRANDSEN, K. D. Effects of threat appeals and media transmission. *Speech Monographs,* 1963, *30,* 101-104.

FREEMAN, J. *The politics of women's liberation.* New York: McKay, 1975.

FRICKE, B. G. Prediction, selection, mortality, and quality of control. *College and University,* 1956, *32,* 34-52.

GAGNE, R. M., & ROHWER, W. D. Instructional psychology. In P. H. Mussen & M. R. Rosenzeig (Eds.), *Annual review of psychology.* Palo Alto, Calif.: Annual Reviews, 1969.

GARRET, H. F. A review and interpretation of investigation of factors related to scholastic success in colleges of arts and sciences and teachers colleges. *Journal of Experimental Education,* 1949, *18,* 91-138.

GARVERICK, C. M. Retention of school learning as influenced by selected affective tone variables. *Journal of Educational Psychology,* 1964, *55,* 31–34.

GEORGE, A. L., & GEORGE, J. L. *Woodrow Wilson and Colonel House.* New York: Dover, 1956.

GIES, F. J., & LEONARD, B. C. The relationship between teacher perception of organizational climate and values concerning disadvantaged pupils. *Negro Educational Review,* 1971, *22,* 152–159.

GOFFMAN, E. *The presentation of the self in everyday life.* Garden City, N.Y.: Doubleday, 1959.

GOFFMAN, E. *Asylums.* Garden City, N.Y.: Anchor Books, 1961.

GOLDSEN, R. K., ROSENBERG, M., SUCHMAN, E. A., & WILLIAMS, R. M., JR. *What college students think.* New York: Van Nostrand, 1960.

GORDON, M. M. *Assimilation in American life.* New York: Oxford University Press, 1964.

GORSUCH, R. L. Rokeach's approach to value systems and social compassion. *Review of Religious Research,* 1969, *11,* 139–143.

GOULD, J., & KOLB, W. L. (Eds.), *A dictionary of the social sciences.* New York: Free Press, 1964.

GOULDNER, A. W. *The coming crisis of western sociology.* New York: Basic Books, 1970.

GREELEY, A. M., & SHEATSLEY, P. B. Attitudes toward racial integration. *Scientific American,* 1971, *225,* 13–19.

GREENSTEIN, F. I. *Personality and politics.* Chicago: Markham, 1969.

GREENSTEIN, T. N. Behavior change through value self-confrontation: A field experiment. *Journal of Personality and Social Psychology,* 1976, *34,* 254–262.

GREENSTEIN, T. N., & BENNETT, R. R. Order effects in Rokeach's value survey. *Journal of Research in Personality,* 1974, *8,* 393–396.

GREENWALD, A. G., & RONIS, D. L. Twenty years of cognitive dissonance: Case study of the evolution of a theory. *Psychological Review,* 1978, *85,* 53–57.

GROSS, B. M., & SPRINGER, M. (Eds.), Political intelligence for America's future. *The Annals of the American Academy of Political and Social Science,* 1970.

GROSS, N., MASON, W. S., & McEACHERN, A. W. *Explorations in role analysis: Studies of the school superintendency role.* New York: Wiley, 1958.

GRUBE, J. W. The role of self-dissatisfaction in value change following self-confrontation: Induction or awareness? Paper presented at the annual meetings of the Western Psychological Association, San Francisco, Calif., April 22, 1978.

GRUBE, J. W., GREENSTEIN, T. N., RANKIN, W. L., & KEARNEY, K. A. Behavior change following self-confrontation: A test of the value mediation hypothesis. *Journal of Personality and Social Psychology,* 1977, *35,* 212–216.

GURIN, P., GURIN, G., LAO, R. C., & BEATTIE, M. Internal–external control in the motivational dynamics of Negro youth. *Journal of Social Issues,* 1969, *25;* 29–53.

GUSTIN, B. H. Charisma, recognition, and the motivation of scientists. *American Journal of Sociology,* 1973, *78,* 1118–1134.

GUTMANN, D. L. An exploration of ego configurations in middle and later life. In B. L. Neugarten & Associates (Eds.), *Personality in middle and late life.* New York: Atherton Press, 1964.

HAGE, J., & DEWAR, R. Elite values versus organization structure in predicting innovation. *Administrative Science Quarterly,* 1973, *18,* 279-290.

HALL, R. H. *Organizations: Structure and process.* Englewood Cliffs, N.J.: Prentice-Hall, 1972.

HAMBLIN, R. L., & SMITH, C. R. Values, status, and professors. *Sociometry,* 1965, *39,* 183-196.

HAMID, P. N., & FLAY, B. R. Changes in locus of control as a function of value modification. *British Journal of Social and Clinical Psychology,* 1974, *13,* 143-150.

HAMMOND, J. L. Revival religion and anti-slavery politics. *American Sociological Review,* 1974, *39,* 175-186.

HARGROVE, E. C. Values and change: A comparison of young elites in England and America. *Political Studies,* 1969, *17,* 339-344.

HARMAN, M., & SIMON, S. B. Values. In S. B. Simon & H. Kirschenbaum (Eds.), *Readings in values clarification.* Minneapolis, Minn.: Winston Press, 1973.

HARTUP, W. W., & LEMPERS, J. A problem in life-span development: The interactional analysis of family attachments. In P. B. Baltes & K. W. Schaie (Eds.), *Life-span developmental psychology: Personality and socialization.* New York: Academic Press, 1973.

HAWKES, N. Science in Europe: Attack on Marxists stirs controversy. *Science,* 1977, *198,* 1230-1231.

HEFFERMAN, E. *Making it in prison: The square, the cool and the life.* New York: Wiley, 1972.

HENSHEL, A. M. (DERMINE). The relationship between values and behavior: An experiment. Ph.D. thesis, Cornell University, Ithaca, N.Y., 1969.

HENSHEL, A. M. The relationship between values and behavior: A developmental hypothesis. *Child Development,* 1971, *42,* 1997-2007.

HESEL, R. Value orientation and pupil control ideology of public school educators. *Educational Administration Quarterly,* 1971, *7,* 24-33.

HODGKINSON, C. Organizational influence on value systems. *Educational Administration Quarterly,* 1971, *7,* 46-55.

HOLLEN, C. C. Value change, perceived instrumentality, and attitude change. Unpublished Ph.D. dissertation, Michigan State University, 1972.

HOLSTI, O. R. Content analysis. In G. Lindzey & E. Aronson (Eds.), *The handbook of social psychology, vol. 2.* Reading, Mass.: Addison-Wesley, 1968.

HOPKINS, S. W., Jr. Behavioral and attitude changes produced from dissonance created between intrapersonal values and attitudes. Unpublished Ph.D. dissertation, University of Texas at Austin, 1973.

HOROWITZ, L. *Foundations of political sociology.* New York: Harper & Row, 1972.

HYMAN, H. The value systems of different classes: A social psychological contribution to the analysis of stratification. In R. Bendix & S. M. Lipset (Eds.), *Class, status, and power,* pp. 426-442. Glencoe, Ill.: Free Press, 1953.

INGLEHART, R. Changing values and attitudes toward military service among the American public. Paper presented to the research seminar on Social Psychology of Military Service, April, 23–25, 1975, Center for Continuing Education, University of Chicago.

INKELES, A. Industrial man: The relation of status to experience, perception, and value. *American Journal of Sociology*, 1960, *66*, 1–31.

INKELES, A., & SMITH, D. H. *Becoming modern.* Cambridge, Mass.: Harvard University Press, 1974.

JACOB, P. E., FLINK, J. J. & SCHUCHMAN, H. L. Values and their function in decision-making. *American Behavioral Scientist*, 1962, *5*, Supplement.

JACOB, P. E., TEUNE, H., & WATTS, T. Values, leadership and development: A four nation study. *Social Science Information*, 1968, *7*, 49–92.

JENNINGS, M. K., & NIEMI, R. G. Continuity and change in political orientations: A longitudinal study of two generations. *American Political Science Review*, 1975, *69*, 1316–1335.

JOHNSON, M., & DANIEL, D. (Eds.) Comprehensive annotated bibliography on the teaching of psychology at the undergraduate level through 1972. *JSAS Catalog of Selected Documents in Psychology*, 1974, *4*, 108 (Ms. No. 735).

JOHNSON, P. What is a socialist? *New Statesman*, September 29, 1972, 421–422.

JONES, A. J. Fascism: The past and the future. *Comparative Political Studies*, 1974, *7*, 107–133.

JONES, E. E., & GERARD, H. B. *Foundations of social psychology.* New York: Wiley, 1967.

KAST, F. E., & ROSENZWEIG, J. *Organization and management theory: A systems approach*, 2nd ed. New York: McGraw-Hill, 1974.

KATZ, D. The functional approach to the study of attitudes. *Public Opinion Quarterly*, 1960, *24*, 163–203.

KATZ, D., & KAHN, R. L. *The social psychology of organizations.* New York: Wiley, 1966.

KATZ, D., & STOTLAND, E. A preliminary statement to a theory of attitude structure and change. In S. Koch (Ed.), *Psychology: A study of a science.* New York: McGraw-Hill, 1959.

KATZ, E., GUREVITCH, M., & HADDASSAH, H. On the use of the mass media for important things. *American Sociological Review*, 1973, *38*, 164–181.

KATZ, M. R. Can computers make guidance decisions for students? *College Board Review*, 1969, *72*, 13–17.

KATZ, M. R., CHAPMAN, W., & GODWIN, W. SIGI—a computer-based aid to career decision-making. *EDUCOM Bulletin*, 1972 (Available from Educational Testing Service, Princeton, N.J.).

KEATING, J. Persuasive impact, attitudes, and image: The effect of communication media and audience size on attitude toward source and toward his position. Unpublished Ph.D. dissertation, Ohio State University, 1972.

KELLER, A. A personal course in psychology. Paper presented at the annual meeting of the American Psychological Association, Philadelphia, 1963.

KELLY, K., SILVERMAN, B. I., & COCHRANE, R. Social desirability and the Rokeach Value Survey. *Journal of Experimental Research in Personality*, 1972, *6*, 84–87.

KELMAN, H. C. Processes of opinion change. *Public Opinion Quarterly*, 1961, *25*, 57–78.

KEMP, C. G. Changes in values in relation to open–closed systems. In M. Rokeach (Ed.), *The open and closed mind*. New York: Basic Books, 1960.

KENNEDY, A. J. Effects of humorous message content upon speaker ethos, persuasiveness, and retention. Unpublished Ph.D. dissertation, University of Michigan, 1972.

KILPATRICK, F. P., CUMMINGS, M. C., JR., & JENNINGS, M. K. *Source book of a study of occupational values and the image of the Federal Service*. Washington, D.C.: Brookings Institution, 1964.

KIRK, R. E. *Experimental design: Procedures for the behavioral sciences*. Belmont, Calif.: Brooks/Cole, 1968.

KLAPP, O. Dramatic encounters. In J. Gusfield (Ed.), *Protest, reform, and revolt*, pp. 337–394. New York: Wiley, 1970.

KLUCKHOHN, C. Values and value-orientations in the theory of action. In T. Parsons & E. A. Shils (Eds.), *Toward a general theory of action*. Cambridge, Mass.: Harvard University Press, 1951.

KLUCKHOHN, C. Have there been discernible shifts in American values during the past generation? In. E. E. Morison (Ed.), *The American style*, pp. 158–204. New York: Harper, 1958.

KLUCKHOHN, F. R. & STRODTBECK, F. L. *Variations in value orientations*. Evanston, Ill.: Row, Peterson, 1961.

KNOWLES, J. H. The responsibility of the individual. *Daedalus*, Winter, 1977, 57–80.

KOHLBERG, L. Moral development. In D. L. Sills (Ed.), *International encyclopedia of the social sciences*, vol. 10. New York: Macmillan and Free Press, 1968.

KOHLBERG, L. Continuities in childhood and adult moral development revisited. In P. B. Baltes & K. W. Schaie (Eds.), *Life-span developmental psychology: Personality and socialization*. New York: Academic Press, 1973.

KOHN, M. L. *Class and conformity: A study in values*. Homewood, Ill.: Dorsey press, 1969.

KOHN, M. L. Social class and parental values: Another confirmation of the relationship. *American Sociological Review*, 1976, *41*, 538–545. (Reply to Wright & Wright, 1976, p. 548.)

KUKURS, I. The assimilation of Latvian immigrants in Australia. Unpublished M.A. thesis, University of Adelaide, 1968.

LANE, R. *Political thinking and consciousness*. Chicago: Markham, 1969.

LARSON, D. N. Rokeach in linguistic perspective. *Review of Religious Research*, 1969, *11*, 146–148.

LASSWELL, H., & KAPLAN, A. *Power and society*. New Haven: Yale University Press, 1950.

LASSWELL, H., & LERNER, D. (Eds.) *World revolutionary elites.* Cambridge. Mass.: MIT Press, 1965.

LAWS, J. L. Work aspirations of women: False leads and new starts. *Signs: Journal of Women in Culture and Society,* 1976, *1,* 33–49.

LEE, C. Improved college teaching: Inquiry and quest. In C. Lee (Ed.), *Improving college teaching.* Washington, D.C.: American Council on Education, 1967.

LEE, R. S. The future of the museum as a learning environment. Paper presented at the Conference on Computers and Their Potential Applications in Museums at the Metropolitan Museum of Art, New York, April 15–17, 1968.

LEFF, H. L. *Experience, environment, and human potential.* New York: Oxford University Press, 1978.

LE LOHÉ, M. J. The National Front and the general election of 1974. *New Community,* 1976, *5,* 292–301.

LENSKI, G. *Power and privilege.* New York: McGraw-Hill, 1966.

LERMAN, P. Individual values, peer values, and subcultural delinquency. *American Sociological Review,* 1968, *33,* 219–235.

LEVINE, R. A. The internalization of political values in stateless societies. *Human Organization,* 1960, *19,* 51–58.

LEWIN, K. *Field theory in social science,* New York: Harper, 1951.

Lewiston Morning Tribune, July 23, 1973, Lewiston, Idaho.

LIPSET, S. M. *The first new nation: The United States in historical and comparative perspective.* New York: Basic Books, 1963.

LIPSKY, M. Protest as a political resource. *American Political Science Review,* 1968, *62,* 1144–1158.

LOCKE, E. A. Job satisfaction and job performance: A theoretical analysis. *Organizational Behavior and Human Performance,* 1970, *5,* 484–500.

LUEPTOW, L. B. Need for achievement and occupational preferences: Some operations with value-orientations as intervening variables in need–goal relationships. *Sociometry,* 1968, *31,* 304–312.

MAAS, H. & KUYPERS, J. *From thirty to seventy.* San Francisco: Jossey-Bass, 1974.

MACKINTOSH, J. P. *The British cabinet,* 2nd ed. London: Methuen, 1968.

MACLEISH, A. The revolt of the diminished man. *Saturday Review,* June 7, 1969, 16–19.

MARSH, J. F., Jr., & STAFFORD, F. P. The effect of values on pecuniary behavior. *American Sociological Review,* 1967, *32,* 740–754.

MARTIN, J. I. *Community and identity: Refugee groups in Adelaide.* Canberra: Australian National University Press, 1972.

MARX, G. T., & WOOD, J. Strands of theory and research in collective behavior. *Annual Review of Sociology,* 1975, *1,* 363–428.

MARX, J. H., & HOLZNER, B. The social construction of strain and ideological models of grievance in contemporary movements. *Pacific Sociological Review,* 1977, *20,* 411–438.

MASLOW, A. H. *Motivation and personality.* New York: Harper, 1954.

MAUSS, A. L. The lost promise of reconciliation: New left vs. old left. *Journal of Social Issues*, 1971, *27*, 1–20.

MAXWELL, W. D. Some dimensions of relevance. *AAUP Bulletin*, 1969, *55*, 337–341.

McCARTHY, J., & ZALD, M. N. *The trend of social movements in America: Professionalization and resource mobilization.* Morristown, N.J.: General Learning, 1973.

McCLOSKY, H. Consensus and ideology in American politics. *American Political Science Review*, 1964, *58*, 361–383.

McCLOSKY, H., & SCHAAR, J. H. Psychological dimensions of anomy. *American Sociological Review*, 1965, *30*, 14–40.

McFALL, R. M., & HAMMEN, C. L. Motivation, structure, and self monitoring: Role of non-specific factors in smoking reduction. *Journal of Consulting and Clinical Psychology*, 1971, *37*, 80–86.

McGUIRE, W. J. The nature of attitudes and attitude change. In G. Lindzey & E. Aronson (Eds.), *The handbook of social psychology*, vol. 3. Reading, Mass.: Addison-Wesley, 1969.

McGUIRE, W. J. Persuasion, resistance, and attitude change. In I. de Sola Pool, et al. (Eds.), *Handbook of communication.* Chicago: Rand McNally, 1973.

McKEACHIE, W. J. Procedures and techniques of teaching: A survey of experimental studies. In N. Stanford (Ed.), *The American college.* New York: Wiley, 1962.

McKENZIE, R. T. *British political parties*, 2nd ed. New York: Praeger, 1963.

McLELLAN, D. D. Feedback of information as a determinant of value change and the implications of cognitive–moral development for value theory. Unpublished Ph.D. dissertation, Michigan State University, 1974.

MEAD, G. H. *Mind, self, and society: From the standpoint of a social behaviorist.* Chicago: University of Chicago Press, 1934.

MEICHENBAUM, D. H., BOWERS, K. S., & ROSS, R. R. A behavioral analysis of teacher expectancy effect. *Journal of Personality and Social Psychology*, 1969, *13*, 306–316.

MENDELSOHN, H. Mass communication and cancer control. In J. W. Cullen, B. H. Fox, & R. N. Isom (Eds.), *Cancer: The behavioral dimensions.* New York: Raven Press, 1976, pp. 197–204.

MERTON, R. K. *Social theory and social structure.* New York: Free Press, 1957.

MERTON, R. K. *On the shoulders of giants.* New York: Harcourt, Brace, & Jovanovich, 1967.

MERTON, R. K., READER, G., & KENDALL, P. L. (Eds.) *The student physician: Introductory studies in the sociology of medical education.* Cambridge, Mass.: Harvard University Press, 1957.

METCALF, G. R. *Black profiles.* New York: McGraw-Hill, 1968.

MEYER, J. *Reflections on values education.* Waterloo, Ontario: Wilfrid Laurier University Press, 1976.

MEYER, J., BURNHAM, B., & CHOLVAT, J. (Eds.) *Values education.* Waterloo, Ontario: Wilfred Laurier University Press, 1975.

MILLER, G. R. A crucial problem in attitude research. *Quarterly Journal of Speech,* 1967, *53,* 235–240.

MILLS, C. W. *The power elite.* New York: Oxford University Press, 1956.

MOORE, W. E. *The professions: Roles and rules.* New York: Russell Sage Foundation, 1970.

MORRIS, C. W. *Varieties of human value.* Chicago: University of Chicago Press, 1956.

MOSTELLER, F., & WALLACE, D. *Inference and disputed authorship: The Federalist.* Reading, Mass.: Addison-Wesley, 1964.

MURRAY, H. A. *Explorations in personality: A clinical and experimental study of fifty men of college age.* New York: Oxford University Press, 1938.

NAMENWIRTH, J. Z., & LASSWELL, H. D. *The changing language of American values: A computer study of selected party platforms.* Sage Professional Papers in Comparative Politics, vol. 1, 1970.

NARDI, A. H. Person-perception research and the perception of life-span development. In P. B. Baltes & K. W. Schaie (Eds.), *Life-span developmental psychology: Personality and socialization.* New York: Academic Press, 1973.

NEAL, M. A. *Values and interests in social change.* Englewood Cliffs, N.J.: Prentice-Hall, 1965.

NEIDT, C., & HEDLUND, D. The relationship between changes in attitude towards a course and final achievement. *Journal of Educational Research,* 1967, *61,* 57–58.

NEUGARTEN, B. L. (Ed.) *Middle age and aging.* Chicago: University of Chicago Press, 1968.

NEUGARTEN, B. L. Personality change in late life: A developmental perspective. In C. Eisdorfer & M. P. Lawton (Eds.), *The psychology of adult development and aging.* Washington, D.C.: American Psychological Association, 1973.

NEWCOMB, T. M., TURNER, R. H., & CONVERSE, P. *Social psychology.* New York: Holt, Rinehart and Winston, 1965.

New perspective on the health of Canadians, A. Ministry of National Health and Welfare, Ottawa, Canada, April, 1974.

OBERSCHALL, A. *Social conflict and social movements.* Englewood Cliffs, N.J.: Prentice-Hall, 1973.

OLSON, M. *The logic of collective action.* Cambridge, Mass.: Harvard University Press, 1965.

Opinion Research Center. *An analysis of the Harris Polls on the October 1974 General Election.* London: Louis Harris International, 1974.

ORNE, M. T. On the social psychology of the psychological experiment: With particular reference to demand characteristics and their implications. *American Psychologist,* 1962, *17,* 776–783.

PALEN, J. J. The education of the senior military decision-maker. *Sociological Quarterly,* 1972, *13,* 145–160.

PARSONS, T. *The social system.* Glencoe, Ill.: Free Press, 1951.

PARSONS, T. Suggestions for a sociological approach to the theory of organizations—I. *Administrative Science Quarterly*, 1956, *1*, 63–85.

PARSONS, T. An approach to psychological theory in terms of the theory of action. In S. Koch (Ed.), *Psychology: A science*, vol. 3, pp. 612–711. New York: McGraw-Hill, 1959.

PARSONS, T. On the concept of value-commitments. *Sociological Inquiry*, 1968, *38*, 135–159.

PEERY, N. S., JR. General systems theory: A critique of its use in administrative theory. *Proceedings of the Mountain-Plains Management Association*, 1973.

PENNER, L. A. Interpersonal attraction toward a black person as a function of value importance. *Personality*, 1971, *2*, 175–187.

PENNER, L. A., HOMANT, R., & ROKEACH, M. Comparison of rank-order and paired-comparison methods for measuring value systems. *Perceptual and Motor Skills*, 1968, *27*, 418–419.

PENNINGS, J. M. Work-value systems of white-collar workers. *Administrative Science Quarterly*, 1970, *15*, 397–405.

PEPPER, S. C. *The sources of value*. Berkeley and Los Angeles: University of California Press, 1958.

PERROW, C. Reality adjustment: A young institution settles for human care. *Social Problems*, 1966, *14*, 69–79.

Phi Delta Kappan. A special issue on moral education, 1975, *56*.

PITTEL, S. M., & MENDELSOHN, G. A. Measurement of moral values: A review and critique. *Psychological Bulletin*, 1966, *66*, 22–35.

PORTER, L. W., & LAWLER, E. E., III. Properties of organization structure in relation to job attitudes and job behavior. *Psychological Bulletin*, 1965, *65*, 24–51.

POSTMAN, L., BRUNER, J. S., & MCGINNIES, E. Personal values as selective factors in perception. *Journal of Abnormal and Social Psychology*, 1948, *43*, 142–154.

POTTER, A. Great Britain: Opposition with a capital "o." In R. A. Dahl (Ed.), *Political oppositions in western democracies*. New Haven: Yale University Press, 1966.

PROSHANSKY, H. M., & EVANS, R. L. The "radical right": A threat to the behavioral sciences. *Journal of Social Issues*, 1963, *19*, 86–106.

PULZER, P. G. *Political representation and elections in Britain*. London: Allen and Unwin, 1972.

PUTNAM, R. D. *The beliefs of politicians*. New Haven: Yale University Press, 1973.

PUTNINS, A. L., & TAFT, R. The Australianism scale revisited: A review of recent data. *Australian Psychologist*, 1976, *11*, 147–152.

RAISON, T. What is a Tory? *New Statesman*, October 6, 1972, pp. 463–464.

RAWLS J., HARRISON, C. W., RAWLS, D. J., HAYES, R. L., & JOHNSON, A. W. Comparison of Wallace, Nixon, and Humphrey supporters along certain demographic, attitudinal, and value-system dimensions. *Psychological Reports*, 1973, *32*, 35–39.

RESKIN, B. Scientific productivity and the reward structure of science. *American Sociological Review,* 1977, *42,* 491–504.

RICHARDS, P. G. *Honourable members.* London: Faber, 1959.

RICHARDSON, A. *British immigrants and Australia: A psycho-social inquiry.* Canberra: Australian National University Press, 1974.

RIEGEL, K. F. Time and change in the development of the individual and society. In H. W. Reese (Ed.), *Advances in child development and behavior,* vol. 7. New York: Academic Press, 1972.

RIMER, I. I. The impact of mass media on cancer control programs. In J. W. Cullen, B. H. Fox, & R. N. Isom (Eds.), *Cancer: The behavioral dimensions.* New York: Raven Press, 1976.

ROBINSON, J. P., & SHAVER, P. R. (Eds.) *Measures of social psychological attitudes.* Ann Arbor: Institute for Social Research, University of Michigan, 1969.

RODHAM, H. Children under law. *Harvard Educational Review, 1973, 43,* 487–514.

RODMAN, H. The lower-class value stretch. *Sociological Forces,* 1963, *42,* 205–215.

ROETHLISBERGER, F. J. DICKSON, W. J., & WRIGHT, H. A. *Management and the worker: An account of a research program conducted by the Western Electric Company, Hawthorne Works, Chicago.* Cambridge, Mass.: Harvard University Press, 1969.

ROGERS, E. M. Mass media and interpersonal communication. In I. de Sola Pool et al. (Eds.), *Handbook of communication.* Chicago: Rand McNally, 1973.

ROKEACH, M. *Value survey.* Sunnyvale, Calif.: Halgren Tests, 1967.

ROKEACH, M. *Beliefs, attitudes, and values: A theory of organization and change.* San Francisco: Jossey-Bass, 1968.

ROKEACH, M. The role of values in public opinion research. *Public Opinion Quarterly,* 1968–1969 (Winter), *32,* 547–559.

ROKEACH, M. Faith, hope and bigotry. *Psychology Today,* 1970, *3,* 33 ff.

ROKEACH, M. Long range experimental modification of values, attitudes, and behavior. *American Psychologist,* 1971a, *26 453459.*

ROKEACH, M. Persuasion that persists. *Psychology Today,* 1971b, *5,* 68–73.

ROKEACH, M. *The nature of human values.* New York: Free Press, 1973.

ROKEACH, M. Change and stability in American value systems. *Public Opinion Quarterly,* 1974a, *38,* 222–238.

ROKEACH, M. Some reflections about the place of values in Canadian social science. In T. N. Guinsburg & G. L. Reuber (Eds.), *Perspectives on the social sciences in Canada.* Toronto: University of Toronto Press, 1974b.

ROKEACH, M. Long-term value change initiated by computer feedback. *Journal of Personality and Social Psychology,* 1975, *32,* 467–476.

ROKEACH, M. Value theory and communication research. In D. Nimmo (Ed.), *Communication Yearbook III.* New Brunswick, N.J.: Transaction Books, 1979.

ROKEACH, M. & COCHRANE, R. Self-confrontation and confrontation with another as determinants of long-term value change. *Journal of Applied Social Psychology,* 1972, *2,* 283–292.

ROKEACH, M., HOMANT, R., & PENNER, L. A. A value analysis of the disputed Federalist Papers. *Journal of Personality and Social Psychology*, 1970, *16*, 245–250.

ROKEACH, M., & McLELLAN, D. D. Feedback of information about the values and attitudes of self and others as determinants of long-term cognitive and behavioral change. *Journal of Applied Social Psychology*, 1972, *2*, 236–251.

ROONEY, R. C. *Equal opportunity in the United States: A symposium on civil rights.* Austin: Lyndon B. Johnson School of Public Affairs, University of Texas, 1973.

ROSE, R. *Politics in England.* Boston: Little, Brown, 1964.

ROSEN, B. C. Race, ethnicity, and the achievement syndrome. *American Sociological Review*, 1959, *24*, 47–60.

ROSENBERG, M. *Occupations and values.* Glencoe, Ill.: Free Press, 1957.

ROSENTHAL, R. *Experimenter effects in behavioral research.* New York: Appleton-Century-Crofts, 1966.

ROSENTHAL, R. Combining results of independent studies. *Psychological Bulletin*, 1978, *85*, 185–193.

ROTTER, J. B. Generalized expectancies for internal versus external control of reinforcement. *Psychological Monographs*, 1966, Whole No. 609, 1–28.

ROUS, G. L., & LEE, D. E. Freedom and equality: Two values of political orientation. *Journal of Communication*, 1978 (Winter), pp. 45–51.

SAMPSON, A. *The anatomy of Britain today,* 2nd ed. New York: Harper & Row, 1966.

SAWYER, T. M. Shift of attitude following persuasion as related to estimate of majority attitude. *Speech Monographs*, 1955, *22*, 68–78.

SCHAIE, K. W., & GRIBBON, K. Adult development and aging. *Annual Review of Psychology*, 1975, *26*, 65–96.

SCHLESINGER, J. A. *Ambition and politics.* Chicago: Rand McNally, 1966.

SCHWARTZ, J. L. A critical review and evaluation of smoking control methods. *Public Health Reports*, Public Health Service, U.S. Department of Health, Education, and Welfare, 1969, *84* (6), 483–506.

SCHWARTZ, S. A survey of guiding principles: The nature of human values. *Science*, 1974, *186*, 436–437.

SCHWARTZ, S. H. Awareness of consequences and the influence of moral norms on interpersonal behavior. *Sociometry*, 1968, *31*, 355–369.

SCOTT, W. A. *Values and organizations.* Chicago: Rand McNally, 1956.

SCOTT, W. E., Jr., & CUMMINGS, L. L. (Eds.) *Readings in organizational behavior and human performance.* Homewood Ill.: Irwin, 1973.

SEARING, D. D. Measuring politicians' values: Administration and assessment of a ranking technique in the British House of Commons. *American Political Science Review*, 1978, *72*, 65–79.

SEEMAN, M. Alienation studies. In A. Inkeles, J. Colomar, & N. Smelser (Eds.), *Annual review of sociology.* Palo Alto, Calif.: Annual Reviews, 1975.

SHERRID, S. D., & BEECH, R. R. Self-dissatisfaction as a determinant of change in police values. *Journal of Applied Psychology*, 1976, *61*, 273–278.

SHOTLAND, R. L., & BERGER, W. G. Behavioral validation of several values from the Rokeach value scale as an index of honesty. *Journal of Applied Psychology*, 1970, *54*, 433–438.

SIEGEL, S. *Non-parametric statistics for the behavioral sciences.* New York: McGraw-Hill, 1956.

SIKULA, A. F. Values and value systems: Relationship to personal goals. *Personnel Journal*, 1971, *50*, 310–312.

SIMON, S. B., & KIRSCHENBAUM, H. (Eds.) *Readings in values clarification.* Minneapolis: Winston Press, 1973.

SMELSER, N. *Theory of collective behavior.* New York: Free Press, 1963.

SMITH, D. H. Communication research and the idea of process. *Speech Monographs*, 1972, *39*, 174–182.

SMITH, M. B. Personal values as determinants of a political attitude. *Journal of Psychology*, 1949, *28*, 477–486.

SMITH, M. B. *Social psychology and human values: Selected essays.* Chicago: Aldine, 1969.

SOCOLOW, R. H. Failures of discourse. *Bulletin of the American Academy of Arts and Sciences*, 1976, *29*, 11–32.

SPRAGUE, D. R. An experimental study of the influence of spoken, audio, and written messages on conferring of resistance to moderately and strongly held beliefs. Unpublished Ph.D. dissertation, Sourthern Illinois University, 1970.

SROLE, L. Social integration and certain corollaries. *American Sociological Review*, 1956, *21*, 709–716.

STEIN, M. J. *Personality measures in admissions.* New York: College Entrance Examination Board, 1963.

STEWART, J. S. Clarifying values clarification: A critique. *Phi Delta Kappan*, 1975, *56*, 684–688.

STRAITS, B. C. Resume of the Chicago study of smoking behavior. In S. V. Zagona (Ed.), *Studies and issues in smoking behavior.* Tucson: University of Arizona Press, 1967, pp. 73–78.

STRAUS, M. A., & HOUGHTON, L. J. Achievement, affiliation, and cooperation values as clues to trends in American rural society: 1924–1958. *Rural Sociology*, 1960, *25*, 394–403.

STRONG, E. K. *Vocational interests 18 years after college.* Minneapolis: University of Minnesota Press, 1955.

SWANSON, D. L. Information utility: An alternate perspective in political communication. *Central States Speech Journal*, 1976, *27*, 95–101.

TAFT, R. Opinion convergence in the assimilation of immigrants. *Australian Journal of Psychology*, 1962, *14*, 41–54.

TAFT, R. *From stranger to citizen.* Nedlands: University of Western Australia Press, 1965.

TAFT, R. Migration: Problems of adjustment and assimilation in immigrants. In

P. Watson (Ed.), *Psychology and race.* Harmondsworth, Middlesex: Penguin Books, 1973.

TAFT, R. Coping with unfamiliar cultures. In N. Warren (Ed.), *Studies in cross cultural psychology,* vol. 1. London: Academic Press, 1977.

TALLMAN, I. *Passion, action, and politics.* San Francisco: Freeman, 1976.

TANNENBAUM, D. A., & KERRICK, J. Effects of newscast items upon listener interpretation. *Journalism Quarterly,* 1954, *31,* 33–37.

TEDESCHI, J. T., SCHLENKER, B. R., & BONOMA, T. V. Cognitive dissonance: Private ratiocination or public spectacle? *American Psychologist,* 1971, *26,* 685.

THEODORSON, G. A., & THEODORSON, A. G. *A modern dictionary of sociology.* New York: Cromwell, 1969.

THOMAE, J. Theory of aging and cognitive theory of personality. *Human Development,* 1970, *13,* 1–16.

THOMAS, C. W., & FOSTER, S. C. Importation model of inmate social roles. *Sociological Quarterly,* 1973, *14,* 225–234.

THOMPSON, J. C. *Organizations in action.* New York: McGraw-Hill, 1967.

THURSTONE, L. L. The method of paired comparisons for social values. *Journal of Abnormal and Social Psychology,* 1927, *21,* 384–400.

TILLY, C. *The Vendée.* Cambridge, Mass.: Harvard University Press, 1964.

TITMUSS, R. M. *The gift relationship: From human blood to social policy.* New York: Random House, 1971.

TRACY, S. L. A content analysis of the values of the Constitution of the United States, Declaration of Independence, and the Federalist Papers. Unpublished manuscript, 1975.

TURNER, R. H. Determinants of social movement strategies. In T. Shibutani (Ed.), *Human nature and collective behavior: Papers in honor of Herbert Blumer.* Englewood Cliffs, N.J.: Prentice-Hall, 1970.

TURNER, R. H., & KILLIAN, L. *Collective behavior,* 2nd ed. Englewood Cliffs, N.J.: Prentice-Hall, 1972.

VICKERS, G. *Value systems and social process.* New York: Basic Books, 1968.

VOLLMER, H. M., & MILLS, D. L. *Professionlization.* Englewood Cliffs, N.J.: Prentice-Hall, 1966.

WAGSCHAL, H. Education and the study of values. *Educational Studies,* 1974, *5,* 205–209.

WALKER, M. *The National Front.* Glasgow: Fontana, 1977.

WALL, V. D., & BOYD, J. A. Channel variation and attitude change. *Journal of Communication,* 1971, *21,* 363–367.

WARNER, L. G., & DEFLEUR, M. L. Attitude as an interactional concept: Social constraint and social distance as intervening variables between attitudes and action. *American Sociological Review,* 1969, *34,* 153–169.

WATERS, L. G. Personality characteristics associated with the inability to quit smoking cigarettes. *Dissertation Abstracts,* 1971, *32,* 1228.

WEBB, E. J., CAMPBELL, D. T., SCHWARTZ, R. D. & SECHREST, L. *Unobtrusive measures: Nonreactive research in the social sciences.* Chicago, Ill.: Rand-McNally, 1966.

WEISS, W. Effects of mass media on communication. In G. Lindzey & E. Aronson (Eds.), *Handbook of social psychology.* Reading, Mass.: Addison-Wesley, 1969.

WELLER, J., & QUARANTELLI, E. Neglected characteristics of collective behavior. *American Journal of Sociology,* 1973, *9,* 665–685.

WHITE, R. K. Hitler, Roosevelt, and the nature of the war propaganda. *Journal of Abnormal and Social Psychology,* 1949, *44,* 157–174.

WHITE, R. K. *Value analysis, the nature and the use of the method.* Glen Gardner, N.Y.: Libertarian Press, 1951.

WICKERT, F. The interrelationships of some general and specific preferences. *Journal of Social Psychology,* 1940a, *11,* 275–302.

WICKERT, F. A test for personal goal-values. *Journal of Social Psychology,* 1940b, *11,* 259-274.

WIENER, N. *The human use of human beings.* Garden City, N.Y.: Anchor Books, 1954.

WIJEYESWARDENE, G. A comparative note on ecology and social structure. *Man,* 1966, *1,* 95–101.

WILLIAMS, R. M., JR. *American society: A sociological interpretation.* New York: Knopf, 1951.

WILLIAMS, R. M., JR. Friendship and social values in a suburban community. *Pacific Sociological Review,* 1959, *1,* 3–10.

WILLIAMS, R. M., JR. *American society: A sociological interpretation,* 2nd ed. New York: Knopf, 1960.

WILLIAMS, R. M., JR. Individual and group values. *The Annals,* 1967, *371,* 20–37.

WILLIAMS, R. M., JR. The concept of values. In D. L. Sills (Ed.), *International encyclopedia of the social sciences,* vol. 16. New York: Macmillan and Free Press, 1968.

WILLIAMS, R. M., JR. *American society: A sociological interpretation,* 3rd ed. New York: Knopf, 1970.

WILLIAMS, R. M., JR. Change and stability in values and value systems. In B. Barber & A. Inkeles (Eds.), *Stability and social change,* pp. 123–159. Boston: Little, Brown, 1971.

WILLIAMS, R. M., JR. Equal opportunity as a societal problem. In R. C. Rooney (Ed.), *Equal opportunity in the United States: A symposium on civil rights,* pp. 104–111. Austin: University of Texas, 1973.

WILLIAMS, R. M., JR. Race and ethnic relations. In A. Inkeles, J. Coleman, & N. Smelser (Eds.), *Annual review of sociology,* pp. 125–164. Palo Alto, Calif.: Annual Reviews, 1975a.

WILLIAMS, R. M., JR. Relative deprivation. In L. A. Coser (Ed.), *The idea of social structure: Papers in honor of Robert K. Merton,* pp. 355–378. New York: Harcourt Brace Jovanovich, 1975b.

WILSON, G. D. (Ed.) *The psychology of conservatism.* New York: Academic Press, 1973.

WILSON, G. D., & PATTERSON, J. R. A new measure of conservatism. *British Journal of Social and Clinical Psychology*, 1968, *7*, 264–269.

WOFFORD, J. C. & WILLOUGHBY, T. L. Attitudes and scholastic behavior. *Journal of Educational Research*, 1968, *61*, 360–362.

WOODRING, P. *The higher learning in America: A reassessment.* New York: McGraw-Hill, 1969.

WOODRUFF, A. D., & DiVESTA, F. J. The relationship between values, concepts, and attitudes. *Educational and Psychological Measurement*, 1948, *8*, 646.

WOODWARD, J. L. Changing ideas on mental illness and its treatment. *American Sociological Review*, 1951, *16*, 443–454.

WOODWARD, J. *Industrial organization: Theory and practice.* London: Oxford University Press, 1965.

WORCHEL, S., ANDREOLI, V., & EASON, J. Is the medium the message? A study of the effects of media, communicator, and message characteristics on attitude change. *Journal of Applied Social Psychology*, 1975, *5*, 157–172.

WRIGHT, J. D., & WRIGHT, S. R. Social class and parental values for children: A partial replication and extension of the Kohn thesis. *American Sociological Review*, 1976, *41*, 527–537. (Reply to Kohn, 1976, pp. 545–548.)

YANKELOVICH, D. The changing values on campus. New York: McGraw-Hill, 1974.

ZALD, M. Comparative analysis and measurement of organizational goals: The case of correctional institutions for delinquents. *Sociological Quarterly*, 1963, *4*, 206–230.

ZANINOVICH, M. G. Elites and citizenry in Yugoslav society: A study of value differentiation. In C. Beck (Ed.), *Comparative communist political leadership.* New York: McKay, 1973.

ZUCKERMAN, H. Interviewing an ultra elite. *Public Opinion Quarterly*, 1972, *36*, 159–175.

Index